Pastor Larry Huch, through his br W9-BNS-785 writings, is a treasured ally of the Jewish people and the State of Israel. It is due to the grassroots support for Israel as demonstrated by Pastor Huch that faith-based diplomacy has been seeing its greatest successes in recent times. The move of the US and Guatemalan embassies from Tel Aviv to Jerusalem, the US recognition of the Golan Heights, and the anti-BDS legislation sweeping throughout the US have been accomplished in a large part due to Christian supporters taking a stand and encouraging their political representatives to support Israel.

At the same time that we have seen dramatic successes in support for Israel, we have also seen rising anti-Semitism throughout the world, reminiscent of the extreme hatred of the Jewish people from the 1930s. It is the same root of hatred as the past, only now masked in a different form. As anti-Semitism masked as anti-Zionism continues to spread around the world, the Jewish community must continue working with Christian leaders and political representatives in order to fight anti-Semitism and strengthen support for Israel. I am grateful for my dear friend Pastor Huch for taking a leadership role in these efforts and wish him continued success in sharing this important message around the world.

—JOSH REINSTEIN
PRESIDENT, THE ISRAEL ALLIES FOUNDATION
DIRECTOR, THE KNESSET CHRISTIAN ALLIES CAUCUS

My dear friend, acclaimed Pastor Larry Huch, has done it again. As the number of published books proliferates, it becomes ever harder to distinguish the wheat from the chaff. But this, his newest, *The Seven Living Prophecies*, is not only wheat—it is delightfully tasty and satisfyingly substantive bread. Pastor Huch's scholarship shines through on every page, bringing life-transforming insights to every reader gazing heavenward for truth.

—RABBI DANIEL LAPIN
AMERICAN ALLIANCE OF JEWS AND CHRISTIANS

I cannot think of anyone better qualified in this generation than Pastor Larry Huch to explain the reality and relevance of prophetic principles to the challenges we face today. Pastor Huch not only seamlessly connects the past to the present; he also points out a path to absolute victory in the days ahead.

—ROD PARSLEY
SENIOR PASTOR, WORLD HARVEST CHURCH

# THE
# SEVEN
# LIVING
# PROPHECIES

## LARRY HUCH

CHARISMA
HOUSE

Most Charisma House Book Group products are available at special quantity discounts for bulk purchase for sales promotions, premiums, fund-raising, and educational needs. For details, call us at (407) 333-0600 or visit our website at www.charismahouse.com.

THE SEVEN LIVING PROPHECIES by Larry Huch
Published by Charisma House
Charisma Media/Charisma House Book Group
600 Rinehart Road, Lake Mary, Florida 32746
www.charismahouse.com

Visit the author's website at https://larryhuchministries.com, larryhuchbooks.com.

Library of Congress Cataloging-in-Publication Data:
An application to register this book for cataloging has been submitted to the Library of Congress.
International Standard Book Number: 978-1-62999-753-7
E-book ISBN: 978-1-62999-754-4

20 21 22 23 24 — 987654321
Printed in the United States of America

## DEDICATION

*To my children and my grandchildren: because of my journey to discover the Jewish Jesus and become grafted into the rich heritage of Abraham, Isaac, and Jacob, and because all of you have stood with me and walked with me in this journey, God says you shall be called blessed. May you always seek the insights, revelations, and wisdom of almighty God. Love Him with all your heart, soul, mind, and strength, and love your neighbor as yourself. Always love Israel and the Jewish people around the world, and be strong and courageous to stand and support them. Every day look for ways to* tikkun olam—*make a difference in the lives of others and change the world. Remember this promise of strength from the Word of our God, who never changes: "I will bless those who bless Israel and curse those who curse Israel." (See Genesis 12:3.)*

*I also dedicate this book to my beautiful, wonderful wife, Tiz. My life and this book would not be possible without you! Not only have you walked with me and stood with me; you also have been my inspiration in everything and in every way. You are wiser than most, stronger than most, and the most loving and caring person I have ever met. It has been a long two years as we have seen the truth of this book unfold in the miracle healing of our baby "grand-sugar" Lion and then in your miracle healing this year. In almost losing you, I realized how much I need and depend on you. Lion's healing and your restoration are evidence of what a mighty God we serve. You are the love of my life, and truly our best is yet to come.*

# CONTENTS

## PART I:
## THE PROPHECIES

## PART II:
## THE PATH FORWARD

# INTRODUCTION

*Every teacher of the law who has become a disciple in
the kingdom of heaven is like the owner of the house who
brings out of his storeroom new treasures as well as old.*
—MATTHEW 13:52, NIV

IZ AND I believe that this is a timely, prophetic, and much-needed message. The growing excitement and hunger we see among Christians who want to connect with their Jewish roots is amazing! We have been in the ministry for forty-five years and have taught on our Jewish roots for almost twenty-five years. We've never felt more excited or inspired about all that we see the Lord doing in our lives and ministries.

During our first fifteen or twenty years in the ministry, we pioneered and pastored seven different churches in different cities, including two in Australia. Opening seven new churches, often in unfamiliar cities and nations with no people and no help apart from what our kids offered, meant that we were in uncharted waters. It was extremely risky as well as exciting.

We studied, taught, preached, prayed, fasted, evangelized, and dedicated our lives to seeing people from all over the world come to the Lord. We saw thousands saved, healed, delivered, and set free. We believed for and saw great miracles every day. By the grace of God we were able to build large, strong churches. We hosted and preached at worldwide Bible conferences and held miracle crusades in many nations. We even launched a TV ministry, which continues today. And we were blessed to write books. God truly granted us global impact!

We also pioneered teachings that were not considered common or orthodox. Nearly thirty-five years ago, because of my background of family and inner-city anger, violence, crime, drug addiction, bondage, and negative generational patterns, I became desperate to find true and lasting freedom. I sought God and dug into the Word to find answers, help, and freedom. He showed me the biblical truth of generational curses, revealing not only how to break them but also how to sever the inner strongholds that keep us bound. This teaching broke the chains off my life and has kept me free, happy, and whole all these years.

Now I've had the privilege of serving Him as He does the same for tens of thousands of other people from every social background, walk of life, ethnicity, and nation. What the Lord did for me, He will do for you too!

## MORE UNCHARTED TERRITORY

Tiz and I pioneered another uncharted area of ministry. From day one of our ministry we refused to accept division or any form of separation between races, nationalities, socioeconomic groups, religions, generations, or genders. Wherever we have lived, pastored, or ministered, we have made breaking down barriers a priority. In cities and nations where this is unheard of and unacceptable, we have torn down walls of division, pride, hatred, prejudice, sin, fear, misconceptions, and lies. In every church we have built, our motto has been "No matter who you are, where you've come from, or what you're going through, Jesus has a new beginning for you!"

We have always made it clear that our churches would look like the united nations for Christ! We have made a stand and lost many people over this idea through the years. But we choose whom we lose. Whether those from the inner city streets or Wall Street, people from the "big house" (prison) or the White House, the Native American tribes or the Australian aborigines, the orphans in Haiti or the politicians and leaders of the world, Tiz and I always have loved, cared for, and opened our hearts and our churches to all. And we always will. We have decided that we will either stand united or fall divided.

People from every sphere of life and the world desperately need to know the love and acceptance of our God. They should experience some of it through those of us who already know His love and acceptance. This is genuinely the greatest way to live a blessed wonderful life! That's why Tiz and I, as well as our family, have always stretched ourselves and pushed ourselves hard. We know what God has done for us, and we want to see Him do it for others. We love the ministry. We love God's people. And we love His Word. We've been extremely honored, excited, and blessed to be part of what God is doing as He changes people's lives.

## A TURNING POINT

After our first twenty years or so in the ministry, we began to feel unrest in our spirits. Something was missing, and my spiritual zeal was going flat. The Word was becoming stale, and we weren't seeing the promises and miracles of God manifested the way we saw them in the Bible. Both Tiz and I felt as though it was time for a change, and we seriously considered leaving the ministry and going into business.

About that time, friends invited us to go to Israel with them. We almost didn't go. But God had a plan, and we said yes. I'll share more about this later; suffice it to say for now that I had a startling revelation while visiting Capernaum: I realized that Jesus was a devout, Jewish Torah believer and follower! It dawned on me for the first time that He had not come to divert the world from Israel, the Jewish faith, or Torah practices. He came to save us and to bring Jewish people and the world back to our Jewish roots and foundations.

That encounter with the Lord completely altered my life, doctrine, and destiny. The Lord not only revealed Jesus as a practicing Jewish man but opened my eyes to the far-reaching impact of His Jewishness on the foundations of Christian faith—past, present, and future.

Changing our thinking changed everything—our lives, family, ministry, and destiny. Our future took a drastic turn, and we knew that we had stepped into our true calling. God told me that He would teach me to read His Word through the eyes of a Jewish Jesus, and I would teach the same truths to the world.

Wow! I was suddenly infused with excitement and a hunger to dig deep into Scripture. I eagerly explored hidden truths, connected to our Jewish roots and ancient foundations, and discovered ancient truths, mysteries, wisdom, and keys to release God's covenant promises and miracles. I knew that my purpose and goal were not just to saturate my mind with biblical truths and history but to discover the missing pieces and connect the dots of our faith. I was to build bridges from God's original Word—the Torah—to the New Testament and to modern Christian theology and practices.

Tiz and I were to connect the dots of faith in yet more uncharted territory. Then we would see God's promises and covenant become reality in our everyday lives. We would learn to take God's Word and promises literally and personally—not as a book of history or an account of what God used to do but as a manual for today's living. Day by day we would learn how to believe Him and take Him at His Word. He would show us how to see the miracles of the Bible become reality today. He would teach us how to live with age-old biblical convictions, tradition, and perspective in a totally modern world. And He would reveal how to build a strong marriage and family on His foundations of faith in a completely contemporary and relevant way.

When we returned to our church and told our staff and congregation what had happened, I said, "This isn't a new teaching series. This is our new direction, foundation, purpose, and future!"

Today, I often share a funny illustration about God in a face-to-face conversation with Moses. God tells him, "I'm going to raise you up as a prophet to the world. But there's good news and bad news."

Moses asks, "What's the good news?"

God replies, "I'm going to show you things in the Word and give you prophetic insight that no one has ever heard before."

Moses says, "Wow! That's awesome! What's the bad news?"

God tells him, "I'm going to show you things in the Word and give you prophetic insight that no one has ever heard before."

That's funny, but it's pretty much what happened as all of this evolved! When we began connecting with and teaching the Jewish roots of our Christian faith, the road was pretty rocky. We had to figure out how everything fit with our conventional Christian lives and church. It was a lot for us and the congregation to process. In the beginning it was not well received, to say the least! This truly was an uncharted course.

Now, twenty-five years later, the message of connecting to our Judeo-Christian roots has become fairly common and well received. Back then, however, it was neither. I don't mean to be negative or dramatic, but we had to plow through thousands of years of religious traditions. We knew we had chosen the road less traveled, and we paid a heavy price in sticking with it. But we were able to condense thousands of years of teachings into a user-friendly guide that we could live in a real-time, real-life way. And we were able to take it to the world.

Tiz and I knew that God had opened our eyes and led us to new ground, so we pressed in deeper and pushed harder to take our church, our TV program, and our books there too. All of it was uncharted territory, and it was very exciting.

## HEARTS TURNING TOWARD ISRAEL AND OUR JEWISH ROOTS

I'm thrilled to say that in the last several years, the teaching of our Jewish roots has taken off like a rocket. Ancient prophecies are unfolding before our very eyes, and hearts are turning and returning to Israel and the Jewish roots and foundations of our faith. This is happening in our church, our global TV program, our books, and our media and streaming ministry. People from every country, nationality, and background are spiritually hungry, fascinated, and searching for deeper truths and revelations in the Word. We're seeing incredible response worldwide. And as our people are pressing in closer to God and His Word, He is pouring out His Spirit in signs, wonders, and miracles.

This is happening because believers are connecting deeply to His Word, His covenant, and His promises. It is fresh, and it is life changing. It is also powerful and anointed. Testimonies continually pour in about the great miracles God is doing in people's lives, health, families, businesses, ministries, and finances. It's not just about gaining more head knowledge. It is about God changing lives and releasing His promises.

As God reveals ancient mysteries in His Word, He is releasing His miracles in the world! The unchurched and churched, businesspeople and street people, young and old, and Christians and the Jewish people are coming together and realizing that we serve the same God—the God of Abraham, Isaac, and Jacob. As we all work together to *tikkun olam* (repair a broken world), we are building bridges and God is restoring broken lives!

We are immensely honored and humbled that God would allow us to be a leading voice and influence in bringing this end-time message to people everywhere. We believe that we are truly in the beginning of the end-time outpouring of salvation and miracles! Without a doubt, this revelation is for "such a time as this" (Est. 4:14).

## A HEART FOR GOD, HIS WORD, AND HIS PEOPLE

Tiz and I have been pastoring for more than forty years. What drives us to press into God's Word through study and prayer is seeing people's lives set free! Our life's calling and purpose have led us to this place in this hour.

My whole life is about studying God's Word and drawing out the meaning, truth, hidden mysteries, and nuggets of revelation—not for the sake of sounding deeply spiritual but to see God's promises become real for us and for others, whether relationally, financially, physically, or in terms of the future.

The amazing thing about God's Word is that it isn't only about spiritual truths and principles. It is also about earthly, physical, and natural wisdom, guidance, and help for everyday life. Ancient biblical truths become today's foundation and path to success. It is where we find victory, equipping, anointing, and miracles.

That is how it is with God. When you take hold and *own* the promises in His Word, they manifest in your life. Truly, when His mysteries are revealed, His miracles are released! That is my prayer for you as we take this journey together.

Regardless of what you might think, God's Word is not legalistic or restrictive. The *Law* is actually the path to all of God's goodness, joy, success, blessings, and miracles. If you place your life and world on this path, get ready to experience His absolute best life for you!

I've never been impressed by people who just spout deep, complex, or long-winded expositions. And I'm certainly not interested in doing it myself. My passion is to dig out deep truths that will change my life, my family, our congregations, and those who are lost, hopeless, desperate, and alone in the world. This book and these teachings are not just for those who know God and are hungry for more. They are also for those who don't have a clue about God, the Bible, or church but have a hunger for more. Whether you are a seasoned believer, a new believer, or an unbeliever, this book and the truths it presents will change your life. How? By revealing how much God loves you and wants to release every blessing into your life and future!

I had no idea how far this journey would take us, but I knew it was the path for me, my family, our ministry, and our destiny. Every day since our first trip to Israel has been an amazing adventure of discovering the Jewish roots and covenants of our Christian faith and sharing them with the world. It has been a time of uncovering ancient mysteries in the Word, which in turn releases the miracles of God. The journey has not been for our personal understanding alone. It was always meant to be shared in order that God's blessings and miracles might also be shared.

Join me on this exciting road! I invite you to open your heart, mind, and soul as we venture into uncharted waters and go treasure hunting in the ancient Word of God. Together we will get to know Jesus—our Jewish Rabbi, Messiah, and Savior. Join the quest to discover and recover the ancient stones and markers of our Jewish faith. Explore the foundations and God's Torah— ancient Jewish wisdom from the prophets of old and from the apostles of our faith.

As God's mysteries and prophecies are revealed to you, His miracles, blessings, and promises will be released into your life, your future, and your destiny.

Welcome! This is the journey of a lifetime!

—Pastor Larry

# PART I

---

## THE PROPHECIES

## CHAPTER 1

# JESUS, OUR JEWISH MESSIAH

*I, Jesus, have sent My angel to testify to you these
things in the churches. I am the Root and the
Offspring of David, the Bright and Morning Star.*
—Revelation 22:16

O NE OF THE Bible's most important questions is the one
Jesus asked His disciples: "Who do men say that I, the
Son of Man, am?" (Matt. 16:13). In verse 14 they answered,
"Some say John the Baptist, some Elijah, and others Jeremiah or
one of the prophets."

Then Jesus asked *the* most important question in Scripture:
"But who do *you* say that I am?" (v. 15).

What would our answer be if Jesus asked us this question? And
why is the answer important? It's because we cannot know all that
Jesus has for us today until we know who He was two thousand
years ago. We already know for certain that He was Jewish. So the
first of our seven living prophecies, and one of the most important
of our time, is rediscovering the Jewishness of Jesus.

---

### LIVING PROPHECY 1

The mystery of God's full intent through our Jewish Jesus
has been hidden until now but will be made known to all the
world and will usher in the great end-time outpouring of God.

In 2008 *Time* contributor David Van Biema wrote about "re-
Judaizing Jesus," one of the "ten ideas that are changing the
world."[1] He described the growing phenomenon that is restoring
the truth of a Jewish Jesus and changing the destiny of the

church. He also quoted New Testament scholar Amy-Jill Levine, who said, "If you get the [Jewish] context wrong, you will certainly get Jesus wrong."[2]

The article claimed that Christianity's journey in this regard began by "cherry-picking Jewish texts," so that Christians separated their idea of Judaism's "dry legalism" from their sense of a Savior who "embodied God's new covenant of love." Once they realized "that Jesus was born a Jew and did Jewish things," Christians acknowledged that both He and the apostle Paul "saw themselves as Jews." Today many Christians admit that although Jesus "rewove" His Jewish ideas, He never rejected them.[3]

I wrote this book because recognizing Jesus' Jewishness is essential, especially for the church. Currently Christians fall into four categories on the issue. One group denies Jesus' Jewishness altogether. Their position, whether they realize it or not, denies scriptural truth and is rooted in a spirit of anti-Semitism. The second group hasn't thought about Jesus as being Jewish and wonders whether it matters or has any relevance. The third group accepts Jesus' Jewishness in much the same way they accept Albert Einstein, Sigmund Freud, or Jerry Seinfeld being Jewish. People in the fourth group, however, realize that Jesus was Jewish not only by blood but by religion, lifestyle practices, and traditions. They also recognize that He never stopped being Jewish in any way.

What difference does it make? All the difference in the world! When we embrace the teachings not of a Protestant or Catholic Jesus but of a Jesus who was born, lived, and died Jewish, we embrace a paramount truth for ourselves and the world. It's a far cry from what most Gentile Christians have been led to believe: that Jesus abandoned Jewish religious practices such as Sabbath keeping, obedience to the Torah, kosher eating, and celebrating the feasts.

Imagine the most famous Jewish person of all time being remembered as a Christian! Even His name was changed from the Hebrew Yehoshua (often shortened to Yeshua) to the Greek form, Jesus.[4] And although followers called Him Rabbi, many Bible translations changed the title to Teacher, which sounds less Hebraic. Even the name of His homeland was changed from Israel to Palestine.

Understanding or rediscovering the Jewishness of Jesus does more than help us understand what Scripture says about the past; it is also the key to a future where Jewish people and Christians walk together.

## A JEWISH JESUS CHANGES US

What does God's Word tell us about a Jewish Jesus and the patriarchs Abraham, Isaac, and Jacob? What are the revelations of Bible prophecy that await our understanding, and how will they change our lives? The Book of Acts shows us what to expect when the Messiah returns:

> It shall come to pass in the last days, says God, that I will pour out of My Spirit on all flesh; your sons and your daughters shall prophesy, your young men shall see visions, your old men shall dream dreams.
>
> —Acts 2:17

This speaks of the latter rain, the great outpouring of God's power and Spirit that every child of God longs to see—a time of signs, wonders, and great miracles of every conceivable kind. Prophecies that are true to God's Word show we are on the threshold of God's anointing being poured out like never before. Haggai 2:9 says, "The glory of this present house will be greater than the glory of the former house" (NIV). It's not a matter of "maybe." The Lord said, it "*will* be greater."

How do we prepare for what God is about to do? I've heard it said that if you know where you came from, there is no limit on what you can accomplish or where you can go. And that is absolutely right. You cannot understand where you are going until you know where you have been. That wisdom is true for the children of God. We need to recognize our Jewish Jesus and our Jewish roots. That is the first step toward restoring unity between Jewish people and the church.

In the article "The New Judaizers" Dan Hummel wrote about how American Pentecostals incorporate "Jewish trappings" into their theology, traditions, and politics. He explains that "incorporating Jewish symbols and practices…has usually been regarded as dangerous to the gatekeepers of Christian orthodoxy" and is therefore called "Judaizing." Hummel adds that the early church father Ignatius said that Judaizing was "absurd" because "Christianity did not embrace Judaism, but Judaism [embraced] Christianity."[5]

Not surprisingly, the term Judaizing became a term of derision.[6] However, this Christian mindset was challenged in the late twentieth century with "outside help" from biblical scholars, including Professor Joseph Klausner, who wrote that "Jesus is the most Jewish of Jews…more Jewish even than Hillel."[7]

Let me pause here to share something amazing that happened while I was writing this book. I was invited to Jerusalem to teach members of parliaments from around the world about Bible prophecy concerning Israel and the Jewish people. At one point our group was invited to Prime Minister Netanyahu's office. When the prime minister opened the floor for questions, all of them involved politics, the West Bank, Judea, Samaria, and other issues concerning his nation.

Before we closed the meeting, my good friend Josh Reinstein (director of the Knesset Christian Allies Caucus and president of the Israeli Allies Foundation) said, "We have time for one more question." He added, "Since Pastor Larry Huch is the only religious leader in our group, I would like him to ask the last question."

I asked Prime Minister Netanyahu, "How important is the discovery of the Pilgrimage Road?" I will talk about this consequential archaeological discovery in a later chapter. For now let me share Mr. Netanyahu's response.

He said, "The Pilgrimage Road is the road my ancestors and Christians walked together two thousand years ago to worship God." Then he talked about his father's best friend, Joseph Klausner, whom I just mentioned. Mr. Netanyahu said that when he was a little boy, he and his brother would visit Professor Klausner's home every week, and the professor would tell them about the books he was writing. Now, as the world was rediscovering a Jewish Jesus, the prime minister of Israel told us about a man who believed Jesus was more Jewish than one of Judaism's great rabbis!

In his must-read article Hummel described the role of Klausner and other scholars, Pentecostalism, archaeology, and discoveries such as the Dead Sea Scrolls in revealing and mainstreaming a Judaized view of Jesus.[8] He mentioned Professor Brad H. Young, who made this important statement: "Though the life of Jesus was originally compiled by the Jewish disciples and for the Jewish disciples, it was preserved by the Gentile church and for the Gentile church."[9]

The mistake the church made was to separate Christianity from its Judaic roots. The Judeo-Christian tradition is real, and Christians by the millions are embracing it. I am thankful for theologians and other scholars who have helped us find our way, but I am even more excited to see a new Judeo-Christian unity in the pews, among everyday Christians.

## WHAT RELIGION WAS JESUS?

This chapter started with Jesus' question: "Who do you say that I am?" (Matt. 16:15). So let's begin by establishing His religion, starting with Matthew 1:16: "Jacob begot Joseph the husband of Mary, of whom was born Jesus who is called Christ." In other words, Jesus was born Jewish, into a Jewish family.

If you're like me, certain portions of Scripture seem uninteresting at first glance. Take the first chapter of Matthew's Gospel, for example: "And so and so begat this guy, and he begat this other guy." That seems boring until you read the Gospel's opening verse carefully: "The book of the genealogy of Jesus Christ, the Son of David, the Son of Abraham" (Matt. 1:1).

This is Jesus' family tree! Although people who were not Jewish, such as Ruth and Rahab, were included in Jesus' earthly bloodline, the list is essentially Jewish. Jesus was born to Mary and Joseph, who lived observant Jewish lives. Jesus was circumcised on the eighth day, and "His name was called Jesus [Yeshua], the name given by the angel before He was conceived in the womb" (Luke 2:21). His circumcision was according to Jewish law. "On the eighth day the flesh of his foreskin [was] circumcised" (Lev. 12:3). The practice of circumcision began when God commanded it as a sign of His covenant:

> This is My covenant which you shall keep, between Me and you and your descendants after you: Every male child among you shall be circumcised; and you shall be circumcised in the flesh of your foreskins, and it shall be a sign of the covenant between Me and you. He who is eight days old among you shall be circumcised, every male child in your generations.
>
> —Genesis 17:10–12

Mary and Joseph lived their Jewish religious roots. Faithful to the Torah, Mary immersed herself in a ritual bath called the *mikvah*, as Luke 2:22 reveals: "When the days of her purification according to the law of Moses were completed, they brought Him to Jerusalem to present Him to the Lord." According to Scripture, a mother is impure for forty days after the birth of a son. After forty days she must bring to the temple an offering for her purification, as prescribed in Leviticus 12:1–8. Mary followed the Law perfectly, and her commitment as a fully observant Jewish woman should speak to our own faith.

## JESSE, THE FATHER OF KING DAVID

Jesus' last recorded words in Scripture were "Surely I am coming quickly" (Rev. 22:20). We all await the coming of the Messiah. But look at what Jesus said four verses earlier: "I am the Root and the Offspring of David, the Bright and Morning Star" (Rev. 22:16).

Why must Jesus remind the church that He descended from King David? It is because, for almost two thousand years, the church seemed to forget it. More than likely Jesus had brown skin. Some would even say he was a Sephardic Jewish man. But the European church presented Him differently. Artists painted Jesus as a light-skinned, blue-eyed, light-haired man in a Roman robe. These images purposefully steal Jesus' true identity from us. He and His disciples were not the only ones whose images were altered. Michelangelo's famous sculpture of an uncircumcised David denies his Jewishness too.

This was not accidental. It seems that Europe's early church leaders did not want to see Jesus or other "good" Bible figures as Jewish. When Jewish-looking people appeared in works of art, they were usually Jesus' enemies, including Judas, the high priest, the Sadducees, and the angry mobs who shouted for Him to be crucified. The message was plain: Jewish people were to be seen as the bad guys. Jesus and His disciples had to be distanced from their Jewish ethnic and religious roots.

Jesus' heritage showed in more than His physical features. Not only was He circumcised, but He was a fully Torah-observant Jewish man and completely obedient to the Scriptures, even down to the tallit (prayer shawl) He wore as a Jewish man and a rabbi.

> Speak to the children of Israel: tell them to make tassels on the corners of their garments throughout their generations, and to put a blue thread in the tassels of the corners. And you shall have the tassel, that you may look upon it and remember all the commandments of the LORD and do them, and that you may not follow the harlotry to which your own heart and your own eyes are inclined, and that you may remember and do all My commandments, and be holy for your God. I am the LORD your God, who brought you out of the land of Egypt, to be your God: I am the LORD your God.
> —NUMBERS 15:38–41

> You shall make tassels on the four corners of the clothing
> with which you cover yourself.
> —DEUTERONOMY 22:12

Such details are important because they are meaningful to all Jewish people. For example, the corners of a tallit have tassels, or fringes, called *tzitzit*, representing the number 613.[10] Only a Jewish person would understand the significance of the tzitzit. They are the reason the woman with the issue of blood wanted to touch the hem of Jesus' garment:

> Behold, a woman, which was diseased with an issue of
> blood twelve years, came behind him, and touched the
> hem of his garment: for she said within herself, If I may
> but touch his garment, I shall be whole.
> —MATTHEW 9:20–21, KJV

Before I personally discovered the Jewishness of Jesus, I pictured the woman reaching for Jesus' plain white robe. But the hem of His garment was the corner of His prayer shawl. Why would this woman tell herself "If I touch the *wing* of His garment, I will be made whole"? I believe it's connected to the Jewish teaching in the Book of Malachi, which speaks of Messiah's coming, saying, "The Sun of Righteousness shall arise with healing in His wings" (Mal. 4:2).

The number represented by the tzitzit, 613, is the number of commandments in the Hebrew Scriptures. It represents God's promises, His Word. When the suffering woman saw Jesus, she knew He had come with "healing in His wings." She was Jewish, and she knew Jesus was Jewish too.

## JEWISH FEASTS, CELEBRATIONS, AND CONNECTIONS TO CHRISTIANITY

Through Scripture we learn about Jesus' upbringing and observance of the Hebrew religious calendar, which marked the Jewish feasts and holy days. Both Jesus and His disciples were faithful to Judaism.

### Jesus and the Passover (Pesach)

Luke revealed that Jesus' "parents went to Jerusalem every year at the Feast of the Passover. And when He was twelve years old, they went up to Jerusalem according to the custom of the feast" (Luke 2:41–42). They were obeying the Torah's command to "observe the month of Abib, and keep the Passover to the LORD your God, for in the month of Abib the LORD your God brought you out of Egypt by night" (Deut. 16:1).

Jesus and His disciples kept the feasts, as Luke's Gospel shows: "Then came the Day of Unleavened Bread, when the Passover must be killed. And He sent Peter and John, saying, 'Go and prepare the Passover for us, that we may eat'" (Luke 22:7–8). Mark's Gospel also shows that the disciples never questioned Jesus' observance of the Passover. They simply asked Him, "Where do You want us to go and prepare, that You may eat the Passover?" (Mark 14:12).

They believed and obeyed the words of Leviticus 23:4: "These are the feasts of the LORD, holy convocations which you shall proclaim at their appointed time."

### Shavuot and Pentecost

The Jewish feasts are connected to Christian events. Did you know that the Hebrew feast of Shavuot and the celebration of Pentecost coincide? My wife Tiz often shares that she grew up believing that the day of Pentecost began in the Book of Acts. But Pentecost did not originate with Christianity; it began in Judaism, as Shavuot.

Pentecost simply means fifty, or "the fiftieth day."[11] Rabbinic thought holds that "Shavuot coincided with…God giving His Torah to Moses on Mt. Sinai."[12] The Exodus began when the Israelites left Egypt, the morning after the first Passover. According to Numbers 33:3, this was on the fifteenth day of the first month. Exodus 19:1 says they arrived in Sinai in the third month. Some believe it was the first day of the third month. Assuming that is accurate, approximately forty days would have passed when Moses ascended Mount Sinai. We know he stayed there for several days before returning with the stone tablets, so Shavuot would have been approximately fifty days after Passover.[13]

Now let's look at God's instructions, first regarding Shavuot:

> You shall count for yourselves from the day after the Sabbath, from the day that you brought the sheaf of the wave offering: seven Sabbaths shall be completed. Count fifty days to the day after the seventh Sabbath; then you shall offer a new grain offering to the LORD. You shall bring from your dwellings two wave loaves of two-tenths of an ephah. They shall be of fine flour; they shall be baked with leaven. They are the firstfruits to the LORD.
>
> —LEVITICUS 23:15–17

The teachings of Moses are connected to the teachings of Jesus. In the passage from Leviticus, the Mosaic Law commanded the Israelites to wait fifty days. Jesus also told His disciples to wait, this time in Jerusalem, for the baptism with the Holy Spirit:

> Being assembled together with them, He commanded them not to depart from Jerusalem, but to wait for the Promise of the Father, "which," He said, "you have heard from Me; for John truly baptized with water, but you shall be baptized with the Holy Spirit not many days from now." Therefore, when they had come together, they asked Him, saying, "Lord, will You at this time restore the kingdom to Israel?" And He said to them, "It is not for you to know times or seasons which the Father has put in His own authority. But you shall receive power when the Holy Spirit has come upon you; and you shall be witnesses to Me in Jerusalem, and in all Judea and Samaria, and to the end of the earth."
>
> —ACTS 1:4–8

Jesus did not suggest that they wait. He commanded them to stay put. This time period was important because it was a time of Shabbat, one of God's appointed times known as *moadim*.[14] It was also critical in birthing the church. You could say that on Shavuot, God birthed Judaism by giving the Torah. On the day of Pentecost, He birthed the church so that "when the Day of Pentecost had fully come, they were all with one accord in one place" (Acts 2:1).

Now let's look at how Scripture describes what happened on Shavuot and Pentecost, beginning with events on Mount Sinai:

> Then it came to pass on the third day, in the morning, that there were thunderings and lightnings, and a thick cloud on the mountain; and the sound of the trumpet was very loud, so that all the people who were in the camp trembled. And Moses brought the people out of the camp to meet with God, and they stood at the foot of the mountain. Now Mount Sinai was completely in smoke, because the LORD descended upon it in fire. Its smoke ascended like the smoke of a furnace, and the whole mountain quaked greatly.
>
> —EXODUS 19:16–18

Notice how similar this is to events on the day of Pentecost:

> Suddenly there came a sound from heaven, as of a rushing mighty wind, and it filled the whole house where they were sitting. Then there appeared to them divided tongues, as of fire, and one sat upon each of them.
>
> —ACTS 2:2–3

Judaism, with the giving of the Law, and Christianity, with the coming of the Holy Spirit, started on the same day. That is no coincidence! There is so much more I could say, but for now I will recommend my books *The Torah Blessing*, *Unveiling Ancient Biblical Secrets*, and *Four Blood Moons*, if you want to hear more.

## Chanukah

Chanukah is a great celebration of a major victory for Israel and the Jewish people. To make a very long story short, it marks the Maccabees' victory over the brutal forces of Antiochus IV Epiphanes, who slaughtered Jewish people and desecrated the temple by sacrificing pigs on the altar.

A group of Jewish men defied and defeated the enemy army, which was a great miracle of God all by itself! But when they reentered the temple to rededicate it to the God of Abraham, Isaac, and Jacob, they only had enough oil to keep the menorah burning for one day. By a miracle of God, the lamp burned for eight days until new, consecrated oil was prepared. You can see why Chanukah is also called the Feast of Dedication, or the Festival of Lights.

Several years ago a very kind rabbi asked me to teach in a synagogue on why I love Israel and the Jewish people. He told me, "I don't know if anyone will show up, but please come."

By the grace of God, the synagogue was filled to capacity. I began by asking the people, "How many of you lit the Chanukah menorah at your home before you came here tonight?"

Everyone's hand went up. Then I asked, "Where does God's Word tell us about Chanukah?"

Everyone looked puzzled, because Chanukah is not mentioned in the Hebrew Bible. So I asked, "Did you know that Scripture speaks of Chanukah only in the New Testament, in John's Gospel?" Then I read the passage: "Now it was the Feast of Dedication in Jerusalem, and it was winter. And Jesus walked in the temple, in Solomon's porch" (John 10:22–23).

I shared this with my Jewish friends to let them know that the Jesus I know never stopped being Jewish. *Never.* When I began to realize this truth all those years ago, it gave me a whole new love for God's Word, the land of Israel, and the Jewish people.

## JESUS' VIEW OF GOD'S COMMANDMENTS

Obviously Jesus not only remained a committed Jewish man but also taught His followers to obey Moses' teachings, saying, "If you want to enter into life, keep the commandments" (Matt. 19:17). Jesus was not talking about eternal life but about a life of blessing—the kind of life He described when He said, "The thief does not come except to steal, and to kill, and to destroy. I have come that they may have life, and that they may have it more abundantly" (John 10:10).

I pray that you understand what the Lord is saying here. He didn't come just so we would enjoy heaven someday. He is inviting us to follow God's Word daily so that heaven can meet us here. Jesus' disciples learned this when they did what Jewish students still do today: they asked their Rabbi for guidance, saying, "Lord, teach us to pray, as John also taught his disciples'" (Luke 11:1).

Part of the prayer Jesus taught them includes these sentences: "Your kingdom come. Your will be done on earth as it is in heaven" (Luke 11:2). In heaven there is no sickness, poverty, or hatred. Jesus showed them that heaven could meet them where they were. They were to say, "Come, kingdom of God. Come, will of God. Come, miracles. Come, healing. Come, blessings of God in every area of our lives. Not someday, but *today!*"

Matthew 7:29 says that when Jesus taught, He did so "as one having authority, and not as the scribes." You might ask, "Do *we* have that kind of authority? Do we have that kind of spiritual power?"

Absolutely! Listen to what Jesus told Peter: "I will give you the keys of the kingdom of heaven, and whatever you bind on earth will be bound in heaven, and whatever you loose on earth will be loosed in heaven" (Matt. 16:19). The key is that our authority is connected to our obedience. When Jesus told His followers to obey, He did not pick and choose from the Law. When He told the rich young ruler to follow the commandments, the man asked, "Which ones?" (Matt. 19:18).

Jesus gave him the list, straight from the Law:

> "You shall not murder," "You shall not commit adultery,"
> "You shall not steal," "You shall not bear false witness,"
> "Honor your father and your mother," and, "You shall
> love your neighbor as yourself."
>                                                    —MATTHEW 19:18–19

Jesus reminded the man that the answer he sought was self-evident to every Jewish person. It's hard to believe that a very dangerous but popular teaching in today's church claims that when we ask Jesus into our hearts, we no longer need to follow God's commandments or laws. This error comes from a misunderstanding of the term *law* as it appears in Scripture. Very simply, the word *law*, as in God's Law, has to do with teaching, instruction, or direction,[15] not legalism. When the Bible commands, "Rejoice in the Lord always" (Phil. 4:4), it is sound instruction because Scripture also says that God inhabits the praises of His people (Ps. 22:3). When Psalm 141:3 says, "Set a guard, O LORD, over my mouth," it is wisdom because "death and life are in the power of the tongue" (Prov. 18:21).

The fact that we are saved by grace and not by works is absolutely true. But that does not mean anything goes. Can you imagine if I told Tiz, "I'm no longer under the curse of the Law; I'm under grace. So whatever the law says about adultery no longer applies to me." Tiz would promptly give a whole new meaning to the laying on of hands and the shedding of blood. It would be her hands and my blood!

My friend, Jesus did not come to remove us from God's Word and instruction. He came to connect us and graft us in. Look at what He said:

> You are the salt of the earth; but if the salt loses its flavor,
> how shall it be seasoned? It is then good for nothing
> but to be thrown out and trampled underfoot by men.
> You are the light of the world. A city that is set on a
> hill cannot be hidden. Nor do they light a lamp and

put it under a basket, but on a lampstand, and it gives
light to all who are in the house. Let your light so shine
before men, that they may see your good works and glorify your Father in heaven. Do not think that I came
to destroy the Law or the Prophets. I did not come to
destroy but to fulfill. For assuredly, I say to you, till
heaven and earth pass away, one jot or one tittle will by
no means pass from the law till all is fulfilled.

—Matthew 5:13–18

We are to be the "salt of the earth" and "the light of the world."
Whether Jewish or Gentile, God's children are supposed to be
different—not better than others but different because we live
according to God's Word.

Jesus said He "did not come to destroy [the Law or the
Prophets] but to fulfill" (Matt. 5:17). His coming did not wipe
away God's Torah. On the contrary, Jesus came to show us the
blessing of God, which is found by following His path. The Law
and the Prophets will not be done away with until the world
as we know it ends and the Messiah rules and reigns from the
temple in Jerusalem.

All of God's Word is relevant to us as His children. The words
*jot* and *tittle* in Matthew 5:18 reveal a powerful secret hidden
in ancient Jewish wisdom. The Hebrew for *jot* is the Hebrew
letter *yod*, which looks like a comma hanging in the air. It's the
smallest Hebrew letter, but it may be the most powerful, because
it signifies God's presence.[16] When Jesus commands us not to
not remove *any* of God's Word, He is telling us not to remove
God's presence from His teachings.

Think about the devil's strategy of removing the Ten
Commandments from American schools and courthouses. It
was designed to remove God's presence! Jesus not only taught
God's Word but cited the Torah to defeat Satan. How? By saying,
"It is written" (Matt. 4:10) and then quoting God's words from the
Book of Deuteronomy. If Jesus used God's Word to defeat the

devil, so should we. We need to *know* His Word—not just the New Testament but also the Old Testament.

## ROOT AND BRANCH

If Jesus was a fully observant Jewish man, where did the term Christian come from, and what does it really mean? The answer is recorded in the story of Barnabas and Saul in Antioch, where "for a whole year they assembled with the church and taught a great many people. *And the disciples were first called Christians*" (Acts 11:26).

Obviously the term Christian did not begin with Jesus. In fact it only shows up three times in Scripture, in Acts 11:26; Acts 26:28; and 1 Peter 4:16. The name seems to have been created by other groups. Some believe it was used "flippantly or even derogatively by [the] powers-that-be—a sort of dismissive wave of the hand to those 'little Christs.'"[17] Personally I am proud to be associated with Christ. If someone wants to mock me for it, that's OK. First Peter 4:16 says, "If anyone suffers as a Christian, let him not be ashamed, but let him glorify God in this matter." I am not ashamed of who I am. I am a Christian.

The larger point here is about Jesus, the most famous Jewish person of all time, who is widely remembered as a Gentile Christian. That is a false separation, but Jesus did not create it. He did not come to separate us from the Jewish people or our Jewish roots. He came to connect us with them. The apostle Paul said it this way: "You [the Gentiles], being a wild olive tree, were grafted in among them [the Jewish people], and with them became a partaker of the root and fatness of the olive tree" (Rom. 11:17). The grafted-in branch does not support the root; the root supports the branch. Through Christ, Christians were joined to the Jewish people; it was not the other way around.

Paul was very clear on this. Even as the apostle to the Gentiles and a true follower of Jesus, Paul never left his Jewish roots and never renounced or converted away from his Judaism. In his book *Paul and Rabbinic Judaism*, W. D. Davies explains Paul's idea of

Christianity "as a form of his ancestral religion or as a further stage of its development, however 'new.'"[18] Here's how Paul said it in Romans 3:31: "Do we then make void the law through faith? Certainly not! On the contrary, we establish the law."

Paul quoted from the Old Testament often to establish the authority of his teachings. He never denigrated the Law. Quite the opposite! Paul said that "the law is holy, and the commandment holy and just and good" and wrote, "I delight in the law of God according to the inward man" (Rom. 7:12, 22). He also warned against lawlessness and said that "the man of lawlessness" would be a sign of the end times (2 Thess. 2:3, NIV).

Some in the church will refuse to recognize God's divine Law. Jesus Himself said that "many false prophets will rise up and deceive many. And because lawlessness will abound, the love of many will grow cold. But he who endures to the end shall be saved" (Matt. 24:11–13).

## THE AVOT

When I thought about writing this book, my focus was on the seven living prophecies that lead us to the latter rain, the great outpouring of God's power, Spirit, and blessings that precedes the Messiah's coming. I believed that showing a Jewish Jesus was the place to start. Everything we learn has a starting place, and that is the starting place of this teaching overall.

In ancient Jewish wisdom the starting point for understanding any mystery of the Bible is the *avot*. The avot is the foundation upon which our understanding of God's Word is built. The Book of Hebrews picks up on this idea when it instructs us to grow in God's wisdom, moving from the "milk" of His word to the "meat" (Heb. 5:12). The starting place in our learning is the avot. The word "literally means 'fathers,' but...it also refers to fundamental principles."[19] It is the most important part of the teaching or revelation. If we miss the avot, we will not understand what God is saying.

Let me give you an example from Paul's epistle to the Ephesians:

> Finally, my brethren, be strong in the Lord and in the power of His might. Put on the whole armor of God, that you may be able to stand against the wiles of the devil. For we do not wrestle against flesh and blood, but against principalities, against powers, against the rulers of the darkness of this age, against spiritual hosts of wickedness in the heavenly places. Therefore take up the whole armor of God, that you may be able to withstand in the evil day, and having done all, to stand.
>
> Stand therefore, having girded your waist with truth, having put on the breastplate of righteousness, and having shod your feet with the preparation of the gospel of peace; above all, taking the shield of faith with which you will be able to quench all the fiery darts of the wicked one. And take the helmet of salvation, and the sword of the Spirit, which is the word of God.
>
> —EPHESIANS 6:10–17

Paul tells us to be strong in the Lord and adds that our battle is not with flesh and blood. Our battle is with principalities, powers of darkness, and the hosts of wickedness. The way we prepare to win the battle is by putting on the "whole armor of God." Then Paul names all the parts of our armor and tells us that they are mighty spiritual weapons.

But what is the avot of the teaching? Well, what is the first piece of armor God names? It's in verse 14: "having girded your waist with *truth*." Where the armor of God is concerned, the avot is truth! That's what gives life and meaning to the remaining armor pieces.

Now think about the avot in terms of the Ten Commandments. We are to embrace all ten, but we cannot do that until we grab hold of the first, which says, "I am the LORD your God, who brought you out of the land of Egypt, out of the house of bondage.

You shall have no other gods before Me" (Exod. 20:2–3). In other words, to walk in God's blessing, you must first know who your Lord is.

The avot is important in every time and teaching. It is certainly important as we approach the threshold of the greatest outpouring of God's love and power that humankind has ever seen. And He has chosen you and me to be a part of it! This is why our starting point is to return to the Jewishness of Jesus. That, in my opinion, is the avot of all living prophecies.

Twenty-five years ago my first trip to Israel was the birth of a journey, the avot that led me here. At that time, I was seriously considering leaving the ministry. Nothing in particular was wrong. Our ministry and church were growing, and our kids were serving God. Yet I felt that something was missing.

I have to admit that I didn't go to Israel to find it. At first I didn't really want to go. But some good friends were going and invited us to join them. I told them I wasn't interested. After all, I was taught the same false teaching that many people have heard. It said that God was finished with the Jewish people as His chosen people and that the church had replaced them. For the record, this replacement theology is the root of much of what the devil has accomplished so far!

Thank God, our friends kept urging us to join them, and we finally relented. One of the first places we visited was ancient Capernaum, where much of Jesus' ministry happened. As our group walked through the gates, almost everyone went straight to where Peter is believed to have lived. But a friend from Jerusalem took us in another direction and showed us the remnants of an ancient synagogue. I noticed some ancient Hebrew writing on one of the synagogue's entry stones and asked my friend what the words said. He answered, "Those are the names."

"Whose names?" I asked.

"The names of some of the apostle's grandchildren or great-grandchildren."

My Jerusalem friend started to walk away, but I stopped him.

"I don't understand. Why are the names of the apostle's grand-children written on a synagogue?"

He answered, "Because they helped build it."

I was baffled. "You mean they weren't followers of Jesus?

"Of course they followed Jesus," he replied.

"Then why," I asked, "did they help build the synagogue? Why were they still part of Judaism?"

That was the moment my life changed forever.

"Larry," my friend said, "Jesus didn't come to separate us from Israel. He came to graft us into Israel."

I was stunned. *Grafted in.* I'd read the Book of Romans many, many times, but on that dirt path in ancient Capernaum the words came alive to me. Next to being born again and filled with the Holy Spirit, it was the most spiritual moment of my Christian life. I clearly heard the voice of God in my heart, saying, "Larry, I'm going to teach you to reread My Word not with American eyes or Western eyes but Jewish eyes."

Little did I know that over the next twenty-five years I would see Israel and the Jewish people from a totally different perspective. I would see the Jewish people as the apple of God's eye, and I would see His Word in many wonderful new ways.

This is the avot of the Christian journey: having our eyes opened to the Jewishness of Jesus. Look at what Dr. Brad Young says about the "new picture" I began to see:

> The religion of the Jews in the first century is the root which produced the fruit of Christian faith. Faith. Faith in Jesus, however, has sometimes made it difficult for Christians to understand and appreciate the faith of Jesus. The religion of Jesus and his people was Judaism. Christian faith in Jesus sometimes has alienated Jesus from ancient Judaism and has exiled him from his people.... Theologians have read the Gospels as Christian literature written by the church and for the church. When Jesus is viewed among the Gentiles, the significance of Jewish culture and custom is minimized

or forgotten altogether. But when Jesus is viewed as a Jew within the context of first-century Judaism, an entirely different portrait emerges.[20]

When I first started teaching on the Jewish roots of our faith, some people thought I'd gone a little crazy. Even some of my best friends asked me if I was still a Christian. My response then is the same now: understanding the Jewishness of Jesus hasn't made me less of a Christian, but it has made me a much stronger and, I hope, better one.

Today Gentile eyes are being opened all around the world. It is just as the prophet Jeremiah said:

> O LORD, my strength and my fortress, My refuge in the day of affliction, the Gentiles shall come to You from the ends of the earth and say, "Surely our fathers have inherited lies, worthlessness and unprofitable things." Will a man make gods for himself, which are not gods? "Therefore behold, I will this once cause them to know, I will cause them to know My hand and My might; and they shall know that My name is the LORD."
> —JEREMIAH 16:19–21

What Jeremiah prophesied is happening around the world, and there's more truth to come. People often say, "The truth will set you free," but that is not exactly what Jesus said. He said, "If you hold to my teaching, you are really my disciples. *Then* you will know the truth, and the truth will set you free" (John 8:31–32, NIV). Jesus was talking about the avot of our armor, which is truth. We can be "more than conquerors" when we know the truth (Rom. 8:37).

Recently I taught on Psalm 37:23: "The steps of a good [or righteous] man are ordered by the LORD, and He delights in his way." I mentioned Noah, whom the Bible says was "a righteous man, blameless in his generation" (Gen. 6:9, ESV). No matter what happened around Noah, he followed God. I explained to the church that God doesn't alter the robe to fit the man; he alters the man to fit the robe.

The same principle applied to the church in Jesus' day. Jewish people and Gentiles came together as one. Gentiles came to faith in Christ and enjoyed themselves with God's chosen people. The Gentiles adjusted to Israel; Israel did not adjust to the Gentiles. In every corner of the globe God is adjusting the church to fit back into our Jewish roots.

If you have ever heard Tiz and me teach, you've heard us say again and again that there is no word for *coincidence* in the ancient Hebrew language. The Lord reveals what He reveals with purpose. That's why Jesus said, "He who has ears to hear, let him hear!" (Matt. 11:15). When He taught in parables, the disciples asked Him, "Why?" (Matt. 13:10). Jesus' answer was profound:

> Because it has been given to you to know the mysteries of the kingdom of heaven, but to them it has not been given. For whoever has, to him more will be given, and he will have abundance; but whoever does not have, even what he has will be taken away from him. Therefore I speak to them in parables, because seeing they do not see, and hearing they do not hear, nor do they understand. And in them the prophecy of Isaiah is fulfilled, which says:
> "Hearing you will hear and shall not understand, and seeing you will see and not perceive; for the hearts of this people have grown dull. Their ears are hard of hearing, and their eyes they have closed, lest they should see with their eyes and hear with their ears, lest they should understand with their hearts and turn, so that I should heal them." But blessed are your eyes for they see, and your ears for they hear.
>
> —MATTHEW 13:11–16

Jesus said that even though they had physical eyes, they could not see what was happening in the spiritual world. In Hebrew one of the differences between eyes that don't see and eyes that do is that tiny letter we talked about earlier—*yod*. Remember that yod signifies the presence of God. Jesus said, "Don't remove the yod (the jot)." In other words, "If you don't remove God from your life or from the understanding of His Word, you will see what He is doing in the world right now!"

It was no coincidence that God took me to Israel that first time. He did it to open my eyes to a Jewish Jesus. It is also no coincidence that you are reading this book. Remember, you can only get to where you're going when you know where you started! So let me ask you one more question before closing this chapter: Have you met your Rabbi?

His name is Jesus! May God open the eyes of our understanding to His Jewishness and to all the wonderful revelations that will follow. I pray that if your journey into the blessings and the power of God has not yet begun, it would begin now.

Your best is yet to come!

## CHAPTER 2

# BREAKING THE CURSE, RELEASING THE BLESSING

*I will make you a great nation; I will bless you and make your name great; and you shall be a blessing. I will bless those who bless you, and I will curse him who curses you.*
—GENESIS 12:2–3

ACK WHEN TIZ and I lived in Portland, Oregon, we had a horse pasture that needed seeding. Being from the inner city, I didn't know much about seeds and horse pastures. But I knew that my field was full of weeds and my tractor had a mower. So I got on my tractor and mowed down every weed I could find.

With the mowing done, I borrowed a neighbor's plow and prepared the field. Then I went to the feed store, bought the best pasture seed I could find, and sowed it evenly throughout the field. Within a couple of days, the rain came. I thought, "This is going to be great—a horse pasture with beautiful grass!"

A week or so later the grass came up and looked perfect—but not for long. Soon I saw weeds coming up with the blades of grass. Before long the weeds were taller than the grass. And within a couple of months the weeds overtook my harvest until the grass was completely wiped out.

I was disappointed and confused. I told the man in the feed store, "I think there's something wrong with the seed I bought." Then I explained what happened to my horse pasture. I still remember the look on the man's face. It was something between pity and "How dumb *are* you?"

Then he asked me a question that radically changed my understanding of farming and of the Bible: "Did you kill the weeds before you planted the seed?"

"Kill the weeds?" I asked. "No! I just cut them down."

"Larry, that's not good enough. Unless you kill the weeds, they will kill your harvest every time!"

I know it sounds simple, but it was a revelation. And just as with everything God teaches us, ancient Jewish wisdom says the lesson had two meanings: one was earthly (or physical), and one was heavenly (or spiritual).

A teaching of Jesus speaks to my seed experience:

> Another parable he put forth to them, saying; "The kingdom of heaven is like a man who sowed good seed in his field; but while men slept, his enemy came and sowed tares among the wheat and went his way. But when the grain had sprouted and produced a crop, then the tares also appeared. So the servants of the owner came and said to him, 'Sir, did you not sow good seed in your field? How then does it have tares?' He said to them, 'An enemy has done this.'"
>
> —MATTHEW 13:24–28

In this parable the Lord said that the tares are a curse from the enemy to steal our blessings and choke the harvests God wants us to reap—the very things Jesus purchased through His blood and life. The question we need to ask ourselves is whether *any* curse is blocking any blessing and destroying our harvest. If so, we need to remove it. In the parable it means killing the tares so the harvest can come forth. But before we can remove the tares, we need to know what caused them.

Let's take this issue all the way back to the avot of blessing, which opened this chapter:

> Now the LORD had said to Abram: "Get out of your country, from your family and from your father's house, to a land that I will show you. I will make you a great

nation; I will bless you and make your name great; and you shall be a blessing. I will bless those who bless you, and I will curse him who curses you; and in you all the families of the earth shall be blessed."

—GENESIS 12:1–3

Remember that God was speaking to Abraham, who died four thousand years ago. But was He speaking *only* to Abraham, or are blessings and curses passed on from Abraham to his descendants? The answer is that everything God spoke to Abraham was passed on to Isaac, Jacob, their entire family, the nation of Israel, and now the church. God will bless anyone who blesses Abraham and Israel.

As Christians we tend to believe in the blessings of God. The Hebrew word for *blessed* is *barak*, which means "to bless, kneel...be blessed."[1] Another Hebrew word that is related to *barak* is *berakhah* (also spelled *b'rakha*), meaning a present, a gift, or a benediction.[2] When God spoke about blessing those who bless Israel, we have no doubt that He wanted to bless us. But what did He mean when He said, "I will curse him who curses you"? Do we believe that too?

When God promised to bless us for blessing Israel, *He meant it*. And when He said He would curse us for cursing Israel, He meant that too. The word translated "curse" in Genesis 12 is *arar*. It also appears in Jeremiah 17:5, when the Lord said, "Cursed is the man who trusts in man and makes flesh his strength, whose heart departs from the LORD."

*Arar* means "to curse...to be cursed."[3] When God warned that those who curse Israel would be cursed, it meant that His presence and protection would no longer be with those who harm Israel or the Jewish people. In Jeremiah 17 *arar* is in the passive voice,[4] meaning the cursing is not an action taken by God but a result of His protective covering being removed.

Are you getting this? When we bless Israel and the Jewish people, God becomes actively involved with blessing and protecting us. But when our words or actions bring harm to Israel or the Jewish people, we become exposed and vulnerable to the enemy's attacks. Both scenarios are real!

## KILLING THE WEEDS, RECEIVING THE BLESSING

Before we talk about how nations become cursed, let's look at how it happens in individual lives. Some years ago I wrote *Free at Last: Breaking Generational Curses* because I realized that even as a Christian and a pastor I had some serious problems that I couldn't seem to break through.

When I first gave my life to the Lord, I was immediately delivered from drug addiction. I was a first-time visitor to a church; I was also a drug addict and dealer. Yet I walked out of that church forgiven and set free. It was supernatural. My drug abuse was so bad at that time that my mother never expected to see me alive again. She thought for sure that I would die in a drug deal or suffer an overdose.

My mother understood the severity of my problem. We both knew what the world says about addicts: "Once a junkie, always a junkie." Thank God, His Word says something else: "If the Son makes you free, you shall be free indeed" (John 8:36).

As I grew in the Lord, drugs and addictions were no longer a problem. But anger and violence were. I was a born-again Christian and the pastor of our second church. We were having great revival, but my anger was explosive. The tares (the weeds or curses) were still growing, choking out my blessing and God's gift of a phenomenal family.

One day, as we pastored our church in Australia, my anger erupted. My son, who is now my associate pastor, was just a little boy. In anger I grabbed and shoved him. When I saw him bounce off the wall, I remembered my dad doing the same thing to me. I told the Lord and myself something that began breaking the curse that was killing my harvest. I said, "I'm just like my dad."

My father later received the Lord into his heart and is in heaven today. But when I was growing up, he was without God and knew nothing about the Bible. When I mistreated my son, I had no such excuse. I was a Christian and a pastor. But when I said, "I'm just like my dad," I wondered, "Can I find an answer to this issue in the Bible?"

Remember: everything in God's Word has a physical side and a spiritual side. Just as the weeds from Jesus' parable choked out the wheat, the curses choke out our spiritual blessings. God's Word speaks specifically about how this is a generational issue:

> I, the LORD your God, am a jealous God, visiting the iniquity of the fathers upon the children to the third and fourth generations of those who hate Me.
> —EXODUS 20:5

> The LORD God…keeping mercy for thousands, forgiving iniquity and transgression and sin, by no means clearing the guilty, visiting the iniquity of the fathers upon the children and the children's children to the third and the fourth generation.
> —EXODUS 34:6–7

You can inherit your physical family's "weeds." Nobody who (God forbid) has had an alcoholic parent wants to become an alcoholic, for example. Yet it happens time and time again. Without going too far into the subject of breaking generational curses, I want you to see that every curse can be broken by the blood of Jesus, which He shed in seven places. Yes, I said seven!

1. In the Garden of Gethsemane
2. At the whipping post
3. From the crown of thorns
4. From the nails in His hands
5. From the nail through His feet
6. From the spear that pierced His side
7. From stomping on the devil's head and bruising His heel at the gates of hell

When we look at the seven places Jesus shed His blood, it reconnects us to His Jewishness. But it also reminds us that He did more than die for our sins; He also broke every generational curse. Now look with me again at the question Jesus asked His disciples: "Who do men say that I, the Son of Man, am?" (Matt. 16:13).

The disciples had several answers, but Peter gave the right one, saying "You are the Christ, the Son of the living God" (Matt. 16:16). He responded in a Jewish way to a Jewish question from a Jewish Jesus: "You are the Christ"! To a Jewish person the Christ was the Anointed One who came to do two things: (1) remove the burden; and (2) break every yoke.

Now let's see the Jewish revelation here, which is about the Day of Atonement, Yom Kippur, the holiest day in the Hebrew calendar. That is when the high priest gave offerings for two different reasons:

> He shall take from the congregation of the children of Israel two kids of the goats as a sin offering, and one ram as a burnt offering. Aaron shall offer the bull as a sin offering, which is for himself, and make atonement for himself and for his house. He shall take the two goats and present them before the LORD at the door of the tabernacle of meeting. Then Aaron shall cast lots for the two goats: one lot for the LORD and the other lot for the scapegoat.
> —LEVITICUS 16:5–8

I believe the two offerings in this Old Testament passage are connected to Peter's response to the burden-removing and yoke-destroying Anointed One of God. Notice what happens with the first offering:

> He [Aaron] shall take some of the blood of the bull and sprinkle it with his finger on the mercy seat on the east side; and before the mercy seat he shall sprinkle some of the blood with his finger *seven* times.... Then he shall sprinkle some of the blood on it with his finger seven

> times, cleanse it, and consecrate it from the uncleanness
> of the children of Israel.
>                              —LEVITICUS 16:14, 19

How many times did the priest sprinkle the blood? Seven. And how many places did Jesus shed His blood? Seven! On the Day of Atonement Jesus came not only to forgive our sin and release every blessing but also to break every curse. When the high priest sprinkled the blood seven times, the whole year's sins were forgiven, and the blessing was ready to be released. But one more thing had to happen, and it involved the other goat.

> Aaron shall lay both his [bloody] hands on the head of
> the live goat, confess over it all the iniquities of the chil-
> dren of Israel, and all their transgressions, concerning
> all their sins, putting them on the head of the goat, and
> shall send it away into the wilderness by the hand of a
> suitable man. The goat shall bear on itself all their iniq-
> uities to an uninhabited land; and he shall release the
> goat in the wilderness.
>                              —LEVITICUS 16:21–22

When the priest touched the animal's head, he confessed all the curses that had come on the Israelites due to their sin that year. He then released the animal, known as the scapegoat, with all those curses. If the goat died in the wilderness, every curse was broken, and because of the blood sprinkled seven times in the holy of holies, the blessing would be released onto the people.

What Jesus did at Calvary is exactly what happened on the Day of Atonement: our sins were forgiven, and He shed His blood seven times. He not only redeemed us by His blood; He also broke every curse that blocked our blessing! Look at this amazing teaching found in the Book of Deuteronomy:

> If a man has committed a sin deserving of death, and
> he is put to death, and you hang him on a tree, his
> body shall not remain overnight on the tree, but you

shall surely bury him that day, so that you do not defile the land which the LORD your God is giving you as an inheritance; for he who is hanged is accursed of God.

—DEUTERONOMY 21:22–23

This is not a book about breaking curses, but I want you to see something here. The passage from Deuteronomy tells us that a person hanging on a tree is cursed. If the person is still hanging there when night falls, that curse is transferred to the land and the people. If all Jesus did was die for our sin, He could have died at the whipping post or anywhere between there and Calvary. But He had to die on the cross. Why? To break every curse off our lives!

Christ has redeemed us from the curse of the law, having become a curse for us (for it is written, "Cursed is everyone who hangs on a tree"), that the blessing of Abraham might come upon the Gentiles in Christ Jesus, that we might receive the promise of the Spirit through faith.

—GALATIANS 3:13–14

Jesus' final words on the cross were "It is finished!" (John 19:30). Our sins were forgiven, the curses were broken, and the blessings of God could be released. He finished the work He came to do.

On the day when I said, "I'm just like my dad," I made it my goal to find the answer to family curses in the Bible. I found it, not once but more than three hundred times. But before we go any further, let's ask ourselves this question: If we need to break the curses of our physical fathers, do we also need to break the curses of our spiritual fathers? Could it be that the church is living under a partially closed heaven and is not experiencing the fullness of the Abrahamic blessing that we inherited through Jesus Christ? Is it possible that a curse over us as the church began with our spiritual fathers and is choking out the harvest of God that we await?

In my opinion the answer in all cases is "Yes!" It is time to break these curses, killing them from the roots up, so the great harvest of God's latter rain and end-time blessings can begin!

## LIVING PROPHECY 2

The curse that came by blaming Jewish people is being broken, and the blessing for standing with Israel is being released. The wall between Jewish and Gentile people is being torn down.

## THE ROOT OF THE PROBLEM

Genesis 12:3 is clear: God promised to bless those who bless Israel and curse those who curse Israel. I believe that curse is blocking the blessing God intends for the church. We have all seen God's blessing to some degree. But He did not promise a sprinkle in the last days; He said there would be a great outpouring.

To talk constructively about the curse of blaming the Jewish people for Jesus' death or about replacement theology overall, we must get to the root. That means asking ourselves whether the responsibility for Jesus' death belongs to Rome or the Jewish people. Cutting down the weeds of the curse is not enough. We must annihilate them. That means diving into the historical facts and uncovering the root system. But before we do, let's establish two facts: (1) nobody should be blamed for Jesus' death on the cross, and (2) He knew all along that dying was His mission. He told His disciples so ahead of time:

> My father loves Me, because I lay down My life that I may take it again. No one takes it from Me, but I lay it down of Myself. I have the power to lay it down, and I have power to take it again. This command I have received from My Father.
> —John 10:17–18

No one took Jesus' life from Him. He *gave* His life as a seed, a ransom for us all. Look at what He told His disciples:

> The Son of Man did not come to be served, but to serve, and to give his life as a ransom for many.
> —Matthew 20:28

> The hour has come that the Son of Man should be glorified. Most assuredly, I say to you, unless a grain of wheat falls into the ground and dies, it remains alone; but if it dies, it produces much grain.
>
> —John 12:23–24

No person or institution had the power or authority to take Jesus' life. Not one! His prayer in the Garden of Gethsemane confirmed it. He said, "O My Father, if it is possible, let this cup pass from Me; nevertheless, not as I will, but as You will" (Matt. 26:39).

Knowing that Jesus said no one could take His life from Him, and knowing that His sacrifice was His mission, how could the church claim Jewish people murdered Him? How did such a doctrine continue for nearly seventeen hundred years? There was no basis for it, yet it persisted. However, I believe that something Jesus said in the Book of Mark can open every Gentile Christian's eyes to the truth and break the curse, once and for all:

> [Jesus] said to them, "All too well you reject the commandment of God, that you may keep your own tradition....making the word of God of no effect through your tradition which you have handed down. And many such things you do."
>
> —Mark 7:9, 13

We must understand this if we are to walk in the fullness of God's blessing. We need to be sure that what we think is true and scriptural actually came from the Bible, as opposed to our own traditions.

Let me give you an example of what I mean. How many stripes (or lashes) did Jesus receive at the whipping post? We know that Isaiah 53:5 says, "By His stripes we are healed." Peter then alluded to Isaiah in his own epistle (1 Pet. 2:24). Almost every Christian knows these scriptures, but what do these and other verses say about the number of stripes the Romans laid on Jesus' back?

When I ask this question, I receive the same answer almost every time. It's the answer I used to give: thirty-nine.

My question is meant to emphasize how our traditions sometimes override the truth. The issue is whether Jesus received thirty-nine stripes according to Scripture or according to a man-made tradition.

To settle the issue, let's start at John 19:1, which says, "Then Pilate took Jesus and scourged Him." Pilate was a Roman governor; therefore it was Rome that laid the whip into Jesus' flesh! Now the question becomes, does it matter who did it?

It does, but let's see why. Pay attention to the details, and the reason will become clear:

> If there is a dispute between men, and they come to court, that the judges may judge them, and they justify the righteous and condemn the wicked, then it shall be, if the wicked man deserves to be beaten, that the judge will cause him to lie down and be beaten in his presence, according to his guilt, with a certain number of blows. Forty blows he may give him and no more, lest he should exceed this and beat him with many blows above these.
>
> —DEUTERONOMY 25:1–3

According to the Torah, no more than forty lashes were allowed. This was very important to Jewish people, who did not want to break God's law accidentally. Therefore they would stop at thirty-nine lashes, just to be sure they did not exceed forty. The apostle Paul confirmed this practice, saying, "From the Jews five times I received forty stripes minus one" (2 Cor. 11:24).

Scripture never says that Jesus received thirty-nine stripes, but we hear it preached all the time. The assumption is that if Paul received thirty-nine lashes, so did Jesus. But Jesus was not beaten by Jewish people. We just saw in John 19:1 that the Romans whipped Him, and there is no reason to believe they would have shown any mercy to someone accused of being a rebellious rabbi. The number of lashes would not have mattered to them because they weren't concerned with what the Torah commanded.

No matter how many stripes Jesus received, by them we are

healed *in every way*—physically, emotionally, psychologically, relationally, and so on. Through Christ we are made whole. I make this point about Jesus' stripes not because it changes the truth of what He accomplished for us through His suffering, death, and resurrection, but to show just one example of men's traditions being passed down generation after generation.

There are many more, and they happen in the church. Blaming Jewish people for killing Jesus is a tradition that has caused unimaginable suffering for the Jewish people, who have been called Christ killers for more than a millennium! Think about this injustice in the light of God's promise to bless those who bless Israel and curse those who curse them. Can you imagine how God views the blaming of Jewish people for what Jesus suffered?

## THE REAL JEWISH RESPONSE TO JESUS

Another tradition is ready to be rooted out! During the Second Vatican Council, in 1965, the Roman Catholic Church published a declaration called "Nostra Aetate," which means "In Our Time." It stated that modern-day Jewish people should and could not be held accountable for Jesus' death, and not all Jewish people alive at the time of the crucifixion were guilty.[5]

Now that's an understatement! Biblical accounts of what happened before Jesus' death say much more about how Jewish people treated Jesus. Remember that He died during Passover, when massive crowds lined Jerusalem's streets. Look what happened just days before He died:

> Then the multitudes who went before and those following cried out, saying: "Hosanna to the Son of David! 'Blessed is He who comes in the name of the LORD!' Hosanna in the highest!"
>
> —MATTHEW 21:9

When Jesus rode into Jerusalem as Zechariah 9:9 prophesied, multitudes of Jewish people praised Him. Matthew's Gospel doesn't say that eleven disciples (twelve minus Judas) praised Jesus. It doesn't even say that a few dozen or a hundred praised Him. Matthew specifically says that, at a time when likely over one million Jewish people were in Jerusalem for the Passover, "the multitudes" praised Jesus.

Now look at the Book of John. Six days before the Passover, Jesus went to Bethany. His friend Lazarus had died, and Jesus raised him from the dead. Notice what happened when the word got out that Jesus was in town.

> Now a great many of the Jews knew that He was there; and they came, not for Jesus' sake only, but that they might also see Lazarus, whom He had raised from the dead. But the chief priests plotted to put Lazarus to death also, because on account of him many of the Jews went away and believed in Jesus. The next day a great multitude that had come to the feast, when they heard that Jesus was coming to Jerusalem, took branches of palm trees and went out to meet Him, and cried out: "Hosanna!"
> —JOHN 12:9–13

There were a few plotters among the powerful, but we see that the multitude of Jewish people followed and believed in Jesus! Scripture proves that these great crowds of worshippers weren't a one-time event. They came out to be with Him again and again.

> Great multitudes followed Him—from Galilee, and from Decapolis, Jerusalem, Judea, and beyond the Jordan.
> —MATTHEW 4:25

> When Jesus saw great multitudes about Him, He gave a command to depart to the other side.
> —MATTHEW 8:18

> Great multitudes followed Him, and He healed them there.
> —MATTHEW 19:2

> Jesus went with [Jairus], and a great multitude followed
> Him and thronged Him.
> —MARK 5:24

> Then He arose from there and came to the region of
> Judea by the other side of the Jordan. And multitudes
> gathered to Him again, and as He was accustomed, He
> taught them again.
> —MARK 10:1

> So it was, as the multitude pressed about Him to hear the
> word of God, that He stood by the Lake of Gennesaret.
> —LUKE 5:1

> Now great multitudes went with Him.
> —LUKE 14:25

I could go on and on, but you get the idea. The masses of Jewish people did not cry, "Crucify Him!" They shouted, "Hosanna!" Yet the tradition of men, which is not scripturally supported, holds that the Jewish people as a whole demanded Jesus' death. That is absolute nonsense!

Although Jesus had enemies among the corrupt Jewish leadership, He was a far greater threat to Rome than to the priests. What Roma feared most was not His teaching, His healing of the sick, or His raising of the dead (although these troubled those in power). What really scared them were the vast crowds of followers who could turn and challenge Roman authority.

Another fact proves that the Romans were responsible for Jesus' death: crucifixion had never been a Jewish form of punishment; it was a Roman custom. The Romans treated God's people harshly, and Jesus wasn't the only Jewish man they crucified. They executed people, Jewish or otherwise, they saw as a threat to their power. When Roman leaders heard the masses shouting, "Hosanna!" (or "Save us!"), they feared Jesus' influence, and they would stop at nothing to destroy Him.

## EARLY CHRISTIAN ANTI-SEMITISM

There is a book titled *Constantine's Sword*, written by a former Catholic priest named James Carroll, which explains how anti-Semitism was birthed in Christianity and grew throughout the church's development, based on blaming Jewish people for killing Jesus.[6] Carroll learned from Mark's Gospel that "the crowd" came against Jesus (15:11, 15). Matthew's Gospel said that "all the people" cried out against Jesus (27:25). But Carroll saw "the crowd" and "all the people" through the eyes of John, who said those who were called the enemies of Jesus were "the Jews":

> When the chief priests and officers saw Him, they cried out, saying, "Crucify Him, crucify Him!"
> Pilate said to them, "You take Him and crucify Him, for I find no fault in Him."
> The Jews answered him, "We have a law, and according to our law He ought to die, because He made Himself the Son of God."
> …But they cried out, "Away with Him, away with Him! Crucify Him!"
> Pilate said to them, "Shall I crucify your King?"
> The chief priests answered, "We have no king but Caesar!"
> —JOHN 19:6–7, 15

While there were Jewish people who played a role in the death of Jesus, it is a tragic distortion to call Jewish people Christ-killers. The trial of Jesus was arranged by a corrupt few. They scoured the land for false testimony against Jesus but found none (Matt. 26:59–60). Most Jewish people saw Jesus as a great rabbi. He did not die because the entire community of Jewish people demanded it. Despite the protests he made in Scripture, Pilate allowed Jesus to be crucified because doing so was in the best interest of Rome. He wanted to prevent an uprising and keep the Jewish people under Rome's control.

The seed of hatred toward the Jewish people was planted

long before Christ. After Christ's death and resurrection some of the church fathers made sure the seed was watered. However, Christian anti-Semitism was not really evident in the first century of the church. Teaching that inspired Christian hatred of the Jewish appeared in the second century and continued from there. Let's look at some examples.

- Justin Martyr (AD 100–165) was a prominent church leader. In *Dialogue With Trypho* (a Jewish man with whom he argued "truth") he wrote that the Scriptures are "not yours, but ours."[7] To Justin, Christians had replaced the Jewish people. The demonic teaching of replacement theology was already in play. Justin also wrote that "those who slandered [Jesus], and said that it was well to preserve the ancient customs, should be miserable."[8] Justin believed that Jewish people rightly suffered because they failed to recognize Jesus as the Christ and instead killed Him.[9] (Imagine church leaders teaching such hate in the name of the Prince of Peace.)

- Sometime around AD 177 Irenaeus, the Bishop of Lyon, declared that Jewish people "are disinherited from the grace of God."[10]

- Origen (AD c. 185–c. 253) said that Jewish people "in the world to come... [will] be converted, on account of their unbelief, from vessels of honour into vessels of dishonour."[11] He also wrote, "And these calamities [the Jewish people] have suffered, because they were a most wicked nation, which, although guilty of many other sins, yet has been punished so severely for none, as for those that were committed against our Jesus."[12]

- The Council of Nicaea (AD 325) was the first worldwide gathering of church leaders, called for by Roman emperor Constantine. Nicaea is now Iznik, Turkey. Three centuries after the time of Jesus the church had done exactly what He commanded: "Go into all the world and preach the gospel to every creature" (Mark 16:15). They did it so successfully that by AD 325 Gentiles led the church and added their own traditions to the original teachings of the apostles.

At Nicaea, Constantine wanted to settle certain doctrines of the church, but his longer-term goals included turning the world's spiritual focus away from Jerusalem and toward the Roman Empire (and eventually Rome itself). How do you accomplish the second goal except by turning Christianity against its birthplace? That was accomplished by making Jewish people the "bad guys," first by blaming them for killing Jesus.

- Gregory of Nyssa (AD c. 331–c. 396) called Jewish people "slayers of the Lord, murderers of the prophets, enemies of God, haters of God, adversaries of grace, enemies of their fathers' faith, advocates of the devil, brood of vipers, slanderers, scoffers, men of darkened minds, leaven of the Pharisees, congregation of demons, sinners, wicked men, stoners, and haters of goodness."[13]

- (This one may shock you!) Martin Luther published "Von den Jüden und Ihren Lügen" ("On the Jews and Their Lies") in 1543. In it he asked, "What shall we Christians do with this rejected and condemned people, the Jews?" His answer: "First, to set fire to their synagogues or schools and to bury and cover with dirt whatever will not burn, so that no man will ever again see a stone or cinder of them....Second, I advise that their houses also be razed and destroyed. For they pursue in them the same aims as in their synagogues....Third, I advise that all their prayer books and Talmudic writings, in which such idolatry, lies, cursing, and blasphemy are taught, be taken from them. Fourth, I advise that their rabbis be forbidden to teach henceforth on pain of loss of life and limb....Fifth, I advise that safe-conduct on the highways be abolished completely for the Jews. For they have no business in the countryside, since they are not lords, officials, tradesmen, or the like....Sixth, I advise that usury be prohibited to them, and that all cash and treasure of silver and gold be taken from them....Seventh, I recommend putting a flail, an ax, a hoe, a spade, a distaff, or a spindle into the hands of young, strong Jews and Jewesses and letting them earn their bread in the sweat of their brow....In brief, dear princes and lords, those of you who have Jews under your rule: if my counsel does not please you, find better advice, so that you and we all can be rid of the unbearable, devilish burden of the Jews."[14]

These words of hate, destruction, violence, racism, theft, slavery, and murder sound more like the perverse beliefs of Adolf Hitler than of those who claim to speak for Christ. I'm reminded of Jesus' own words: "Truly I tell you, whatever you did for one of the least of these brothers and sisters of mine, you did for me" (Matt. 25:40, NIV).

It is hard to imagine that these church leaders read the same Bible we are reading. They called for unbelievable hatred and abuse of those whom God calls "the apple of His eye" (Zech. 2:8). According to Matthew 25:40, saying these things to Jewish people is like saying them to Jesus. It is unimaginable and inexcusable for the church to have provided a platform for almost two thousand years of Jewish suffering.

## FROM THE CRUSADES TO THE HOLOCAUST

When you think about the horrors of the Holocaust, you can almost rationalize the existence of a handful of psychopaths such as Hitler, Göring, Himmler, and Eichmann. But how could such insanity spread across the European continent? To understand how it was possible, let's go back to the Crusades.

### The Crusades

Although the Crusades were essentially religious wars between Christians and Muslims seeking control of sacred sites in the Holy Land, Jewish people became victims. The First Crusade, in 1095, started out from France. Jewish people in France attempted to preserve friendly relations with the pope and the church, providing both food and funds for the Crusaders. Yet some of the Crusaders attacked Jewish people in several communities in Germany, including Cologne, Mainz, and Speyer, and were offered the terrible choice of converting to Christianity or dying Jewish. Most of them—men, women, and children—chose death.[15]

Once the crusaders reached Jerusalem in 1099, they brought local Jewish people "into the central synagogue and set it afire. Other Jews...were caught and beheaded."[16] One firsthand account said, "In the Temple and porch of Solomon, men rode in blood up to their knees and bridle reins. Indeed, it was a just and splendid judgment of God that this place should be filled with the blood of the unbelievers."[17]

Jewish casualties in the Crusades were precedent setting. Entire families and whole towns were destroyed by those representing the church. These actions released a curse and forecast what Hitler and the Nazis would eventually do. On the eve of Rosh Hashanah, to this day, Jewish people remember those who sacrificed their lives, and they ask God to remember the blood of "fathers and sons...merciful women and their children...brothers and sisters...grooms and brides...wise men and wise women" and others.[18]

The Second Crusade started in 1146. Again, Jewish people

suffered persecution and death in some of the same European towns as in the First Crusade. A monk named Radulf incited the Crusaders to kill the Jewish people of Europe, telling them to "avenge the crucified one upon his enemies who stand before you; then go to war against the Muslims."[19] The Third Crusade began four decades after the start of the second and greatly impacted Jewish people in England. During the twelfth century, anti-Semitism in England led to Jewish people being fined and subjected to blood libel.[20]

Remember: anti-Semitism is a curse. Like a weed, it must be eradicated. Otherwise it keeps growing and infecting everything around it. Look at what Jesus said about lying prophets: "Many false prophets will rise up and deceive many. And because lawlessness will abound, the love of many will grow cold" (Matt. 24:11–12). I believe this also applies to lies about the Jewish people. The curse isn't just passed on from one generation to the next. Jesus said it abounds, which means "to increase, to multiply."[21]

The curse of anti-Semitism is still abounding. The masses in early church times had no Bibles and were at the mercy of those who taught them. It is somewhat understandable that the unlearned might believe anti-Semitic lies. But for such lies to spread among educated people in modern society—that is truly unbelievable!

## Pogroms

For most people, the word *pogrom* is a reminder of anti-Semitism in the World War II era. However, the devastation for which pogroms are now known began much earlier, especially during the Crusades. The term means "to destroy, to wreak havoc, to demolish violently."[22] It was first used in the nineteenth century to describe attacks on Jewish people in Russia, but pogroms include various forms of violence against people because of their ethnic identity. The term, however, is mostly used in reference to attacks against Jewish people. Pogroms include massacres, violent confiscations and destruction of property, and other acts of terror. The movie *Fiddler on the Roof* has an excellent example of a pogrom. Although most pogroms are much more violent than what the movie portrays,

Jewish people in the movie had property stolen and were forced off their land for one reason: they were Jewish.

**Jewish life, the church, and government**

Throughout history Jewish people have faced special government restrictions and taxes. In some cases monarchs seized the estates of deceased Jewish people. Sometimes the church got involved in the confiscation process. For example, English financier Aaron of Lincoln (c. 1125–1186) loaned large sums of money to build English monasteries and abbeys. When he died, his property was seized by Henry II as "the escheat of a Jewish usurer," and because of the enormity of his estate, a special government office was created.[23]

Other forms of persecution worsened the plight of Jewish people. At the Fourth Lateran Council in 1215, the pope enacted four anti-Jewish decrees, which included the requirement that all Jewish people were "to be distinguished in public from other people by the character of their dress."[24] The law echoed an Islamic decree from several centuries earlier and was intended to "prevent friendships, and possibly intermarriage, from occurring between Christians and Jews." As a result local dress for Jewish people included "a so-called badge of shame, a yellow circle symbolizing the Jews' alleged love of gold."[25] (Remember the badge the Nazis required Jewish people to wear!) Jewish people in England were made to wear an insignia of the tablets Moses received on Mount Sinai. The Council also forbade Jewish people from holding public positions that placed them over any Christian, a strategy the Nazis also implemented.[26]

## NEVER FORGET

Can you see how the curse of anti-Semitism perpetuates itself and multiplies anti-Jewish myths? Yosef Eisen's article "Ten Anti-Semitic Myths" provides stunning examples, listing blood libel; ritual murder; accusations that Jewish people desecrated stolen communion wafers and poisoned wells; claims that Jewish people are devils and give off a sulfuric odor; the belief that

Jewish blood is polluted; and claims that Jewish people run a worldwide conspiracy.[27]

These myths are still alive today! For example, *The Protocols of the Elders of Zion* (a document Hitler cited in *Mein Kampf*) speaks to the world-domination myth and has since been used as fodder in Arab regimes.[28] I could go on and on about how the curse of anti-Semitism has endured all the way to today's anti-Israel movement.

The point is that we must never forget. So, whenever I take a group to Israel, we visit Yad Vashem, the World Holocaust Remembrance Center in Jerusalem. The memorial does more than remember six million Jewish victims who died for being Jewish; it remembers six million individuals who had mothers, fathers, children, and siblings.

Seeing the face of someone who was murdered is an unforgettable experience. The memory of the Children's Memorial is especially moving and always fresh for me. There are no pictures or suitcases—just 1.5 million lighted candles and the spoken name of each child.[29] Hearing the names of Jewish children who were taken from their parents and killed by brutal people, I cannot help but cry and wonder, "How could this happen?" During a particular visit, I heard the names of two little boys, Asher and Judah. The sound hit my heart and soul like never before. I have two "grand sugars," identical twin grandsons named Asher and Judah. Hearing their names made the Holocaust personal to me.

I pray that I state this correctly and don't offend anyone: it is hard for the number six million to register for most of us. That's almost the size of the Dallas-Fort Worth-Arlington metro area where I live and pastor our church. Imagine every resident of such a city being exterminated. It's hard to visualize. Think instead of one person—your mom, your dad, your brother, your sister, your child—being murdered six million times just for being Jewish. That will register.

My friend, the curse of anti-Semitism started with the church, and its end must begin with the church! Before writing this book, I debated with myself and talked with others (both Jewish and

Christian) about whether I should focus on the root and curse of anti-Semitism, replacement theology, and their connection with the teachings of the early church fathers. Everyone with whom I sought counsel said, "Absolutely! It must be taught so we can kill this disease at its root."

If we are to please God and walk in the fullness of His blessings, we must understand where the curse started. Then we can fight it.

Let me add this timely thought: in our politically correct society, very few people would openly say, "I hate the Jews." Instead today's anti-Semitism hides behind a veil—the claim that "we are not anti-Semitic or anti-Jewish but anti-Israel." The BDS movement for boycott, divestment, and sanctions against Israel is modern anti-Semitism in action. The terminology of the movement—calling Israel *Palestine*, labeling it an *apartheid* state, and citing the Jewish *occupation* of Palestine are the current ways that anti-Semitism is framed.[30] I will address these topics and provide historical, political, and (most importantly) biblical answers later on in this book. We will look at questions such as:

- What is the history of the land of Israel, and to whom does it belong?
- Where did the name Palestine originate, and where did the Palestinian people come from?
- Is there any history of a Palestinian nation?
- What are the roots of the BDS movement, and how have its principles been used by previous generations of anti-Semites?

We Christians cannot be duped into complicity with anti-Semites any longer. There are no first-century documents blaming the Jewish people for killing Jesus, which tells me the idea was fabricated after the fact. We cannot continue saying things that are not true.

## THE HOLOCAUST SURVIVORS' HOME

During a recent visit to Israel, Tiz, our daughters, and I were privileged to visit a very special home for Holocaust survivors. There we met some of the most beautiful people we have *ever* met. Their stories are amazing. We had coffee and tea with the ladies, who ranged in age from ninety-four to one hundred three. They are precious and beyond kind. Tiz calls them her "angels."

We are very strong believers of these teachings from Matthew chapter 6:

> Therefore I say to you, do not worry about your life, what you will eat or what you will drink; nor about your body, what you will put on. Is not life more than food and the body more than clothing?... Therefore do not worry, saying, "What shall we eat?" or "What shall we drink?" or "What shall we wear?" For after all these things the Gentiles seek. For your heavenly Father knows that you need all these things. But seek first the kingdom of God and His righteousness, and all these things shall be added to you.
>
> —MATTHEW 6:25, 31–33

This passage changed our lives when we read it through the eyes of a Jewish Jesus. In it He told us not to worry anything, because He will care for us. We only need to seek first His kingdom and His righteousness. He will handle the rest.

When Jesus told us to seek after righteousness, the earthly side of His command was about acts of kindness and charity. Tiz and I always pray, especially when we're in Israel, for God to show us where we can be a blessing. Ancient Jewish wisdom tells us that whenever God is ready to bless us, He first gives us an opportunity to be a blessing.

When Tiz and I visited with these "angels," I asked one of the ladies, "Is there anything we can do for you?" Her response totally caught me by surprise. I thought she would say they needed more food or furniture or she could use a TV in her apartment. Instead she took my hand and looked into my eyes with her ninety-five-year-old ones that had witnessed things no one ever should. As her eyes flooded with the tears of remembering, she said, "Tell our story to everyone you can so that our story will never happen to anyone ever again—not to anybody."

This chapter is my response to that dear lady's request. It is time to end seventeen hundred years of lies. The Jewish people did not kill Jesus. The church has not replaced Israel. We are not the new Israel. God has fulfilled prophecies that are more than two thousand years old, and Israel is a sign to us all—a nation born in one day!

I also wrote this chapter because a change is happening worldwide among Christians. If you are a Christian, it is vitally important to heed what God said in Genesis 12:3: "I will bless those who bless you [Israel], and I will curse him who curses you." I believe with all my heart that we are close to the Messiah's coming. If that is true, then we are already at the threshold of the latter-rain blessings God promised us. He wants you and me to be ready for that.

So are you ready for the greatest outpouring of God's might and power? Are you ready to live under the open windows of heaven? Then let's reverse the curse right now and receive the blessing. It is *time*.

Your best is yet to come!

## CHAPTER 3

# THE RETURN: GOD'S GREATEST SIGN

*Who has heard such a thing? Who has seen such things? Shall the earth be made to give birth in one day? Or shall a nation be born at once?*
—ISAIAH **66:8**

THROUGHOUT HISTORY DOUBTERS have said that it could never happen. No nation or people lacking land and a common language could possibly be reborn as a nation—not after two thousand years! It had never happened before, and most of the world was convinced that it would never happen again.

So they said, "Your Bible is a bunch of fairy tales!"

Yet the impossible did happen, exactly the way God said it would. Nothing is impossible for God (Luke 1:37). Yet I can understand the world's skepticism. Their disbelief was not illogical. Even God's Word acknowledged the sense of impossibility:

> "Who has heard such a thing? Who has seen such things? Shall the earth be made to give birth in one day? Or shall a nation be born at once? For as soon as Zion was in labor, she gave birth to her children. Shall I bring to the time of birth, and not cause delivery?" says the LORD. "Shall I who cause delivery shut up the womb?" says your God...."As one whom his mother comforts, so I will comfort you; and you shall be comforted in Jerusalem."
> —ISAIAH 66:8–9, 13

On April 13, 2002, when Rabbi Lord Jonathan Sacks (then the United Kingdom's Chief Rabbi) testified to Israel's return, he opened with Isaiah's words. He then described the difference between false prophets and real ones, saying,

> Isaiah's words…are more than a simple vision. They tell us what it is to be a prophet. No one was more severe in his criticisms of Israel than Isaiah.…Yet when Israel was in crisis, Isaiah didn't say, "I told you so." He didn't say, "You are to blame." He brought his people comfort. He gave them strength. More than strength, he gave them hope.[1]

False prophets are fair-weather friends who disappear in tough times. True prophets address the people's complacency when times are good, but during the dark days they encourage and comfort them. True prophets stand with the people in their distress and give them the courage to fight on. Rabbi Sacks reminded his hearers that God never takes us to the brink of the breakthrough only to desert us. He walks with us and brings us through every challenge.[2]

Isaiah's passage, written thousands of years ago, speaks to what Israel faces even today. Yet, no matter what comes, the Jewish people's continued return to the land is a sign to the world, perhaps the greatest sign concerning God's promises. First it proves that His Word is true. Second it speaks to the end of the age. That's exactly what His disciples wanted to know when Jesus sat on the Mount of Olives. They said, "What will be the sign of Your coming, and of the end of the age?" (Matt. 24:3).

## REBIRTH OF A NATION

Two very significant days fall back to back on Israel's calendar: Remembrance Day and Independence Day. The first is a national day of mourning, honoring all who have died in Israel's struggle to exist.[3] The second is a national celebration marking the people's return to the homeland after two millennia in exile.

I have been in Jerusalem on both occasions. On Remembrance

Day a two-minute siren sounds across the nation at 11:00 a.m. Everywhere—in cafés and on highways—everyone stops what they are doing to stand at attention.[4] It is a sign of respect for more than twenty thousand Israeli military personnel killed in the line of duty, as well as more than three thousand who died in terrorist attacks.[5] On Independence Day the mood completely shifts, and celebrations erupt nationwide. Though the two days are different, both testify to the miracle that is Israel.

In Tel Aviv on May 14, 1948, David Ben-Gurion proclaimed the State of Israel, thus establishing the first Jewish state in two thousand years. The next day, the *New York Times* reported that "the declaration of the new state…was delivered during a simple and solemn ceremony at 4 P.M., and new life was instilled into his people."[6] Israel was reborn in a day!

## LIVING PROPHECY 3

God will gather the Jewish people from around the world and will return them to Israel.

If you think back to the days of the ancient prophets, you can grasp in some small way the miracle of Israel's impossible rebirth. The path was complicated. The very Holocaust that decimated the world's Jewish population also helped Israel's rebirth along. Ben-Gurion, who became Israel's first prime minister, "saw the horrors of the Holocaust as paving for the way to the birth of a Jewish State, and he was not alone" in thinking so.[7] This idea showed up in the proclamation establishing the newly reborn nation, quoted here from newspaper archives:

> The Nazi holocaust which engulfed millions of Jews in Europe proved anew the urgency of the re-establishment of the Jewish state, which would solve the problem of Jewish homelessness by opening the gates to all Jews and lifting the Jewish people to equality in the family of nations.[8]

Romans 8:28 says that "all things work together for the good to those who love God… [and] are called according to His purpose." God purposed to gather the Jewish people from the four corners of the earth and return them to the land of promise. Would it have happened without the murder of six million Jewish people? Who can say? But we know that God took something more horrible than we can comprehend and used it in the fulfillment of prophecy. What Satan meant for evil, God used for good.

God said more than once that He would replant His people in the land He chose for them. The questions posed in Isaiah 66 challenge our human ideas about divine possibility: "Shall the earth be made to give birth in one day? Or shall a nation be born at once?… Shall I bring to the time of birth, and not cause delivery?… Shall I who cause delivery shut up the womb?" (Isa. 66:8–9). In other words, "Such a thing has never happened in human history, but I always keep My Word!"

Think about how Jewish people felt when they had a national homeland again! In 1917 the Balfour Declaration urged the re-creation of Israel's homeland in what it called Palestine. Balfour's letter led the League of Nations to give Britain the mandate over Palestine in 1922. In November of 1947, Britain announced its intention to and the mandate, effective May 15, 1948. That was Israel's first day as a sovereign state.

We will see more of God's perfect timing playing out later, but remember that God told us about it long ago, saying, "The revelation awaits an appointed time; it speaks of the end and will not prove false. Though it linger, wait for it; it will certainly come and will not delay" (Hab. 2:3, NIV).

In other words, "Hang on! God's promise is coming."

## THE ERROR OF REPLACEMENT THEOLOGY

Waiting for God's promise can keep us from the error of replacement theology. The church fathers struggled to interpret the Scriptures in which Israel's becoming a nation was involved. The prophecies had already gone unfulfilled for hundreds of years, and the Jewish people had been scattered to the four corners of the earth after the destruction of the second temple. With every passing century the idea of their returning to Israel seemed more impossible.

I believe that the church fathers "solved" the discrepancy of unfulfilled prophecy not by waiting for its fulfillment but by transferring Israel's promises to the church. They reasoned that Israel had rejected the Messiah, and God had therefore rejected them. With Israel out of the picture the only possible candidate for God's blessing was the church.

But here is what the apostle Paul said: "I ask then: Did God reject his people? By no means!" (Rom. 11:1, NIV) These words strongly refute the replacement-theology line of thinking.

In all fairness, it would have been easy to assume that Israel's return would never happen. And when early church leaders failed to explain the delay, I believe the people just gave up. There's a great lesson here for all of us. We need to hold on to God's promises and never let go. Habakkuk said that even if the promise tarries, we are not to give up. Whatever God said would happen *will* happen.

After two thousand years of diaspora, Israel was resurrected! Since 1948 the nation has contributed to humanity in unimaginable ways. From mathematics to optics, medicine to robotics, digital technologies to agriculture, this tiny nation has contributed on an outsized level.[9] Even Israel's innovation is part of God's promise to Abraham:

> I will make you a great nation; I will bless you and make your name great; and you shall be a blessing. I will bless those who bless you, and I will curse him who curses you; and in you all the families of the earth shall be blessed.
>
> —GENESIS 12:2–3

> Blessing I will bless you, and multiplying I will multiply your descendants as the stars of the heaven and as the

sand which is on the seashore; and your descendants
shall possess the gate of their enemies. In your seed all
the nations of the earth shall be blessed, because you
have obeyed My voice.

—Genesis 22:17–18

## A PROMISE WITH ROOTS

The prophecy of Israel's rebirth is not found in just one scripture.
God repeated His promise over and over again. One example is
a vision in Ezekiel 37, where the Lord started by showing the
prophet Israel as heaps of dead, dry bones.

The hand of the Lord came upon me and brought me out
in the Spirit of the Lord, and set me down in the midst
of the valley; and it was full of bones. Then He caused me
to pass by them all around, and behold, there were very
many in the open valley; and indeed they were very dry.

—Ezekiel 37:1–2

To me this vision is powerfully connected to the miracle of
Israel's rebirth. Ezekiel tells us that the Spirit of God set him
down not among newly dead bodies but among the dried-out,
dismembered skeletons of people who were long dead. As Ezekiel
moved through the bleak scene, God asked him a question.

"Son of man, can these bones live?"
So I answered, "O Lord God, You know."
Again He said to me, "Prophesy to these bones, and
say to them, 'O dry bones, hear the word of the Lord!'"

—Ezekiel 37:3–4

A little about Ezekiel's personal history: He was born in Judah,
and his father was a priest. In 597 BC Ezekiel was exiled along
with King Jehoiachin (Jeconiah) and ten thousand others.[10] He
spent the rest of his life in Babylon.[11]

Some assume on first reading Ezekiel 37 that it prophesies the
return of the Jewish people from Babylon. I believe that is the

lesser teaching of the passage and ignores the greater teaching. God did bring His people out of Babylon, and they did rebuild the temple. However, the dryness of the bones suggests a far more miraculous return to Israel—not after seventy years of exile but after two thousand years! I believe it speaks to the modern-day return of the Jewish people and is a sign to those whose spiritual eyes are open to the Messiah's soon coming.

The Book of Ezekiel ends with a prophetic vision the prophet saw on Yom Kippur, fourteen years after the destruction of Jerusalem and the first temple (Ezek. 40:1). Here Ezekiel saw himself being taken to the Temple Mount, where an angel with a measuring rod revealed the details of what I and many others believe is the third temple.

> In the twenty-fifth year of our captivity, at the beginning of the year, on the tenth day of the month, in the fourteenth year after the city was captured, on the very same day the hand of the Lord was upon me; and He took me there. In the visions of God He took me into the land of Israel and set me on a very high mountain; on it toward the south was something like the structure of a city. He took me there, and behold, there was a man whose appearance was like the appearance of bronze. He had a line of flax and a measuring rod in his hand, and he stood in the gateway.
>
> And the man said to me, "Son of man, look with your eyes and hear with your ears, and fix your mind on everything I show you; for you were brought here so that I might show them to you. Declare to the house of Israel everything you see."
> —EZEKIEL 40:1–4

In verse four the angel told Ezekiel to look with his eyes and hear with his ears, meaning his spiritual eyes and ears. Our physical eyes and ears are not enough, especially when a promise tarries. The Lord certainly understood His people's weakness during the Babylonian captivity and was gracious to promise repeatedly that they would be freed and returned to Israel. Two scriptures plainly encouraged the exiles:

> "Then it will come to pass, when seventy years are completed, that I will punish the king of Babylon and that nation, the land of the Chaldeans, for their iniquity," says the LORD; "and I will make it a perpetual desolation."
> —JEREMIAH 25:12

> Thus says the LORD: After seventy years are completed at Babylon, I will visit you and perform My good word toward you, and cause you to return to this place.
> —JEREMIAH 29:10

Seventy years is a long time. I wonder how many Jewish people gave up believing that God would return them to their land. I'm sure many felt as though Jerusalem was lost forever. Now imagine when the Jewish people were exiled for two thousand years! No wonder God's question to Ezekiel was perplexing: "Son of man, can these bones live?" (Ezek. 37:3).

Sometimes when I am teaching, I ask the people, "What does this question really mean? What is God saying here?"

I can see the answer in their eyes and their silence: "Pastor, is this another trick question?"

I sense the same thing in Ezekiel's answer, "O Lord GOD, *You* know" (Ezek. 37:3).

Maybe that was the prophet's politically correct way of saying, "God, You know everything. Answering that question is way above my pay grade."

Maybe. But I really think Ezekiel was telling God, "I don't see how it would even be possible for these bones to live. Plus the people haven't had their own land for two thousand years. Their common language is gone, and the world has tried to destroy them every step of the way. In all honesty, Lord, no, I don't think they can live. But only You know for sure."

God then pushed Ezekiel past the realm of rational thinking so he could partner with God in fulfilling the vision: "Again He said to [Ezekiel], 'Prophesy to these bones, and say to them, "O dry bones, hear the word of the LORD!"'" (Ezek. 37:4). Centuries later the bones obeyed.

## THE FIRST EXODUS

Genesis 1:27 tells us that God made us in His image and likeness. Have you ever asked yourself what that means? I could write a whole book on that verse, but allow me to give you the short version, which speaks to what God told Ezekiel to do about the dry bones.

When God created the world, He didn't use tools, machinery, or lasers. He used words. Because He made us in His image, we can create with our words. It is extremely important for us to understand this truth. Let's look at it in both the New Testament and the Old:

> For we all stumble in many things. If anyone does not stumble in word, he is a perfect man, able also to bridle the whole body. Indeed, we put bits in horses' mouths that they may obey us, and we turn their whole body. Look also at ships: although they are so large and are driven by fierce winds, they are turned by a very small rudder wherever the pilot desires. Even so the tongue is a little member and boasts great things. See how great a forest a little fire kindles!
>
> —JAMES 3:2–5

> Death and life are in the power of the tongue, and those who love it will eat its fruit.
>
> —PROVERBS 18:21

This is not a chapter about the power of our faith and our words. But I do want you to understand that you are made in God's image and have life-changing, situation-changing power in your words. So where does that power fit into this study?

One of the greatest Bible accounts is of what I call the first exodus, when God led the Israelites out of Egypt and into the Promised Land. He told them the land flowed with milk and honey. They had not seen the place yet, but He wanted them to trust whatever He said. He wanted them to have faith and believe that He is a God of miracles.

There are two basic kinds of faith in the Hebrew. The first is *emunah*, a very powerful, basic form of faith. This is not blind faith but an "innate conviction" based on "wisdom, understanding and knowledge."[12] *Emunah* has the same Hebrew root as the word *amen*. The second kind of faith is called *bitachon*, which is "a powerful sense of optimism and confidence." We might call it childlike faith. It is super-rational, meaning it is faith beyond reason.[13]

Recently my son-in-law, who heads our worship team, participated in a conference in California. He and my daughter Anna decided that their whole family would fly out and visit Universal Studios when the conference was over. My ten-year-old grand sugar, Aviva, was especially excited and couldn't wait to go. She didn't worry about a thing. She wasn't concerned about how the airplane worked. She never worried about renting a car or having money for food or a place to stay. She never had a care about any of that. She only knew that Mom and Dad said, "We're going to Universal Studios." That was all the information she needed.

She had bitachon.

The children of Israel should have had both kinds of faith. They saw miracles such as the ten plagues in Egypt. They saw the parting of the Red Sea and the destruction of Pharaoh's army. They drank water out of a rock and ate manna from heaven. They saw it all. So when God said, "You're going to Universal Studios"—oops!—I mean "the Promised Land," that should have been the end of it. Instead they questioned what God said and decided to spy out the land for themselves.

Now here's a question for you: Have you ever heard it taught that Israel was lost in the wilderness for forty years? I hear it preached all the time. But if you have visited the Red Sea area, you know it is geographically impossible to get lost while walking from Egypt to Israel. Not only that, but Moses' father-in-law, Jethro, visited their camp at least twice during their wandering. If the Israelites were lost, don't you think Moses would have asked to follow Jethro out?

The ten spies were even greater proof that they weren't lost. They went into the Promised Land and returned to the Israelites' camp with a cluster of grapes so big that it took two men to carry it on a pole.

> They went up and spied out the land from the Wilderness of Zin.... And they went up through the South and came to Hebron....(Now Hebron was built seven years before Zoan in Egypt.) Then they came to the Valley of Eshcol, and there cut down a branch with one cluster of grapes; they carried it between two of them on a pole. They also brought some of the pomegranates and figs....
>
> Now they departed and came back to Moses and Aaron and all the congregation of the children of Israel in the Wilderness of Paran, at Kadesh; they brought back word to them and to all the congregation, and showed them the fruit of the land. Then they told him, and said: "We went to the land where you sent us. It truly flows with milk and honey, and this is its fruit. Nevertheless the people who dwell in the land are strong; the cities are fortified and very large; moreover we saw the descendants of Anak there."
>
> —NUMBERS 13:21–23, 26–28

God "is able to do exceedingly abundantly above all that we ask or think" (Eph. 3:20), but the ten spies weren't so sure. When they reported back to Moses and the people, they said, "Yes, we saw the land. It definitely flows with milk and honey, and the fruit is beyond anything we have ever seen. Just one problem—there are giants in the land!" Translation: "It's exactly what God promised, but if we go in there, we will surely die."

Joshua and Caleb saw the situation differently. They saw

everything the other ten spies saw. And they heard the same promises from God. But they believed God and told the Israelites to go in and take the land, because God was with them.

Now, look at how God responded to the two groups of spies. I want you to see this because it changed my life, and I believe it can change yours.

> The LORD spoke to Moses and Aaron, saying, "How long shall I bear with this evil congregation who complain against Me? I have heard the complaints which the children of Israel make against Me. Say to them, 'As I live,' says the LORD, 'just as you have spoken in My hearing, so I will do to you: The carcasses of you who have complained against Me shall fall in this wilderness, all of you who were numbered, according to your entire number, from twenty years old and above. Except for Caleb the son of Jephunneh and Joshua the son of Nun, you shall by no means enter the land which I swore I would make you dwell in.'"
>
> —NUMBERS 14:26–30

We know that "God is no respecter of persons" (Acts 10:34, KJV). So why did Joshua and Caleb get to enter the Promised Land when everyone else who was twenty years old or older fell in the wilderness? Answer: There is power in our words! Joshua and Caleb came back and said, "We can take the land," which they did. The spies came back and said, "We are going to die." So God told the naysayers, "I promise to do to you exactly what you said would happen."

No wonder God told us to put a guard on our mouths! There is either death or life in our words. That's why God told Ezekiel to prophesy to the bones. Like Ezekiel, Joshua, and Caleb, we are not to be ruled by what we see or what seems logical; we are to speak whatever God's Word says. He is a miracle God, and He is waiting for us to come into agreement with Him and partner with Him in His great work.

## TWO STORIES OF CREATION

We know that God's question "Can these bones live?" challenged Ezekiel. It would challenge any of us. But Ezekiel followed God's instruction anyway and prophesied to a field piled high with parched bones. Though he hedged at first, there was a childlike faith in Ezekiel's obedience.

> So I prophesied as I was commanded; and as I prophesied, there was a noise, and suddenly a rattling; and the bones came together, bone to bone. Indeed, as I looked, the sinews and the flesh came upon them, and the skin covered them over; but there was no breath in them.
> —EZEKIEL 37:7–8

Look closely at what Ezekiel said: "And *as* I prophesied, there was a noise." When Ezekiel said what God told Him to say, the miracle began. Bear with me, because I must repeat myself: everything God teaches us has both a physical and a spiritual side. If we allow Him to give us eyes to see, what comes next will become clear.

Now look carefully at the end of verse 8: "but there was no breath in them," meaning the bones. As Ezekiel prophesied, he heard the bones rattling and saw them coming together. Sinew and flesh and skin came on the bones, but they had no breath. Where have we seen this before?

It's in the story of creation, in Genesis. In that account God repeated Himself. It's not because He forgot what He said. God is never redundant. When He repeats Himself, there is a secret or mystery that He wants us to understand. Let's look at what He said when He created humankind.

> Then God said, "Let Us make man in Our image, according to Our likeness; let them have dominion over the fish of the sea, over the birds of the air, and over the cattle, over all the earth and over every creeping thing that creeps on the earth." So God created man in His

own image; in the image of God He created him; male
and female He created them.

—GENESIS 1:26–27

"Male and female He created them." It was a done deal, and it
was described in way that is easy for us to understand. So why,
after describing humankind's creation in Genesis chapter 1, did
God return to the subject in chapter 2?

The LORD God formed man of the dust of the ground,
and breathed into his nostrils the breath of life; and man
became a living being.

—GENESIS 2:7

God was revealing a mystery in the repetition. In the earlier
text He created the physical man, but here He breathed into the
man "the breath of life." He was giving the physical being a soul.
Ancient Jewish wisdom and many Christian scholars say that
when God blew into man's nostrils, He breathed a part of Himself
into all of us. As a result we are more than physical beings. We
are spiritually part of God and His great plan for humankind.

Keep that in mind, and let's return to God's conversation with
Ezekiel:

Also [God] said to me, "Prophesy to the breath, prophesy,
son of man, and say to the breath, 'Thus says the Lord
GOD: "Come from the four winds, O breath, and breathe
on these slain, that they may live."'" So I prophesied as
He commanded me, and breath came into them, and
they lived, and stood upon their feet, an exceedingly
great army.

—EZEKIEL 37:9–10

What is God telling us? Can bones that have been dead and
dried out for a long, long time live again? Yes! Absolutely nothing
is impossible for God. He made it clear that through Ezekiel's
prophesying, a dead nation would breathe again. By bringing
back the Jewish people from the four corners of the world and

gathering them to the land of Israel, God gave a sign to those with spiritual eyes and ears. It was a sign that He is about to do great things for us all.

> Then say to them, "Thus says the Lord GOD: 'Surely I will take the children of Israel from among the nations, wherever they have gone, and will gather them from every side and bring them into their own land; and I will make them one nation in the land, on the mountains of Israel; and one king shall be king over them all; they shall no longer be two nations, nor shall they ever be divided into two kingdoms again.'"
>
> —EZEKIEL 37:21–22

## THE SECOND EXODUS

Most people who have never picked up a Bible have heard of the first exodus, if only from movies such as *The Ten Commandments*. As epic as the first exodus was, the Bible prophesies a second, more spectacular exodus. Here's what the prophet Jeremiah said about it:

> "Therefore, behold, the days are coming," says the LORD, "that they shall no longer say, 'As the LORD lives who brought up the children of Israel from the land of Egypt,' but, 'As the LORD lives who brought up and led the descendants of the house of Israel from the north country and from all the countries where I had driven them.' And they shall dwell in their own land."
>
> —JEREMIAH 23:7–8

The first exodus was a profound miracle of God, but it will pale by comparison to the second. How can that be? When Moses led God's people out of Egypt, they were all in one land and had been there for approximately four hundred years. Even on foot the journey from Egypt to Israel was short. But the second exodus is very different. Jewish people are still scattered across the globe, and they have been for more than two thousand years.

Listen to what God said about it through the prophet Isaiah:

> Since you were precious in My sight, you have been honored, and I have loved you; therefore I will give men for you, and people for your life. Fear not, for I am with you; I will bring your descendants from the east, and gather you from the west; I will say to the north, "Give them up!" and to the south, "Do not keep them back!" Bring My sons from afar and My daughters from the ends of the earth.
>                                        —Isaiah 43:4–6

That is how God described the massive second exodus. Now here is what Amos said about it:

> "I will bring back the captives of My people Israel; they shall build the waste cities and inhabit them; they shall plant vineyards and drink wine from them; they also shall make gardens and eat fruit from them. I will plant them in their land, and no longer shall they be pulled up from the land I have given them," says the LORD your God.
>                                        —Amos 9:14–15

Amos said this return of the Jewish people to their land would never be undone. That is so important because they were pulled up from their land repeatedly by the Babylonians, Romans, Greeks, Persians, and others. Even when they tried to live outside of Israel, nations such as Spain, Russia, England, Germany, and France forced them out by decree or by persecution. They have been driven out of their homeland and almost every other place that they have lived.

Earlier I mentioned *Fiddler on the Roof*, one of my favorite movies. It depicts Jewish people being forced from their land simply because they were Jewish. The attempt to uproot the Jewish people is not only in the past however. There are people, organizations, and nations calling for the Jewish people to be pushed out of their country today. Anti-Semites seem to believe that everybody has a right to their homeland except the Jewish people.

God, however, will have the final word. Whether the United Nations, Iran, Iraq, or anyone else tries to uproot the Jewish people, He has prophesied otherwise. The God who said that the bones of the whole house of Israel shall live is the same God who told Pharaoh, "Let My people go" (Exod. 8:1). In Ezekiel 11:17 and 36:24 He promised to gather His people from the nations of the world. He fulfilled those prophecies on May 14, 1948. And in the Book of Amos He said, "No longer shall they be pulled up" (9:15).

So what makes this time different from all the other times? Simply the power and promises of almighty God. His great presence rests upon the Jewish people and upon their nation, Israel. They will never be removed again. God said, "I will put My Spirit in you, and you shall live, and I will place you in your own land. Then you shall know that I, the LORD, have spoken it and performed it" (Ezek. 37:14).

We are already seeing God's mighty hand of blessing bringing this to pass. The moving of the US Embassy from Tel Aviv to Jerusalem was a marker, and now other nations are following the United States' example. I believe the United States' formal recognition of Israel's sovereignty over the Golan Heights and its updated position on the settlements also reflect the moving of God's hand.[14] I feel the same way about the United States and other nations standing up for Israel against its opposers, such as Iran, Iraq, and Hamas. Recently I watched President Trump on TV as he presented a peace plan that I pray will bring peace to Jerusalem and all of Israel.[15]

Before we move on, let me show you something about the connection between the first exodus and the second. I want you to understand that the first exodus was about much more than giving the people a land of milk and honey. God explained what He was really after:

The LORD said to Moses, "Go to Pharaoh and say to him,
'This is what the LORD says: Let my people go, so that
they may worship me.'"

—EXODUS 8:1, NIV

It is interesting how words and phrases catch on and are
appropriated by completely different causes. "Let my people go"
has become a catchphrase for many situations and causes that
have nothing to do with why God said it. Whether it is by acci-
dent or design (I suspect it is the latter), the rest of God's statement gets lost. He caused Pharaoh to let His people go so they
could worship Him. They were to go to Mount Sinai, receive
the Torah, and come into covenant with God. This was part of
fulfilling Israel's destiny not only for their benefit, but so they
would bring God's words and ways to all humankind. The world
was to see God's power and blessings through the Jewish people.

Both exodus events testify to the power and glory of the God of
Abraham, Isaac, and Jacob. They are signs to the nations. Whether
you call the current day the time of the Messiah or the beginning
of the latter rain, it is God's moadim, an appointed time and a
time of His great outpouring. Later I will show you signs that are
shouting at us, but I believe no sign speaks more loudly than the
rebirth of Israel and the return of the Jewish people.

## THE FIG TREE AND THE GENERATION

The prophet Hosea wrote, "I [God] found Israel like grapes in
the wilderness; I saw your fathers as the firstfruits on the fig tree"
(Hos. 9:10). Could this fig tree, which Hosea suggests is Israel, be
the same fig tree that Jesus mentioned in Matthew's Gospel?

Now learn this parable from the fig tree: When its
branch has already become tender and puts forth leaves,
you know that summer is near. So you also, when you
see all these things, know that it is near—at the doors!
Assuredly, I say to you, this generation will by no means
pass away till all these things take place. Heaven and

earth will pass away, but My words will by no means
pass away.
                                        —MATTHEW 24:32–35

Over the years, this passage has been heavily debated, especially since Israel's 1948 rebirth. Personally I believe the fig tree
in Matthew 24 is the fig tree in Hosea 9, the nation of Israel.
However, a second question comes up concerning the generation
mentioned in the Matthew passage. Jesus said that when Israel
puts forth its leaves, the generation that sees it won't pass away
before the Messiah comes. But how long is a generation?

Moses may have given us a hint in these words: "The days
of our lives are seventy years...by reason of strength they are
eighty years.... So teach us to number our days, that we may gain
a heart of wisdom" (Ps. 90:10, 12). Was Moses saying that a generation is seventy or eighty years long? Also, was the nation of
Israel fully born in 1948 (i.e., "in one day"), or did the generation
begin in 1967 when Jerusalem was returned to Jewish hands?

Also, what does Luke 21:24 mean when it says, "Jerusalem will
be trampled by Gentiles until the times of the Gentiles are fulfilled"? In Luke 21 Jesus prophesied the destruction of Jerusalem,
saying, the city would be "surrounded by armies" as Judeans
"flee to the mountains" (Luke 21:20–21). He said people would
"fall by the edge of the sword, and be led away captive into all
nations" (Luke 21:24).

Notice He said they would be led captive "into all nations," not
just Babylon or Rome. Verse 20 speaks of when Rome destroyed
the city, but in verse 24 Jesus seemed to jump forward to 1967,
when the Gentile rule of Jerusalem would end. That was a hugely
significant event. I have a famous photo of a rabbi blowing a
shofar at the Western Wall, surrounded by Israeli soldiers.[16] It is
believed by some to be the first time that had happened since AD
70. At the very least it was the "first Jewish prayer session at the
Western Wall since 1948."[17]

In my opinion the generation Jesus mentioned in Matthew 24
began in 1948 when Israel was quite literally born in one day.

Whether it began in 1948 or 1967, you and I are living in that generation. We know that no man can be privy to the day of the Messiah's coming. That might be why the generation question remains unsettled. That is OK, because I believe the time of the Messiah is clearly at hand. Paul compared His day to a woman's sudden transition into labor and warned us to be vigilant:

> The day of the Lord so comes as a thief in the night. For when they say, "Peace and safety!" then sudden destruction comes upon them, as labor pains upon a pregnant woman. And they shall not escape. But you, brethren, are not in darkness, so that this Day should overtake you as a thief. You are all sons of light and sons of the day. We are not of the night nor of darkness. Therefore let us not sleep, as others do, but let us watch and be sober.
>
> —1 Thessalonians 5:2–6

Tiz and I learned about birth pangs the hard way. When she was pregnant with our second child, we didn't take the signs of labor seriously enough. Suddenly it was too late for the hospital. I had to deliver our son, Luke, at home! Trust me when I tell you that we paid better attention when our third child was born. I took Tiz to the hospital maybe twelve times before she gave birth!

That's what prophetic signs are all about. God loves us so much that He doesn't want us to miss the most important events in our lives and in history. My great friends in the Holy Land and I have a running joke. We say, "When the Messiah comes, we will say to Him (remember, we are *joking*), 'Have You been here before? Or can we show You around?'"

There's some truth in our joke. We can disagree about whether this will be the Messiah's first coming or His second. But we agree 100 percent that when He comes, He will come to the Holy Land. There is absolutely no question about that.

That is why we must stand together for an undivided Israel and an undivided Jerusalem. God promised the land to the Jewish people forever.

The Lord said to Abram, after Lot had separated from him: "Lift your eyes now and look from the place where you are—northward, southward, eastward, and westward; for all the land which you see I give to you and to your descendants forever."

—Genesis 13:14–15

So they will say, "This land that was desolate has become like the garden of Eden; and the wasted, desolate, and ruined cities are now fortified and inhabited." Then the nations which are left all around you shall know that I, the Lord, have rebuilt the ruined places and planted what was desolate. I, the Lord, have spoken it, and I will do it.

—Ezekiel 36:35–36

God said He would "raise a banner for the nations and gather the exiles of Israel… [and] assemble the scattered people of Judah from the four corners of the earth" (Isa. 11:12, niv). Where? In their homeland, Israel. Only God could have rebirthed a nation that was dead for two thousand years. It is a fulfillment and a sign to those with eyes to see it.

How incredible is it that you and I get to be a part of what God is doing in the world in these last days! My friend, our best is yet to come!

CHAPTER 4

# PROOF AND THE
# PROMISED LAND

*Though one may be overpowered, two can defend them-*
*selves. A cord of three strands is not quickly broken.*
—ECCLESIASTES 4:12, NIV

I N 1960, AFTER hearing the orchestral theme from the movie
*Exodus*, our good friend Pat Boone was moved to write the
lyrics of "The Exodus Song (This Land Is Mine)." Tiz and I
were privileged to hear the story while sitting with Pat and his
late wife, Shirley, in their living room. I can still see his eyes
lighting up as he shared the memory with us.

Pat has also shared the details in media interviews. He talks
about when he first sang the lyrics to Shirley. They knew the song
was for the Jewish people in the land of Israel. "It was like the
melody was singing to me," Pat said.[1] Today the Christmas card
on which Pat jotted down the lyrics is displayed at Yad Vashem,
the Holocaust Memorial in Jerusalem, and the song has become
almost another Jewish national anthem.[2]

"The Exodus Song" speaks powerfully to Israelis about their
promise from God. Yet many in the world continue to ask, "Can
the Jewish people *really* say that Israel belongs to them?"

This chapter will prove beyond a shadow of a doubt that it
does. Yet the case needs to be made because much of the world
is determined to prove otherwise. They claim that Jewish people
are "occupiers" of the land. Even former UN Secretary General
Ban Ki-Moon "made the outrageous assertion that the slashing
of innocent Israeli civilians by knife-wielding Palestinians is

justifiable as a response to the 'weight of half a century of (Israeli) occupation.'"[3]

The anti-Semitic voice is strong, but the proof regarding Israel is stronger. Scripture says that "a cord of three strands is not quickly broken" (Eccles. 4:12, NIV). That is what this chapter is about: three braided strands that connect the land of Israel directly to the Jewish people. When you see how God has woven them together, you will rest assured that man cannot break the cord.

---

## LIVING PROPHECY 4

A three-strand cord is not easily broken. Biblical, political, and archaeological proof confirms that the land of Israel belongs to the Jewish people.

## THE FIRST STRAND: THE BIBLE

The first strand is God's Word, the biblical evidence of God's covenant with the Jewish people, which is both spiritual and physical. In terms of the physical, it addresses a certain people and place. The place is Israel, a tiny country approximately 290 miles long and 85 miles wide, with a total area of about 8,630 square miles. That is comparable in size to New Jersey, a small US state.

Why would a nation of insignificant size be so important in the world's eyes? The answer is God! The world knows the biblical history that traces Israel's origins back to Abraham. Remember the avot in this matter: God's unchanging covenant reveals His intent regarding Israel, the Jewish people, and the world's response to both:

> Now the LORD had said to Abram: "Get out of your country, from your family and from your father's house, to a land that I will show you. I will make you a great nation; I will bless you and make your name great; and you shall be a blessing. I will bless those who bless you,

and I will curse him who curses you; and in you all the
families of the earth shall be blessed."

—GENESIS 12:1–3

God revealed Himself as the one true God and told Abram
(later named Abraham) to leave Mesopotamia for a land that God
would show him. The revelation of the God who is not a false
god is central to Jewish thought and to the promise. Probably
the most important prayer in Judaism is called the *Shema*, which
in Hebrew means "hear or listen."[4] The prayer comes from
Deuteronomy 6:4 and calls Israel to attention, saying, "Hear O
Israel: the LORD our God, the LORD is one!"

As we continue, please bear in mind that leading Abraham
to the Promised Land was key to the promise of Genesis 12:2–3.
Now let's take a good look at this promise.

## God's three-part promise to Abraham

The first part of God's promise to Abraham involved blessing
him and making a nation of his lineage. In other words,
Abraham would be a father to the generations after him. Gentile
believers in Jesus would become part of this blessing, but that
would come much later, when they were grafted in. (See Romans
11:17–18). In fact the Gentiles would have to understand that the
church is not the root but the branch being grafted into the lineage of Abraham, Isaac, Jacob, Moses, David, and others. The
first Christian martyr, Stephen, affirmed this, saying, "The
God of glory appeared to *our father Abraham* when he was in
Mesopotamia" (Acts 7:2).

The second part of the promise to Abraham involved his
descendants and the land of Israel. God said, "I am the LORD,
who brought you out of Ur of the Chaldeans, to give you this
land to inherit it" (Gen. 15:7). The land was given not only to
Abraham but also to his descendants. God specifically said, "To
your descendants I have given this land, from the river of Egypt
to the great river, the River Euphrates" (Gen. 15:18).

Notice that God did not speak in general terms. He described very specific borders and boundaries "from the river of Egypt to the great river, the River Euphrates—the Kenites, the Kenezzites, the Kadmonites, the Hittites, the Perizzites, the Rephaim, the Amorites, the Canaanites, the Girgashites, and the Jebusites" (Gen. 15:18–21). God named many different peoples in these verses, but in no way, shape, or form did He mention the people known today as Palestinians.

The name Palestinian is not mentioned in the Bible, although it is believed to be related to the Philistines (who were not an Arabic people, as we'll see shortly). Nor does Scripture record the history of a Palestinian people. I don't say that to be cruel or uncaring but to prove what history shows: there is no evidence that they as a people inhabited the land when God made His everlasting covenant with Abram and his lineage.

The Hebrew word for *covenant* is *berit*, a "solemn, formal agreement between two parties."[5] In Abraham's case God made a covenant between Himself and the entire Jewish race. It is an everlasting and unbreakable covenant, a *berit olam*. When God makes such a covenant, He does not take it back.

The third part of God's promise was that Abraham would bless the world. When God made this promise, the tiny nation of Israel existed only in His heart. Yet one day that nation would bless the entire world, even if the world despised it. We saw earlier the many ways in which Israel's excellence has benefited the planet. That is God's promise being fulfilled!

**Does God's covenant still apply?**

In my opinion we can address questions about the covenant's standing by understanding the term Promised Land. We can agree that the land promised to Abraham is the biblical land known as Israel. The question being raised today is about who promised the land and whether a promise from four thousand years ago is still valid.

Let's examine the proof and advance the story by several hundred years. Joshua was about to lead the Israelites into the

Promised Land, and God reiterated the promise He'd made to Abraham, Isaac, and Jacob:

> After the death of Moses the servant of the LORD, it came to pass that the LORD spoke to Joshua the son of Nun, Moses' assistant, saying: "Moses My servant is dead. Now therefore, arise, go over this Jordan, you and all this people, to the land which I am giving to them—the children of Israel. Every place that the sole of your foot will tread upon I have given you, as I said to Moses....Be strong and of good courage, for to this people you shall divide as an inheritance the land which I swore to their fathers to give them."
>
> —JOSHUA 1:1–3, 6

To paraphrase verse 6, God said, "I know you're going to face great obstacles and fight many battles. But stay strong and courageous. I was the One who promised this land to your forefathers, and it will be the Jewish people's homeland forever." God restated the promise in Deuteronomy 4:40, where He referred to the territory as "the land which the LORD your God is giving you for *all time*."

Notice that God promised the land to Abraham and then repeated the promise to Isaac, Jacob, and Moses. Then, after the Israelites spent forty years in the wilderness and were about to step into the land, God reiterated His promise to Joshua. God never changed His mind.

Later, in the Book of Ezekiel, God spoke about the land being divided among Israel's twelve tribes and called it their inheritance:

> These are the borders by which you shall divide the land as an inheritance among the twelve tribes of Israel. Joseph shall have two portions. You shall inherit it equally with one another; for I raised My hand in an oath to give it to your fathers, and this land shall fall to you as your inheritance.
>
> —EZEKIEL 47:13–14

I encourage you to read all the way to verse 20 to see the details that God provided concerning the land and its borders. We hear today about how Israel is being pressured to change its borders, but God already defined them. Many Scripture references reiterate God's promise to Abraham. Here are just a few:

> The LORD said to Abram, after Lot had separated from him: "Lift your eyes now and look from the place where you are—northward, southward, eastward, and westward; for the land which you see I give to you and your descendants forever. And I will make your descendants as the dust of the earth; so that if a man could number the dust of the earth, then your descendants also could be numbered. Arise, walk in the land through its length and its width, for I give it to you."
>
> —GENESIS 13:14–17

> When Abram was ninety-nine years old, the LORD appeared to Abram and said to him, "I am Almighty God; walk before Me and be blameless. And I will make My covenant between Me and you, and will multiply you exceedingly." Then Abram fell on his face, and God talked with him, saying: "As for Me, behold, My covenant is with you, and you shall be a father of many nations. No longer shall your name be called Abram, but your name shall be Abraham; for I have made you a father of many nations. I will make you exceedingly fruitful; and I will make nations of you, and kings shall come from you. And I will establish My covenant between Me and you and your descendants after you in their generations, for an everlasting covenant, to be God to you and your descendants after you. Also I give to you and your descendants after you the land in which you are a stranger, all the land of Canaan, as an everlasting possession; and I will be their God."
>
> —GENESIS 17:1–8

Then the LORD said to [Moses], "This is the land of
which I swore to give Abraham, Isaac, and Jacob, saying,
'I will give it to your descendants.'"
                                        —DEUTERONOMY 34:4

He remembers His covenant forever, the word which He
commanded, for a thousand generations, the covenant
which He made with Abraham, and His oath to Isaac,
and confirmed it to Jacob for a statute, to Israel as an
everlasting covenant, saying, "To you I will give the land
of Canaan as the allotment of your inheritance."
                                        —PSALM 105:8–11

The LORD has chosen Zion; He has desired it for His
dwelling place: "This is My resting place forever; here I
will dwell, for I have desired it."
                                        —PSALM 132:13–14

This should settle the question of whether Israel belongs to the
Jewish people. God's Word has never wavered. I would also note
that Scripture mentions places such as Judea and Samaria but
not the West Bank and Palestine.

## THE SECOND STRAND: POLITICS

The second strand in the cord connecting the Jewish people to
their land is politics and where it meets biblical prophecy. While
the first cord should be sufficient to prove the Jewish people's
case, it is not enough for some. So let's unpack their claims that
Israel is "occupying" Palestinian land.

The origins of the word *Palestine* are uncertain. Many believe it
comes from the Hebrew and Egyptian *peleshet*, meaning "rolling
or migratory," and refers to people who lived northeast of Egypt.
These were the Philistines, an Aegean people not associated "eth-
nically, linguistically, or historically with Arabia." In fact a deriv-
ative of the word Palestine—Palaistin—"first appear[ed] in Greek
literature in the 5th Century BCE."[6]

Amazing, isn't it? A 1967 UN Security Council resolution that was unfavorable to Israel did not refer to Palestinians but only to "refugee[s]."[7]

This is where politics and prophecy begin to coincide. In the first century the Romans held Israel and the Jewish people, and they were true occupiers of the land. Yet even Rome's mighty armies could not break the spirit of the Jewish people, as we see at Masada, Herod's fortress in the Judean desert. In AD 73 Rome used fifteen thousand men and women, including around eight thousand soldiers, to capture Masada.[8] In the end nine hundred sixty Jewish men, women, and children were dead.[9]

Rome was not satisfied with ruling Israel; they wanted to crush the Jewish people. In AD 132, decades after Rome sacked Jerusalem in AD 70, a Jewish revolt led by Shimon Bar Kokhba [also spelled Kochba], known as the Bar Kokhba Revolt, was the third and final revolt against the Roman Empire. The revolt was initially successful, but the Romans ultimately laid waste to ancient Judea. This decimated Judean society, with most of the Jewish population either dead, enslaved, or exiled.[10] All hope seemed lost, and the Jewish people would not see an independent state until 1948.

Rome's hatred of the Jewish people and the land of Israel seemed to have no end. Determined to wipe out Israel's name and identity, the Roman Emperor Hadrian renamed the nation Syria Palaestina.[11] Later, when the Ottoman Empire ruled the land (1517–1917), the name Palestine was used to describe the land south of Syria. However, during the British Mandate (which ended when Israel regained its independence in 1948), press reports often referred to Jewish people, not Arabs, as Palestinians.[12]

### The words of politicians

You have seen the biblical evidence of God's promises regarding Israel. Now we will see how politicians, lawyers, and international law confirmed its Jewish ownership. In 1917 the British government endorsed the establishment of a Jewish homeland in Palestine (as the land was called under the British

Mandate). The endorsement went public on November 2, 2017, in a letter from British foreign secretary Arthur James Balfour to Lord Rothschild. In 1922 the League of Nations responded to the Balfour Declaration by entrusting the land's administration to Britain, which had been granted the mandate in 1920, at the San Remo Conference.

At San Remo the Allied victors of World War I had acted on the Balfour Declaration and divided the previous Ottoman Empire into three territories—Syria, Mesopotamia, and Palestine—and established mandates for their government. It was the first time in two thousand years that the world's nations agreed about the existence of a Jewish homeland. The conference was attended by the British Empire, France, Italy, and Japan, with the United States as a neutral observer. Later, when the League of Nations endorsed the San Remo Resolution, the Jewish people received exclusive legal and political rights to the land of Israel.[13]

Despite these international proclamations, the State of Israel did not yet exist. In late 1947 the United Nations General Assembly drafted a resolution calling for Palestine to be partitioned between Arab and Jewish people. This brought Israel's rebirth closer and put fifty-six nations on record. UN Resolution 181 was adopted on November 29, 1947, with 33 countries voting in favor, 13 countries against, and 10 abstentions.

On May 14, 1948, the day the British Mandate expired, at midnight, the provisional government officially declared the independent State of Israel. Eleven minutes after this proclamation President Harry S. Truman made the United States the first nation to grant Israel de facto recognition. On May 11, 1949, Israel was admitted to the United Nations as its fifty-ninth member.

Decisions made at San Remo, the League of Nations, and the United Nations continue to be challenged but only in regard to Israel's existence. No one challenges the right of Syria, Lebanon, or any other nation to exist. The borders of Jordan and Egypt are not questioned, and no other lawfully established nation's sovereignty has been disputed. The San Remo Conference laid the political foundation for all the Arab League states and one

Jewish one—the State of Israel. If the world is OK with all those Arab states, why can't the Jewish people have just one?

Another point is rarely mentioned: the Arabs never resisted San Remo's re-creation of a Jewish state. Their main goal was establishing independent Arab states. They were not concerned about the Jewish people getting a tiny, mostly abandoned sliver of land. Listen to what His Royal Highness the Emir Faisal (representing the Arab side) and Dr. Chaim Weizmann (representing the Zionists) agreed publicly at the time: "In the establishment of the Constitution and Administration of Palestine all such measures shall be adopted as will afford the fullest guarantees for carrying into effect the British Government's Declaration of the 2nd of November, 1917."[14]

In other words, an Arab leader and a Jewish leader publicly supported the Balfour Declaration! It gets even better: Faisal agreed that "All necessary measures shall be taken to encourage and stimulate immigration of Jews into Palestine on a large scale, and as quickly as possible to settle Jewish immigrants upon the land through closer settlement and intensive cultivation of the soil."[15]

Does that shock you? Here is another amazing fact: The Arab nation-states did not challenge Israel's right to exist until after they had secured 99 percent of the former Ottoman Empire as Arab territory.[16]

Now, let me braid the second strand of our cord a little tighter. On July 24, 1922, the entire League of Nations and all fifty-one of its members unanimously declared, "Whereas recognition has thereby been given to the historical connection of the Jewish people with Palestine and to the grounds for reconstituting their national home in that country..."[17] Two key points must be stressed: First the League unanimously recognized the historical connection between the Jewish people and Palestine, underscoring the preexisting right of the Jewish people to the land. Second the agreement called for "reconstituting" the Jewish national home. All fifty-one nations supported Israel's rebirth!

This great merging of biblical and political mandates confirms that the Jewish people belong in their Promised Land. The Word of God and the words of international legal documents agree: Israel is the national homeland of the Jewish people.

## THE THIRD STRAND: ARCHAEOLOGY

The third strand linking the Jewish people to their land is historical. Several years ago I was asked to do a small documentary in Israel encouraging tourism to the Holy Land. Today the Israeli national park and archaeological site known as the City of David is full of tourists, but back then its excavation was just underway. I remember standing next to what some archaeologists believe to be King David's palace. Later one archaeologist discovered a rare clay seal and a twenty-six-hundred-year-old stone stamp bearing biblical names engraved in ancient Hebrew. The items were in the ruins of a magnificent building from the first temple period that was thought to have been destroyed by the ancient Babylonians.[18]

Dr. Anat Mendel-Geberovich of the Hebrew University of Jerusalem and the Center for the Study of Ancient Jerusalem deciphered the writing on the stamp and found these words: "(belonging) to Nathan-Melech, Servant of the King."[19] Nathan-Melech's name is found only once in the Hebrew Bible:

> Then he removed the horses that the kings of Judah had dedicated to the sun, at the entrance to the house of the Lord, by the chamber of Nathan-Melech, the officer who was in the court; and he burned the chariots of the sun with fire.
>
> —2 Kings 23:11

Nathan-Melech served under King Josiah, six hundred years before the time of Jesus. Yet many people still insist that the Jewish people were not in the land. They claim that Bible history is false and no Jewish temple or City of David ever existed. But I have stood among the newly discovered ruins of the City of David, and I have seen pictures of the artifacts I just described. I heard the Lord speak these words afresh to my spirit: "But He answered and said to them, 'I tell you that if these should keep silent, the stones would immediately cry out'" (Luke 19:40).

Another stamp-seal was found in the ruins, this one bearing the Hebrew name "Ikar son of Matanyahu," which appears in most English Bible translations as "Mattaniah."[20] I could go on and on about coins, seals, stamps, pottery, and other discoveries—not only at the City of David but everywhere in Israel. The stones really are crying out! They are proving the truth of God's Word and of the ancient Jewish presence in the Promised Land.

To skeptics none of this seems to matter. They say the pottery could be fake, the coins and other items could be counterfeits, and the sites are fabrications. But something happened in 2004 that no one could have faked. A discovery changed everything when a sewage pipe failed in Silwan, an East Jerusalem neighborhood known in Scripture as Shiloah, or Siloam. Because of Israel's ancient historical roots, both a construction team and archaeologists examined the site. What they found was stunning: some long, wide stairs just meters from where the ancient pool, or mikvah, of Siloam stood until AD 70.[21]

The pool is well-documented in Scripture. Isaiah 8:6 describes "the waters of Shiloah that flow softly." The pool also appears in John's account of Jesus healing the blind man:

> [Jesus] spat on the ground and made clay with the saliva; and He anointed the eyes of the blind man with the clay. And He said to him, "Go, wash in the pool of Siloam"....So he went and washed, and came back seeing.
>
> —JOHN 9:6–7

Some rabbinic traditions identify the pool as the "Messiah's pool," which King Hezekiah built in the eighth century BC to provide water to Jerusalem.[22] Scripture confirms that such a structure existed:

> Now the rest of the acts of Hezekiah—all his might, and how we made a pool and a tunnel and brought water

into the city—are they not written in the book of the chronicles of the kings of Judah?

—2 KINGS 20:20

The pool had a special role during the Feast of Tabernacles, when a priest would fill a vessel at the pool and carry it up the Pilgrim's Road to the temple courts. As the priest poured the water on the altar, the crowds chanted the Hallel (Psalm 113–118).[23] Isaiah tells us that the Feast of Tabernacles was a time of great joy:

> Therefore with joy you will draw water from the wells of salvation. And in that day you will say: "Praise the LORD, call upon His name; declare His deeds among the peoples, make mention that His name is exalted. Sing to the LORD, for He has done excellent things; this is known in all the earth. Cry out and shout, O inhabitant of Zion, for great is the Holy One of Israel in your midst!"
>
> —ISAIAH 12:3–6

Finding the pool's steps led to two more great discoveries. The first was ancient Jerusalem's central water drainage channel, through which today's visitors can now walk. The second was the ancient Pilgrim's Road, or Pilgrimage Road. Archaeologists believe that millions of Jewish people walked this road on Pesach (Feast of Unleavened Bread, or Passover), Shavuot (Feast of Weeks, or Pentecost), and Sukkot (Feast of Tabernacles).[24] Scripture says that all Jewish males came to Jerusalem for these three feasts:

> Three times a year all your males shall appear before the LORD your God in the place which He chooses: at the Feast of Unleavened Bread, at the Feast of Weeks, and at the Feast of Tabernacles; and they shall not appear before the LORD empty-handed.
>
> —DEUTERONOMY 16:16

Many times I have been privileged to film our television show on the Pilgrimage Road. My good friend Ze'ev Orenstein

(Director of International Affairs at the City of David Foundation) has walked the ruins with me—stones that were hidden from sight for almost two thousand years. He showed me where archaeologists found a golden bell that would have hung from the high priest's robe. Archaeologists also found a place full of the exact coins the money changers would have used, which a respected source told me proves that Jesus walked this road! The places, events, and people that make Jerusalem what it is were here, exactly the way the Bible says. Ze'ev calls the road the location of "the beating heart of Jerusalem."[25] The Pilgrimage Road links the Pool of Siloam, Mount Moriah and the Temple Mount, and the City of David!

Friend, this is happening right before our eyes. Even as I wrote this chapter, my phone lit up with texts and calls from friends around the world telling me that another first temple seal had been found! Its inscription says, "Belonging to Adoniyahu, the Royal Steward." Adoniyahu means "the Lord is my Master."[26] The archaeological third strand is proving the living prophecies true!

## THE STONES SPEAK ANYWAY

On Sunday, June 30, 2019, Israeli and American dignitaries gathered to commemorate the finding of the Pilgrimage Road.[27] A few days later US Ambassador David Friedman shared his reaction with Christians United for Israel:

> How incredible to be involved, even ceremonially, in this once in a century discovery. To immerse oneself in the ancient history of the Jewish people; to stand on the footsteps of the beginning of Christianity. Not just to see in a museum a shard of glass, an ancient coin or a piece of parchment. But to stand at the crossroads of history itself![28]

Not everyone agreed with the ambassador. "Saeb Erekat, the chief Palestinian negotiator, said…'[The Pilgrimage Road] has nothing to do with religion, it is fake.'"[29] His remarks remind me of an expression that is sometimes funny but also sad: "My mind is made up. Don't confuse me with the facts." The prophet Jeremiah said it this way: "Behold, you trust in lying words that cannot profit" (Jer. 7:8).

No matter what the world says, the stones will cry out, and those who have ears to hear will hear. In chapter 1 I mentioned a meeting in which Prime Minister Netanyahu answered my question about the Pilgrimage Road. He said that Jewish and Christian people walked that road together two millennia ago. Today, as those stones cry out, Jewish and Christian people are walking side by side on that road again—a miracle of God! What God has in store is more exciting and powerful than you can imagine, so let's go!

Your best is still ahead!

## CHAPTER 5

# THE SPIRITUAL RETURN (STEP OUT OF LINE!)

*"Return to Me, and I will return to you," says the LORD of hosts.*
—MALACHI 3:7

EVER SINCE WRITING the outline for this book, I had planned to call this chapter "The Spiritual Return." Recently, however, my daughters, Anna and Katie, told me about an acceptance speech by actress Alex Borstein, who talked about her grandmother, an immigrant and Holocaust survivor. While waiting in line to be shot and thrown into a ditch, Borstein's grandmother asked a guard, "What happens if I step out of line?"[1]

The guard assured her that he would not shoot her, but someone else would. Borstein's grandmother stepped out of line anyway. She lived to tell the story and, according to Borstein, is the reason the actress and her children are here today.[2]

To step out of line in such dire circumstances took unimaginable courage. Going against the tide is difficult even when your life is not at stake. But if you are willing to break with man's traditions, you can play your part in prophetic history. In a way that is what this chapter is all about.

---

## LIVING PROPHECY 5

The greater return—the spiritual return—has begun. The church will return to its Jewish roots and a Jewish understanding of God's Word.

## RETURN OF THE HEART

Earlier we focused on the miracle return of the Jewish people to the land of God's promise. As I have already mentioned, there is another return—the spiritual return of the Gentile Christians, in which every Christian has a part.

The word *aliyah* is about ascent and literally means elevation or going up. It is used to refer to the return of the Jewish people to Israel, but it is also used in the synagogue, when a person is called up to the *bimah* (usually an elevated platform) to present a reading from the Torah.[3] Whether it is physical or spiritual, aliyah requires that you step out of where you are.

I'm asking you to have courage, not to defy Nazi guards, but to make your personal aliyah back to your Jewish roots. Believe it or not, your spiritual return is linked to the return of the Jewish people to the land. The prophet Jeremiah showed us the connection in a passage I have divided into two parts. I believe each word is a paving stone that will bring you closer to your spiritual promised land. Take your time reading it.

> "Therefore behold, the days are coming," says the LORD, "that it shall no more be said, 'The LORD lives who brought up the children of Israel from the land of Egypt,' but, 'The LORD lives who brought up the children of Israel from the land of the north and from all the lands where He had driven them.' For I will bring them back into their land which I gave to their fathers."
> —JEREMIAH 16:14–15

This is obviously about the physical return to the land. Jeremiah referenced the original Exodus but also spoke to the more profound physical return from the four corners of the globe. In my opinion what he described next is the spiritual return of the Gentiles:

> O LORD, my strength and my fortress, my refuge in the day of affliction, the Gentiles [the church] shall come

to You from the ends of the earth and say, "Surely our
fathers have inherited lies, worthlessness and unprofitable
things." Will a man make gods for himself, which are not
gods? Therefore behold, I will this once cause them to
know, I will cause them to know My hand and My might;
and they shall know that My name is the LORD.

—JEREMIAH 16:19–21

Notice that Jeremiah depicted Gentile Christians realizing that
they have inherited certain man-made traditions from their spiritual fathers. We have seen that these traditions include replacement
theology, the blaming of the Jewish people for killing Jesus, and the
belief that the land of Israel does not belong to the Jewish people.

We develop untruths when our knowledge of God—our
*knowing* God—wanes. So, let's focus now on Jeremiah's use of
the word *know*, which appears three times in verse 21: "I will this
once cause them to *know*, I will cause them to *know* My hand
and My might; and they shall *know* that My name is the LORD."
Notice how the Lord connects the word *know* to the experience
of His hand, might, and power. In the ancient Hebrew language
*knowing* is very personal and intimate. As English-speaking
people, we claim to know people when we are merely aware of
their existence. In Hebrew thought, however, you cannot know
someone without sharing a depth of relationship. This is the
kind of knowing that Jeremiah is pointing to. The Hebrew word
is *yada*, which was also used to describe the intimate relationship between God and Abraham:[4]

> For I have *known* him, in order that he may command
> his children and his household after him, that they
> keep the way of the LORD, to do righteousness and jus-
> tice, that the LORD may bring to Abraham what he Has
> spoken to him.
>
> —GENESIS 18:19

God said that He trusted Abraham because He had "known"
him, meaning they shared a very personal relationship. We develop

that kind of intimacy with God through an accurate understanding of His Word. Through this intimate *knowing*, He is able to reveal and release His powerful hand in every area of our lives.

Jesus explained it this way: "You shall know the truth, and the truth shall make you free" (John 8:32). Only the truth you *know* can make you free. The divine power contained in Scripture is not released until we understand and own the truth. That's the last thing the devil wants, which is why he feeds us lies and encourages us to pass them down, as some of our spiritual fathers did.

Let me give you an example. We believe that we have been redeemed by the blood. For those who have accepted Christ's sacrifice, that is absolutely true. But just saying, "I've been redeemed by the blood," has little power. We need to *know* what it means and how Jesus purchased our redemption. We need to understand the seven places He shed His blood for us and how those places directly affect us, especially when we need a miracle.

We have already talked about how this relates to the breaking of generational curses. It is also relevant to the end-time outpouring of God's power, the coming transfer of wealth, the rapture, and the second coming. *Knowing* is important.

## WHAT RETURNING LOOKS LIKE

It is so interesting that I wrote this chapter during the Hebrew month of Elul, which begins the "liturgical season of returning and repentance."[5] That is no coincidence! So let's begin with a look at Malachi 3:7: "Return to Me, and I will return to you."

The Hebrew word for *return* is *shuwb*, the root word of *teshuva*, which means repentance.[6] *Shuwb* means "to turn back."[7] The English word *repent* comes from the Latin *penitire*, which means to regret.[8] The Hebrew goes beyond regret and includes action.

We need to consider Malachi's perspective when we read his writings. He was a Jewish thinker writing to the Jewish people who returned from the Babylonian exile. Malachi was a prominent figure, one of 120 Jewish men in the *Anshei Knesset HaGedolah*— Men of the Great Assembly. This was a pretty impressive bunch of people! Included in its ranks were Ezra, Nehemiah, Mordecai, Zerubbabel, Haggai, Zechariah, and others. Today's Israeli Knesset was modeled after the Anshei Knesset HaGedolah and also has 120 members.[9]

Why did these great men of God assemble? They were seeking God's guidance "when Jewish life in the Land of Israel was crumbling."[10] They asked the difficult questions we ask today:

- How do we keep the enemy from defeating us?
- How do we stop losing?
- Why have we been conquered over and over again?
- What's up, Lord?

What God revealed to these men not only answered their questions; it answers ours. When God said, "I am the LORD, I do not change" (Mal. 3:6), it was meaningful. Imagine what it meant to men who were leading a completely broken nation. And imagine how it calmed the people's fears.

Now let's pick up in Malachi from the second part of that verse:

> Therefore you are not consumed, O sons of Jacob. Yet from the days of your fathers you have gone away from My ordinances and have not kept them. Return to Me, and I will return to you.
> —MALACHI 3:6–7

What was God saying here? Remember that the text was originally written to the Jewish people who returned from Babylon. God told them that because He does not change, He did not allow the enemy to totally destroy them. They may have walked away from their part of the covenant, but He never walked away from His!

How exactly had they walked away, and how have we? God said, "You have gone away from My ordinances and have not kept them" (Mal. 3:7). So He encouraged His people to return to the center of His path for them. That is what the Law is about—not

legalism but the path. When we drift, God draws us back by His
Spirit. Then, if we obey and return to Him, He returns to us and
releases His power and might on our behalf.

That is what God promised in this passage from Malachi:

> "Bring all the tithes into the storehouse, that there may
> be food in My house, and try Me now in this," says the
> Lord of hosts, "if I will not open for you the windows
> of heaven and pour out for you such blessing that there
> will not be room enough to receive it."
> —Malachi 3:10

The Hebrew word translated "windows" here is 'arubbah, a
window or opening—in other words, a place where the light can
come in and blessing can flow. The window opens when we get
to *know* God and His Word.

## KNOWING THE TRUTH IS KNOWING GOD

Returning to God means getting to know Him by understanding
the true meaning of His Word. That is why He urged us to get
wisdom, knowledge, and understanding.

> My son, if you receive my words, and treasure my
> commands within you, so that you incline your ear to
> wisdom, and apply your heart to understanding; yes, if
> you cry out for discernment, and lift up your voice for
> understanding, if you seek her as silver, and search for
> her as for hidden treasures; then you will understand
> the fear of the Lord, and find the knowledge of God. For
> the Lord gives wisdom; from His mouth come knowl-
> edge and understanding; He stores up sound wisdom for
> the upright; He is a shield to those who walk uprightly.
> —Proverbs 2:1–7

> Wisdom is the principal thing; therefore get wisdom.
> And in all your getting, get understanding.
> —Proverbs 4:7

> The protection of wisdom is like the protection of money, and the advantage of knowledge is that wisdom preserves the life of him who has it.
> —ECCLESIASTES 7:12, ESV

The Scriptures are clear: we need to find and *know* the truth of God's Word. That means finding the deeper meaning in what God says. Doing this spiritually is no different from looking for deeper meanings in science. The process is virtually the same.

Do you remember when we talked about the woman with the issue of blood? She understood the deeper meaning in touching the hem of Jesus' garment. We need to understand similar secrets. We need to know why God told His people to write His words on their doorposts and gates (Deut. 6:9). We need to know what happens when we "remember the Sabbath day, to keep it holy" (Exod. 20:8). We need to understand how "the Son of Man is Lord of the Sabbath" (Matt. 12:8, NIV). Knowing these things will bring blessings to our homes, marriages, children, and grandchildren.

In his second letter to Timothy, Paul shared a key that applies to us today: "Study to shew thyself approved unto God, a workman that needeth not to be ashamed, rightly dividing the word of truth" (2 Tim. 2:15, KJV). In other words, *study and know God's Word!* Some Christians might think that Paul was referring to the New Testament books. Yes, we should study those, but please remember that when Paul wrote to Timothy, there was no New Testament. He was pointing Timothy to the same texts that Jesus taught from, and all of them were in the Old Testament.

Paul said that we are to study *so that we are not ashamed*. When we miss the true meaning of God's Word, we miss out on His power and lose sight of His path. If we passively accept the lies that have been handed down to us, we miss out on the fullness of God's promises and good intentions. Yet, even if we have made this mistake, we need only to spiritually return. Just as our Jewish brothers and sisters are returning to the physical land, we can return to the spiritual truth of God's Word and really *know Him*.

## THE OPEN HAND

Several years ago Tiz and I stayed at the King David Hotel in Jerusalem. One night, as we left for dinner with friends, we spotted a ring in a shop window near the lobby. It was a beautiful gold band with only some Hebrew letters engraved on it, which when translated said: "When you open your hand, it draws God near. When you close your hand, it sends God away."

I pray that what I am about to explain stirs in you a hunger to go deeper into your Jewish roots. The Hebrew word for *knowledge* comes from the word *yada*, the word for *know*.[11] Remember that *yada* is an intimate knowing that implies deep relationship. The word consists of three Hebrew letters, and the first two spell the word *hand*, or *yad*.[12] The last letter in *yada* is *ayin*, which means eye.[13] So, in the Hebrew, hand and eye are both involved in knowing.

Think about this: if I asked you to show me your hand, you would most likely stretch it out palm up with your fingers apart. When beggars do this, they don't have to say a word. You know exactly what they are asking.

Now imagine that you have just committed the sin of gluttony at a buffet restaurant, and someone offers you more food. Because you're stuffed, you stretch out your hand with your palm outward, like a police officer stopping traffic. Everybody knows exactly what you mean: "I've had enough, thank you. No more."

Two letters in Hebrew say, "Give me," but when you reverse the order, they say, "Enough. No thank you." *Yada* is a composite of both hand and eye. When your hand is open, God's wisdom, knowledge, and understanding are available so you can know Him better. But a closed hand tells God, "No thanks. I've had enough."

You see, in Hebrew thought, giving and receiving are not entirely separate ideas. The Hebrew verb *nathan* means to give.[14] In Hebrew the word is a palindrome, which means that it reads the same forward and backward. In Jewish thought our giving also means that we receive. An open hand draws God's blessing; a closed hand rejects it.

Remember that ring in the King David Hotel? Tiz, who is a real truth and treasure in my life, bought it for me for my birthday! Every time I wear it, I am reminded that when I open my hand to help others, God opens His hand to help me.

## FIRST COMING OR SECOND?

Before I close this chapter, let's look at another way in which our spiritual return is connected to supernatural wisdom. We know that God said, "Return to Me, and I will return to you" (Mal. 3:7). God is talking teshuva here, but we need to know exactly whom He was addressing. Many believe that Malachi was preparing the Jewish people for the first coming of the Messiah. They are right. But if you said, "No, I think God is telling the church to return and prepare for the second coming," you would be right too.

Let me explain by doing something we Christians need to do more: check the context. Instead of reading the most popular lines from Malachi, let's look at the beginning of chapter 3, where the Lord said: "Behold, I send My messenger, and he will prepare the way before Me" (Mal. 3:1).

Now ask yourself, "Who is this messenger?" Most people would agree that God was talking about John the Baptist—"the voice of one crying in the wilderness: 'Prepare the way of the LORD; make straight in the desert a highway for our God'" (Isa. 40:3). Matthew's Gospel seems to confirm it:

> In those days John the Baptist came preaching in the wilderness of Judea, and saying, "Repent, for the kingdom of heaven is at hand!" For this is he who was spoken of by the prophet Isaiah, saying: "The voice of one crying in the wilderness: 'Prepare the way of the Lord; make His paths straight.' ".
> —MATTHEW 3:1–3

We can agree that Malachi is speaking of John the Baptist, but remember that many teachings convey both a lesser and greater meaning. The concept of the lesser and the greater is seen often in Scripture:

> Then God made two great lights: *the greater light to rule the day, and the lesser light* to rule the night.
> —Genesis 1:16

> Let us now fear the Lord our God, who gives rain, both *the former and the latter*, in its season. He reserves for us the appointed weeks of the harvest.
> —Jeremiah 5:24

> For He has given you the former rain faithfully, and He will cause the rain to come down for you—*the former rain, and the latter rain* in the first month.
> —Joel 2:23

> "The glory of this latter temple shall be *greater* than the former," says the Lord of hosts.
> —Haggai 2:9

> Assuredly, I say to you, among those born of women there has not risen *one greater than John the Baptist; but he who is least in the kingdom of heaven is greater than he.* And from the days of John the Baptist until now the kingdom of heaven suffers violence, and the violent take it by force. For all the prophets and the law prophesied until John. And if you are willing to receive it, he is Elijah who is to come.
> —Matthew 11:11–14

> There were also women looking on from afar, among whom were Mary Magdalene, Mary the mother of *James the Less* and of Joses, and Salome.
> —Mark 15:40

> Consider how great this man [Melchizedek] was, to whom even the patriarch Abraham gave a tenth of the spoils. And indeed those who are of the sons of Levi,

> who receive the priesthood, have a commandment to
> receive tithes from the people according to the law, that
> is, from their brethren, though they have come from the
> loins of Abraham; but he whose genealogy is not derived
> from them received tithes from Abraham and blessed
> him who had the promises. Now beyond all contradic-
> tion *the lesser is blessed by the better.*
> —HEBREWS 7:4–7

> Likewise, you younger people [of lesser rank and expe-
> rience], submit yourself to your elders [those of higher
> rank and experience].
> —1 PETER 5:5

Understanding the lesser and the greater is one of the great
secrets of rabbinical Bible study. For example, Elijah was one of
the greatest prophets in all of Scripture. Yet Jesus said that John
the Baptist was an even greater prophet. The same is true of the
first exodus and the second. The first was phenomenal, but the
second was even more miraculous, as we read in Jeremiah 16:14–15.

You just saw where Malachi wrote, "Behold, I send My messenger, and he will prepare the way before Me" (Mal. 3:1), speaking
of John the Baptist, "the voice of one crying in the wilderness" (Isa.
40:3). This wilderness was a physical desert, and the messenger
was calling the people to prepare for the coming of the Messiah!
As amazing as this was, it was the lesser event, the early rain.

Allow me to explain. Four hundred fifty years earlier God
warned the people, saying, "From the days of your fathers you
have gone away from My ordinances and have not kept them.
Return to Me, and I will return to you" (Mal. 3:7). So the Jewish
people returned. We know this because in Jesus' time Jewish
people came from every nation to worship in Jerusalem and
bring their offerings to the temple at Passover, Shavuot, and
Tabernacles. John even baptized people in the wilderness. It was
a sign of their return done in preparation for the holiest day on
the Jewish calendar, the Day of Atonement, which was about to
be fulfilled in Christ.

When God called for the Jewish people to return in Malachi, they asked Him, "How shall we return?...How have we robbed You?" He answered very plainly: "In tithes and offerings" (Malachi 3:7–8, NASB), which God had commanded centuries earlier:

> And all the tithe of the land, whether of the seed of the land or of the fruit of the tree, is the LORD's. It is holy to the LORD.
>
> —LEVITICUS 27:30

> Three times a year all your males shall appear before the LORD your God in the place which He chooses: at the Feast of Unleavened Bread, at the Feast of Weeks, and at the Feast of Tabernacles; and they shall not appear before the LORD empty-handed.
>
> —DEUTERONOMY 16:16

Obviously God brought correction to the Jewish people within Malachi's call to return. But I am making a larger point. The Jewish people responded to God's call and were worshipping together in Jerusalem when John the Baptist prepared them for the Messiah's first coming. Today's call to teshuva comes before the Lord's *second* coming, which is the greater event!

## SUDDENLY

Now let's look at a characteristic that distinguishes the second coming from the first. Remember that Malachi 3:1 says the Lord "will *suddenly* come to His temple." I emphasize the word *suddenly* because there was nothing sudden about Jesus' advent and earthly walk.

To see what I mean, let's touch on some highlights in Jesus' story, beginning with the angelic messages delivered to Mary the virgin and Joseph, her betrothed.

> In the sixth month the angel Gabriel was sent by God to a city of Galilee named Nazareth, to a virgin betrothed to a man whose name was Joseph, of the house of David. The virgin's name was Mary. And having come in, the

> angel said to her, "Rejoice, highly favored one, the Lord
> is with you; blessed are you among women!...And
> behold, you will conceive in your womb and bring forth
> a Son, and shall call his name Jesus."
>
> —Luke 1:26–28, 31

An angel also visited Joseph.

> The birth of Jesus Christ was as follows: After his
> mother Mary was betrothed to Joseph, before they came
> together, she was found with child of the Holy Spirit.
> Then Joseph her husband, being a just man, and not
> wanting to make her a public example, was minded to
> put her away secretly. But while he thought about these
> things, behold, an angel of the Lord appeared to him in
> a dream, saying, "Joseph, son of David, do not be afraid
> to take to you Mary your wife, for that which is con-
> ceived in her is of the Holy Spirit."
>
> —Matthew 1:18–20

After Jesus was born, because He was Jewish, He underwent
the ritual circumcision when He was eight days old.

> When eight days were completed for the circumcision
> of the Child, His name was called Jesus, the name given
> by the angel before He was conceived in the womb. Now
> when the days of [Mary's] purification according to the
> law of Moses were completed, they brought Him to
> Jerusalem to present Him to the Lord.
>
> —Luke 2:21–22

Months after Jesus was born, wise men from far away visited
Him and gave Him gifts.

> After Jesus was born in Bethlehem of Judea in the days
> of Herod the king, behold, wise men from the East came
> to Jerusalem, saying, "Where is He who has been born
> King of the Jews? For we have seen His star in the East

and have come to worship Him."...And when they had come into the house, they saw the young Child with Mary His mother, and fell down and worshiped him. And when they had opened their treasures, they presented gifts to Him: gold, frankincense, and myrrh.

—MATTHEW 2:1–2, 11

Later, because of Herod's rage, an angelic messenger told Joseph to take the family to Egypt.

When they had departed, behold, an angel of the Lord appeared to Joseph in a dream, saying, "Arise, take the young Child and His mother, flee to Egypt, and stay there until I bring you word; for Herod will seek the young Child to destroy Him." When he arose, he took the young Child and His mother by night and departed for Egypt.

—MATTHEW 2:13–14

When Jesus was twelve, He and His parents celebrated the Passover in Jerusalem. On the way home Jesus separated Himself from them and lingered in the temple.

His parents went to Jerusalem every year at the Feast of the Passover. And when He was twelve years old, they went up to Jerusalem according to the custom of the feast. When they had finished the days, as they returned, the Boy Jesus lingered behind in Jerusalem....Now so it was that after three days they found Him in the temple, sitting in the midst of the teachers, both listening to them and asking them questions.

—LUKE 2:41–43, 46

Scripture is virtually silent about Jesus' life between the ages of twelve and thirty. The following passage describes a very significant event when Jesus was a fully grown man—His baptism by his cousin, John:

> When all the people were baptized, it came to pass
> that Jesus also was baptized; and while He prayed, the
> heaven was opened. And the Holy Spirit descended in
> bodily form like a dove upon Him, and a voice came
> from heaven which said, "You are My beloved Son; in
> You I am well pleased." Now Jesus Himself began His
> ministry at about thirty years of age.
> —LUKE 3:21–23

These scriptures are only a sampling of the events in Jesus' life. Obviously there were countless others, including the wedding feast in Cana of Galilee, the Sermon on the Mount, the Samaritan woman at the well, the raising of Lazarus from the dead, the triumphant ride into Jerusalem on a borrowed donkey, His final Passover meal with His disciples, the Garden of Gethsemane, His brutal death, His glorious resurrection, and His ascension.

My point is that there was absolutely nothing sudden about the Lord's first coming. But Malachi said that He will *suddenly* come to His temple. Therefore Malachi could not be talking about His first coming. It has to be His second coming, which Paul and Peter described so beautifully.

> ...in a moment, in the twinkling of an eye, at the last
> trumpet. For the trumpet will sound, and the dead will
> be raised incorruptible, and we shall be changed.
> —1 CORINTHIANS 15:52

> The day of the Lord will come as a thief in the night,
> in which the heavens will pass away with a great noise,
> and the elements will melt with a fervent heat; both the
> earth and the works that are in it will be burned up.
> —2 PETER 3:10

Malachi's call to teshuva in chapter 3 verse 7 preceded the first coming of Jesus. That return took from the time of Malachi and the Great Assembly to the time of Jesus—approximately 400 to 450 years to be fulfilled. From the time the angel visited Mary to the time that Jesus hung on the cross was approximately thirty-three years. But Jesus' second coming, mentioned in Malachi 3:1, could happen before you finish reading this page.

So who is the latter rain messenger who will prepare the way for the Lord's return to the temple in Jerusalem? I believe with all my heart that it is you!

One final thought before we close this chapter: it is no coincidence that I wrote this book and you are reading it in the season when the Pilgrimage Road has reopened after two thousand years. Is it possible that some of us will be walking that road in the instant of the Messiah's coming?

Yes, it is absolutely possible!

Meanwhile you and I are on the most amazing, exciting, and powerful journey the world has ever seen. Let us return to Him now! Let's go!

## CHAPTER 6

# SIGNS AND WONDERS: GOD IS SPEAKING

*Then God said, "Let there be lights in the firmament of
the heavens to divide the day from the night; and let them
be for signs and seasons, and for days and years."*
—GENESIS 1:14

BACK WHEN I was a hippie in college, the Five Man Electrical Band had a popular song called "Signs." It was about how we lose sight of the signs all around us, as they blend into the scenery.

Have you ever felt like God was speaking, but you weren't quite getting the message? I have. Sometimes it's because we are not fully aware that He speaks in many different ways. But whichever way God speaks—through a sermon, a prophecy, or a life experience—we know when He has touched our hearts.

One of the best "sermons" I ever heard was delivered by my then five-year-old daughter Anna. We sat down to dinner about an hour before I had to leave for a meeting, and I was running late. We bowed our heads, and I said one of those "Rub-a-dub-dub, thanks for the grub" prayers all of us are guilty of praying sometimes.

When I looked up, Anna was staring at me with her big, brown eyes.

"What?" I asked.

I will never forget her response. "Daddy, don't you think we ought to thank the Lord better than that?"

Talk about out of the mouths of babes!

Sometimes God speaks to me in that still, small voice, but when He wants to awaken me to what's ahead, He sometimes shouts. It's like the Book of Joel says, "Blow the trumpet in Zion, and *sound an alarm* in My holy mountain! Let all the inhabitants of the land tremble; for the day of the LORD is coming, for it is at hand" (2:1).

That is God's shout!

When I wrote this chapter, we were in the Hebrew month of Elul, during which the shofar is blown every day except for one.[1] The month after Elul is Tishri, which starts on Rosh Hashanah (the Head of the Year). God said that day is "a day of blowing the trumpets" (Num. 29:1). These are appointed times (moadim) that connect us to the miracles and blessings of God. He uses them in part to say, "Wake up! Get ready for what I am doing! Don't miss what I have prepared for you."

Last year, on the Sunday morning our Dallas church celebrated Rosh Hashanah, our twin grand sugars, Asher and Judah, were asleep at our house, having slept over the night before. Normally Tiz awakens them with a gentle, "Boys, it's time to get up and get ready for church." But this time, I tiptoed into their room ever so quietly and blew my shofar. They went from a sound sleep to a jarring state of full alert instantly.

I know it was a little mean, but I couldn't resist. Plus I wanted to use the experience as a sermon illustration. (We preachers will do anything for a good message!) It was a great example of when God sounds the alarm. There's no time to rub your eyes or snooze. It's time to launch! He is preparing us for the ultimate event, when He will sound the alarm that changes everything:

> Behold, I tell you a mystery: We shall not all sleep, but we shall all be changed—in a moment, in the twinkling of an eye, at the last trumpet. For the trumpet will sound, and the dead will be raised incorruptible, and we shall be changed.
>
> —1 CORINTHIANS 15:51–52

The word *mystery* here is connected with sleep and the sounding of the trumpet. You can feel the drama of the scene. But we have to pay attention. God is not only speaking but shouting to us, often through profound signs and wonders. Our job is to learn the language of His signs and wonders.

We will talk primarily about signs and wonders in this chapter, but they often overlap with His miracles. This is true in the Hebrew also, in which certain words can mean all three. The two words I will focus on are *owth* which means "sign, signal,"[2] and *mowpheth*, which means "wonder, sign, miracle, portent."[3] They are virtually synonymous and often occur together in verses like the following:

> The LORD showed signs [*owth*] and wonders [*mow-pheth*] before our eyes, great and severe, against Egypt, Pharaoh, and all his household.
> —DEUTERONOMY 6:22

> …the great trials which your eyes saw, the signs [*owth*] and the wonders [*mowpheth*], the mighty hand and the outstretched arm, by which the LORD your God brought you out. So shall the LORD your God do to all the peoples of whom you are afraid.
> —DEUTERONOMY 7:19

Many Old Testament scriptures speak of God's power being demonstrated through signs and wonders. Deuteronomy 4:34; 26:8; 34:11; Nehemiah 9:10; and Psalm 105:27 are just a few. The New Testament also mentions signs and wonders involving the Holy Spirit and the apostles:

> Truly the signs of an apostle were accomplished among you with all perseverance, in signs and wonders and mighty deeds.
> —2 CORINTHIANS 12:12

...God also bearing witness both by signs and wonders, with various miracles, and gifts of the Holy Spirit, according to His own will.

—HEBREWS 2:4

Signs, wonders, and miracles are God's manifested power at work. Miracles of healing, deliverance, provision, and victory are all signs and wonders. Because "Jesus Christ is the same yesterday, today, and forever" (Heb. 13:8), miracles are for every era (although they seem to be on the rise today). You may already know that our family experienced two lifesaving miracles from God's hand within a year's time. When I say "lifesaving," I mean it! I'll save those for later. For now we have some amazing signs and wonders to explore!

## LIVING PROPHECY 6

God said, "I will show wonders in heaven above and signs in the earth beneath: blood and fire and vapor of smoke. The sun shall be turned into darkness, and the moon into blood, before the coming of the great and awesome day of the Lord. And it shall come to pass that whoever calls on the name of the Lord shall be saved" (Acts 2:19–21).

## THE SIGN OF THE BLOOD MOONS

God's signs and wonders are plain, if our spiritual eyes and ears are open to them. One of the most amazing signs *ever* happened not once but four times in 2014 and 2015. I'm talking about the blood moons that occurred on April 15 and October 8 in 2014, and on April 4 and September 27 in 2015. While in Jerusalem I had eyes to see what God was saying, both in the physical and spiritual sense with these amazing sights.

Before we explore further, remember what God said as He created the heavenly bodies:

> Let there be lights in the firmament of the heavens to
> divide the day from the night; and let them be for signs
> and seasons, and for days and years.
> —GENESIS 1:14

God created the heavens to speak to us. In Genesis 1:14 the word translated "signs" is *owth*. Signs appear much the way "a flag, beacon, monument, omen, prodigy, evidence… [or] token" does.[4] Remember that the 2014 and 2015 blood moons coincided with Jewish feast days. Signs like that should get our attention. They are God's shout in a language only He can speak!

Allow me to clarify something: when God talks about signs in the heavens, He is talking in terms of astronomy, *not* astrology. Astronomy is the science that guides observation and research into everything outside the earth's atmosphere. It is one of the oldest sciences, and many of the world's earliest civilizations studied the skies.

The Bible is filled with astronomical references such as the one we just read in Genesis 1:14. When God called Abraham, he used the stars to illustrate the limitlessness of Abraham's legacy, saying, "Look now toward heaven, and count the stars if you are able to number them" (Gen. 15:5). God used "the sun, the moon, and the eleven stars" in a dream to show Joseph the greatness of his destiny (Gen. 37:9).

I have to smile as I remember a preacher on TV who said that if we have Jesus, signs in the sky have nothing to do with us. But signs in the heavens have a lot to do with us. In fact God used heavenly signs to announce the birth of Jesus, which is definitely New Testament.

> After Jesus was born in Bethlehem of Judea in the days
> of Herod the king, behold, wise men from the East came
> to Jerusalem, saying, "Where is He who has been born
> King of the Jews? For we have seen His star in the East
> and have come to worship him."
> —MATTHEW 2:1–2

The wise men who came seeking Jesus had a keen knowledge of biblical prophecy and understood that the star signaled the birth of a king—*the* King. They trekked all the way to Bethlehem because they understood the significance of what was happening.

> When they had come into the house, they saw the young Child with Mary His mother, and fell down and worshiped Him. And when they had opened their treasures, they presented gifts to Him: gold, frankincense, and myrrh.
>
> —MATTHEW 2:11

The wise men knew prophetically that the world was about to change. They were right: the first coming of Jesus changed everything. Today's signs are announcing Jesus' second coming; therefore they are even greater and cannot be ignored. Tremendous change has happened since the four blood moons of 2014 and 2015—arguably more than had previously happened worldwide since 1948. We need to reopen our eyes toward the signs in the heavens and read them!

First let's cover some of the practical aspects of the four blood moons we recently experienced. Their sequence is pretty amazing. NASA experts explained that lunar eclipses tend to come in no particular order, but "occasionally...the sequence is more orderly. When four consecutive lunar eclipses are all total [as opposed to penumbral or partial], the series is called a tetrad."[5]

Blood moons are total lunar eclipses and are fairly common. But the tetrad of 2014 and 2015 was uncommon, according to scientists. The fact that all four eclipses coincided with the feasts of the Lord tells me that they were a sign to be reckoned with. From the time of Jesus through 2013 only seven tetrads coincided with Jewish feasts.[6] It's very important to recognize that science is proving the prophetic fulfillment of God's Word. NASA is helping to blow the shofar and sound the alarm.

There is a certain numerical significance about the seven tetrads that happened prior to 2014. Seven is the biblical number of perfection and completion. In 2014 and 2015 we saw the eighth tetrad of blood moons that occurred on biblical feast days.[7] Biblically the number eight signifies a new beginning. One more profound thought before we dive into the details of tetrads: four blood moons coinciding with Jewish feasts will not happen again until 2582–2583.

There were many more tetrads in history, but we are focusing on those that happened around the Jewish feasts. Let's do a quick overview of the first seven that have occurred since Jesus' day.

### Summary of seven blood-moon tetrads

The following are the dates of the seven tetrads we are interested in, with certain details about each period. We will take a deeper dive into three of them afterward.

- AD 162–163: a time of famine and the persecution of Christians under the Roman Emperor Marcus Aurelius
- AD 795–796: halt of the Arab invasion of Western Europe, facilitated by Charlemagne's buffer zone
- AD 842–843: division of the Holy Roman Empire by the Treaty of Verdun
- AD 860–861: heating up of the Arab-Byzantine wars, with the Byzantines being successfully raided multiple times; but then the Abbasids began to decline leading to a decisive Byzantine victory in 863 at the Battle of Lalakaon
- AD 1493–1494: expulsion of Jewish people from Spain and Spanish territories in 1492; Christopher Columbus' return from first expedition to the New World and departure on second expedition in 1493
- AD 1949–1950: signing of armistice agreement to end the Arab-Israeli war; Israel admitted to the United Nations
- AD 1967–1968: the Six-Day War and the return of Jerusalem to Jewish hands; Jesus' prophecy about the "day of the Gentiles" ending is fulfilled[8]

These world-changing events marked history because they coincided with significant spiritual, political, and economic shifts. Kingdoms and nations were turned upside down and in some cases transferred into other hands. Many books have been written about the events coinciding with all seven tetrads. Let's focus on the last three.

### The blood moons of 1493–1494

When I was in elementary school, my schoolmates and I learned a poem to help us remember an important event in American history. The first two lines are "In fourteen hundred ninety-two, Columbus sailed the ocean blue."[9] Is it ringing a bell?

I believe our teachers taught us this rhyme to commemorate a very important event for America and the world. What we did not learn was the backstory to why Columbus came. Unfortunately, terrible anti-Semitism had gripped Spain. The nation's rulers, King Ferdinand and Queen Isabella, conspired with Pope Sixtus IV to expel Jewish people and launch the brutal Inquisition under the guise of maintaining religious unity. The Inquisition was a "powerful office set up within the Catholic church to root out and punish heresy." In other words, the church sponsored the intimidation, beatings, confiscation of possessions and property, torture, and burning alive at the stake of Jewish people (and others), simply because they were Jewish (or not Catholic).[10]

In 1492 Ferdinand and Isabella issued a decree to banish all Jewish people from Spain. An entry in Christopher Columbus' personal diary confirms the timing:

> So, after having expelled all the Jews from all of your Kingdoms and Dominions, in the same month of January Your Highnesses commanded me to go, with a suitable fleet, to the said regions of India.[11]

The deadline of the expulsion decree was the ninth of Av, or Tisha b'Av. This is a very significant date in Jewish history, because both the first and second temples were also destroyed on that day.[12] Because of the expulsion decree, Jewish people in Spain and other Spanish territories had to sell their possessions and property for practically nothing in an attempt to fund their departures, and some "unscrupulous captains threw Jews overboard or robbed them of all their possessions."[13]

Many believe that what was essentially a confiscation of Jewish wealth made the Columbus expedition to the Indies possible. Some historians suggest that wealthy Jewish people who had previously financed Ferdinand and Isabella's projects offered great sums of money to reverse the expulsion order and allow the Jewish people to stay in Spain. One financier, Don Isaac Abarbanel, is said to have "offered his entire enormous fortune to the Catholic kings if they would rescind the decree."[14]

Some people see these painful events as accidents of history. But it is possible that the wealth confiscated from the Jewish people (as despicable as that injustice was) played a part in Columbus finding what would become the United States—Israel's best and most powerful friend in the entire world!

### The blood moons of 1949–1950

The miracle of Israel's rebirth would give us more than enough to talk about here. But there was another amazing prophecy, and it connects this tetrad to the one that occurred in 1967 and 1968.

The story begins in 1215, when Rabbi Judah ben Samuel prophesied the future history of a nation that no longer existed: Israel. Although some question the validity of the prophecy, I believe it is true. Here's the gist of what he said: The Ottoman Empire would rule Jerusalem over the course of eight jubilees, which is four hundred years. Jerusalem would then change hands but would be called a "no man's land" for one jubilee, or another fifty years.[15] After that, the Jewish people would again rule Jerusalem, and the city would never be in Gentile hands again. Ben Samuel prophesied *another* jubilee after that, which would prepare the world for the coming of the Messiah. At its end we would enter the Messianic era, a time of signs, wonders, and miracles.[16]

Rabbi ben Samuel was not predicting the date of the Messiah's coming; he spoke of the Messianic era that would lead to His coming.[17] Also, when he prophesied that the Ottoman Turks would rule for eight jubilees, there were no Ottomans. A man named Osman was born not long after Rabbi ben Samuel died, and his people increased in size and strength over the next several hundred years. By 1517 they were powerful enough to invade Israel and take control of Jerusalem.

Here is the connection between the Ottomans and Osman: Apparently, Europeans pronounced *Osman* in a way that became *Ottoman*,[18] the people Rabbi ben Samuel had named hundreds of years beforehand. For the record, ben Samuel died two years after he gave these prophecies.[19] Yet what he prophesied affects the world even today. And he got it exactly right! The Ottomans ruled Jerusalem for *exactly* four hundred years.

The Ottoman Empire was formidable and replaced the Byzantine Empire as the major force in the Eastern Mediterranean. It reached its apex under the rule of Suleman the Magnificent (1520–1566), and it ultimately included what is now Bulgaria, Egypt, Greece, Hungary, Jordan, Lebanon, Macedonia, Palestine, Romania, Syria, Turkey, parts of Arabia, and parts of the North African coast.[20]

In 1917, four hundred years after the Ottomans took control of Jerusalem, the Allied Forces sent General Edmund Allenby to oppose the Ottoman Turks and restore Israel. Allenby read the Scriptures every day, and after the surrender of Jerusalem, he approached the Holy City with reverence, even in the midst of war.[21] Allenby understood "that the moral significance of Jerusalem's capture 'was even greater than its military importance.'"[22]

Jerusalem surrendered on the first day of Chanukah, the Festival of Lights that celebrates the miraculous rededication of the temple after the successful Maccabean revolt. Without a single bullet being fired in the Holy City, the Ottomans surrendered it.

Remember that according to Rabbi ben Samuel's prophecy, Jerusalem would be designated a no-man's-land for one more fifty-year period, after the Turks lost the land. The League of

Nations designated a strip of land in Jerusalem that belonged to no nation and was under international control—a no-man's-land:

> Even after the war of 1948–49, Jerusalem was still divided by a strip of land running right through the heart of the city, with Jordan controlling the eastern part of the city and Israel controlling the western part of the city. That strip of land was called "no-man's land" by both the Israelis and the Jordanians![23]

### The blood moons of 1967–1968

Rabbi ben Samuel's "final" jubilee period began in 1917 and ended in 1967. So what happened on June 5, 1967? The Six-Day War, between Israel and the surrounding Arab nations, started. As fighting forces go, the Israelis were outmatched: they had 275,000 troops compared with the Arabs' 456,000; they had half as many tanks as the Arabs and one-quarter the number of aircraft.[24]

The Arab nations' goal was to wipe Israel off the face of the earth. So they surrounded the tiny nation with almost half a million troops and over two thousand tanks. In parts of the Sinai and the Gaza Strip, the Egyptians alone had hundreds of artillery pieces.[25] But by a miracle of God and according to the prophecies, Israel prevailed and all of Jerusalem was retaken. The no-man's-land was no more. The times of the Gentiles were fulfilled, as Luke's Gospel promised:

> They will fall by the edge of the sword, and be led away captive into all nations. And Jerusalem will be trampled by Gentiles until the times of the Gentiles are fulfilled. And there will be signs in the sun, in the moon, and in the stars.
> —LUKE 21:24–25

As amazing as this was, ben Samuel said that one more jubilee was still ahead. It was the fifty-year period of preparation for the Messianic era. Remember, the Rabbi did not say that the Messiah would come fifty years after 1967. He said the age leading to the coming of the Messiah would begin in 2017, according to the math—not 2015 when the most recent series of blood moons ended.

So how does this all fit together? Watch!

Most people agree that the early prophets observed a 360-day calendar based on the moon and the feasts of the Lord. The Egyptians also observed lunar months. For example, a calendar in the fifth century BC consisted of twelve months of thirty days each. Daniel 7:25 and 12:7, and even Revelation 12:6 and 12:14, also hint at the 360-day calendar. So there is precedent for it.

But whichever way we count the months, the period between 2015 and 2017 is in range for the ben Samuel prophecy. The inexactness of the date is not a problem in my opinion. Jesus said: "But of that day and that hour no one knows, not even the angels of heaven, but My Father only" (Matt. 24:36). We cannot know the exact time of Jesus' return, but we are to be mindful of the signs God gives us. Just as a mother's birth pangs come closer and closer together and become more intense as the birth nears, so the signs of Jesus' return are coming more quickly and with more intensity. It is a rapid acceleration of signs, wonders, and miracles.

## PRESIDENT TRUMP

On June 16, 2015, toward the very end of the jubilee period that began with the return of Jerusalem to the Jewish people, Donald Trump announced his run for the US presidency. On November 9, 2016, he was elected, and on Friday, January 20, 2017 he was sworn in as the nation's forty-fifth president.

Since then the world has changed spiritually, politically, and economically in ways that are truly epic. I won't list all the outstanding events during the Trump presidency so far, but I will concentrate on the signs concerning Israel or pointing to the Messiah's return.

Remember that no one thought Donald J. Trump had the slightest chance to win. The evangelical vote played a huge part in his victory, but not all evangelicals were on board at first. I remember a New York meeting of evangelical leaders in which former governor Mike Huckabee fielded questions for candidate Trump. Someone asked what Trump would do about Syria. His response was something along the lines of, "I will blow the heck out of them."[26] ("Heck" is not exactly what he said!)

Personally I thought, "Finally! Somebody's going to do something about the ISIS killers."

But some people were offended by Mr. Trump's choice of words. The following year my good friend Rabbi Daniel Lapin, who voiced his support for Donald Trump on a May 2016 radio program,[27] came to our church. While interviewing him on Sunday morning, I asked why he had supported Mr. Trump. He said that when the streets are full of wild dogs, we need more than someone who'll pray about the problem. We need a dog-catcher who knows how to handle wild dogs.[28]

This is not a chapter about politics, but you have to admit that the United States, Israel, and the entire world have changed dramatically since Donald Trump was elected. I personally feel that he is an answer to prayer, a gift from God "for such a time as this."

**President Trump and Israel**

To understand what has happened in Israel since the last blood moon tetrad, we need to look back to the 1995 Jerusalem Embassy Act, which recognized Jerusalem as Israel's capital and called for the city to remain undivided.[29] The bill passed by overwhelming majorities in both the US House and Senate and became law on November 8, 1995, despite the fact that President Bill Clinton never signed it.

The word *undivided* is more important than I can explain here. Suffice to say that an undivided Jerusalem is crucial to the fulfillment of Bible prophecy and the coming of the Messiah. The law's purpose was to relocate the US Embassy from Tel Aviv to Jerusalem by May 31, 1999.[30] Of course Israel had always claimed Jerusalem as its capital, but the claim was not internationally recognized. Imagine if other countries told the United States that Washington, DC, is not the rightful capital of the United States. What would Spain, France, or the United Kingdom say if we

decided that Madrid, Paris, and London were not their legiti-
mate capital cities? The idea is ludicrous. But that is exactly what
Israel was up against.

Although the 1995 Jerusalem Embassy Act made an important statement, it allowed sitting American presidents to waive
its provisions every six months, delaying enactment on the basis
of national security.[31] Presidents Clinton, Bush, and Obama used
the waiver every six months, and, for a time, Trump did too.

But watch this sign: President Trump signed the waiver in
June 2017. On the fifth day of that month, the US Senate unanimously passed a resolution commemorating the Jubilee (Fiftieth)
Anniversary of Jerusalem's reunification.[32] Remember that
during Mr. Trump's campaign, he promised to take care of ISIS
(which he did) and stand behind Israel (which he has). One of
the greatest prophetic signs was when he made good on the 1995
Embassy Act by officially recognizing Jerusalem as Israel's capital and moving the US embassy from Tel Aviv to Jerusalem. The
presidential proclamation of recognition happened on December
6, 2017. On February 23, 2018, President Trump announced the
plan to move the embassy. The actual relocation was completed
on May 14, 2018, coinciding with the seventieth anniversary of
the Israeli Declaration of Independence.

God has done many more amazing things for Israel and its
people since President Trump took office. The Taylor Force Act
forbids US economic aid to the Palestinian Authority until certain
anti-terrorist conditions are met.[33] The United States reversed its
position on West Bank settlements.[34] And President Trump has
recognized Israel's sovereignty over the Golan Heights.[35] Despite
its challenges, the Middle East is experiencing more peace and
unity than perhaps ever before.

These are critical times. As David Ben-Gurion once said, "Five
years are nothing next to eternity, but not all years in history are
alike, and in the next five years the fate of our generation may
be decided, if not the fate of generations."[36] I believe these words
apply today.

I was privileged to attend the opening of the US Embassy in

Jerusalem in May of 2018. My friend Josh Reinstein had us over for Shabbat dinner. During the meal with Josh and his beautiful family, he said something that touches my heart and soul to this day: "We in Israel have seen more miracles with the moving of the US Embassy and so many other things in the last year than we thought we would ever see until the coming of the Messiah."

The Scriptures tell us to pay attention to God's signs and wonders. But remember what Jesus said about why He taught in parables: "...because seeing they do not see, and hearing they do not hear, nor do they understand" (Matt. 13:13). The people's physical eyes and ears were not the issue. Their need was spiritual. One of the things I pray every day is for God to make me sensitive to what He is doing, saying, and showing me. I ask Him for spiritual eyes and ears and the clarity to perceive His signs and wonders. I want to hear His alarm. I want to be awake so I can be a part of whatever He is doing. May I never miss His signs the way I missed the signs of our son's birth!

Friend, our God is not a hard taskmaster who wants to "get us." His eyes "run to and fro throughout the whole earth, to show Himself strong on behalf of those whose heart is loyal to Him" (2 Chron. 16:9). It is His "good pleasure to give [us] the kingdom" (Luke 12:32).

I believe that Jerusalem is in Jewish hands so that we can hear the trumpet in Zion shouting, "Wake up!"

When the people living around Jerusalem heard the shofar from the Temple Mount in Jesus' day, they grabbed their own shofars, turned away from Jerusalem, and passed along the good news, from town to town. Likewise, our victory in God is not complete until we share what He shows us. Some people are too far to hear the initial trumpet blast. They need us to send the sound forward. We can only do that if we are paying attention. God wants us to be a big part of everything He is about to do.

Our best is yet to come!

## CHAPTER 7

# DEFEATING THE SPIRIT OF AMALEK

*Therefore it shall be, when the L*ORD *your God has given you rest from your enemies all around, in the land which the L*ORD *your God is giving you to possess as an inheritance, that you will blot out the remembrance of Amalek from under heaven. You shall not forget.*
—DEUTERONOMY 25:19

THIS CHAPTER IS not about people but about the spirit that drives people to seek the destruction of the Jewish people. I am talking about the spirit of Amalek, whose history we are about to explore. Amalek has infiltrated nations, organizations, and even the church. Yet God's Word promises its end, and we are seeing signs of a shift.

### LIVING PROPHECY 7

The anti-God, anti-Jewish spirit of Amalek will be destroyed. For the first time in two thousand years the church is defeating the spirit of Amalek from within.

One of the most amazing stories I've heard is about a little boy who survived the Holocaust and became the Chief Rabbi of Israel. Israel Meir Lau was about five years old when he saw the SS beating his father for refusing an order to shave his beard. At the time, Rabbi Lau's father was the chief rabbi in Piotrków, Poland. The town's Jewish men had asked the rabbi whether they should follow the Nazi order to cut their beards. He told them to "do it in order to save [themselves] from punishment." However, he kept his own beard to "safeguard tradition" and "preserve the honor of the town rabbinate."[1]

Young Israel Lau was sent to the concentration camp at Buchenwald. He and his brothers Naphtali and Yehoshua were the only members of their immediate family not to be murdered. You can see why Rabbi Lau wrote the following:

> We must not speak of the six million who were butchered, or of the million and a half children who were murdered. The human mind cannot process—either emotionally or experientially—the concept of millions of people. Rather we must speak of little Shloimy and Moshe, young Leah-le and Sarah-le.[2]

Rabbi Lau believes that the tally of murdered Jewish people is not entirely accurate. "Physically," he said, "the Nazis did kill six million Jews in acts of indescribable cruelty. But in terms of emotion, faith, and consciousness, they killed far more than that."[3]

## BE VIGILANT

In chapter 2 I told you about a dear woman I met in a home for Holocaust survivors. Her only request was that we tell the survivors' story everywhere, in hopes there would be no more holocausts. Yet even reasonable people look back to the Holocaust and convince themselves that it could never happen again. But is that true? Didn't the unthinkable happen in our modern era? Didn't evil triumph because millions of reasonable people did nothing?

We must remain vigilant. Some are saying that today's anti-Semitism is even more virulent than it was in Hitler's time because technology can "spread vile thoughts globally instantaneously."[4] What a sobering thought that is!

There is no doubt that the spirit of Amalek is still present, but the label has changed. The term *anti-Semitism* became a "nice" way to describe the hatred for Jewish people. It's a euphemism that was coined by a nineteenth-century political writer to replace the term *Jew-haters*, which was thought to be too vulgar. The new term deemphasized religion and seemed more acceptable to the masses.[5] But now the vocabulary continues to evolve. Today those who want to sound politically correct reject the word *anti-Semitism* and say instead that they are "anti-Israel" or "anti-Zionist."

Whatever the terminology, anti-Semitism is on the rise, and I am about to show you disturbing examples. Before I do, let me challenge you to stand up for Israel and for the Jewish people. You and I are not only responsible for what we do and say; we are also responsible when we do and say nothing about injustice. Scripture is clear on this: "You must not stand idly by when your neighbor's life is at stake. I am the LORD" (Lev. 19:16, NET). Jewish tradition says that one who watches and does nothing is as guilty as one who commits the crime. We are obligated by God to do all we can do to stop evil. Imagine how different history would look if someone such as Pope Pius XII had boldly spoken against Hitler's "Final Solution."

At the Wannsee Conference of January 20, 1942, the Nazis planned the extermination of eleven million Jewish people.[6] They did not fully succeed, but neither did they fully fail. We cannot stand idly by. "To him who knows to do good and does not do it, to him it is sin" (Jas. 4:17).

## TODAY'S ANTI-SEMITISM

To grasp what we see today, we need reflect on history. Anti-Semitism began with Pharaoh's genocide of newborn Israelite boys. It showed up when Balak and Balaam planned to curse Israel, when Haman planned to wipe out the Jewish people, when the Crusades raged, when the Inquisition's oppression surged, and when Hitler enacted extermination policies. Anti-Semitism was not only in the past, but it is also on the rise!

There are too many examples to cover here, but the following demonstrate what today's Jewish people face.

- In 2018 France experienced a 74 percent increase in offenses against Jewish people, as compared with the previous year. Germany also reported an increase, with violent attacks against Jewish people up 60 percent.[7]

- In May 2019 a Jewish cemetery was vandalized in Bordeaux, France.[8] In the same month, Germany's government warned Jewish men not to wear kippahs in public, following spikes in anti-Semitic attacks.[9] Friends from Israel have also told me that it is no longer safe to wear their kippahs in European cities.

- More than 10 percent of Orthodox and Catholic Christians in Eastern Europe state that they would not be willing to accept Jewish people as fellow citizens.[10]

- Fifty-six percent of Austrians are unaware that six million Jewish people perished in the Holocaust, with 12 percent believing the number of Jewish people killed was fewer than 100,000.[11]

- The Weather Channel in the United States recently listed Jerusalem as "the State of Palestine."[12]

- During a five-month period in New York City, 110 of 184 reported hate crimes were committed against Jewish people.[13]

- In April 2019 the *New York Times* international edition published a vile, anti-Semitic cartoon depicting President Trump as a blind man wearing a kippah and being led by a dog. The dog had the face of Prime Minister Benjamin Netanyahu and wore the Star of David on its collar.[14] The cartoon was reminiscent of propaganda pieces under the Third Reich.

- An Islamic man, Mohammed Merah, shot soldiers in Toulouse and Montauban, France, and attacked innocents at a Jewish school in Toulouse.[15]

- Dr. Sarah Halimi, a retired physician, was beaten to death and thrown from her Paris balcony in 2017.[16] Witnesses report that after the killer threw her body off the balcony into the building's courtyard, he said, "I killed the *shaitan*" (demon).[17]

- In 2018 a shooter murdered eleven and injured six during Shabbat services at the Tree of Life Synagogue in Pittsburgh, Pennsylvania.[18]

- On the last day of Passover in 2019, a shooter killed one woman and injured three others during services at a Poway, California synagogue.[19] The shooter had posted an open letter in which he professed to be a Christian and blamed the Jewish people for the "genocide of the European race" and "the murder of Jesus."[20]

- In May 2019 a Neo-Nazi group disrupted a peaceful Holocaust memorial event in Russellville, Arkansas by "waving swastikas and chanting as they marched down the street."[21]

- In 2019 Minnesota Congresswoman Ilhan Omar made openly anti-Semitic statements that went unchallenged by the Democrat Party and much of the mainstream media. In 2012 she claimed that Israel had "hypnotized the world," and she expressed the hope that Allah would "awaken the people and help them see the evil doings of Israel."[22]

That is just a small sample of terrible acts, but it's enough to convey the crisis. We can all agree that something must be done and that standing silent on the sidelines is not an option. The question is, What else can we do?

1. Refuse to be silent! For example, when you hear someone say, "The Jews killed Jesus," bring them to the truth in a loving but compassionate way. Remember that anti-Semitism is Christianity's original sin. Then choose to become part of the solution. Show misinformed people the facts, as I have done in these pages. It is unfair and illogical to blame all the Jewish people for what a few corrupt leaders and the Roman Empire did two thousand years ago.

2. Stand up for the nation of Israel and be aware of the issues.

## BOYCOTT, DIVEST, SANCTION

To stand up, you have to know what you are standing for and against. Overt violence and verbal attacks are only part of today's anti-Semitism. Currently the Boycott, Divest, Sanction movement (BDS) has taken aim at Israel and the Jewish people, "wrapped in a cloak of social justice," and is gaining support across from students, businesses, and even some religious denominations.[23] The movement supports an Israel-Palestine two-state solution and is bringing pressure to bear on Israeli commerce and trade.

BDS is not a new concept. In 1933 the Nazis instituted boycotts of Jewish businesses.[24] The first began on April 1 of that year when storm troopers "stood menacingly in front of Jewish-owned department stores and retail establishments," as well as doctors' offices.[25] These actions reached a crescendo by November 9–10, 1938, when Nazis "torched synagogues, vandalized Jewish homes, schools, and businesses and killed close to 100 Jews."[26] The Star of David and anti-Semitic slogans were painted on doors and windows to discourage Jewish commerce and blame the Jewish people for Germany's troubles.[27] The police did almost nothing to stop the terror.

The attack in November 1938 was known as *Kristallnacht*, the Night of Broken Glass. Thousands of businesses and hundreds of synagogues burned in Germany, Austria, and the Sudetenland.[28] Waves of violence ensued, as did the mass arrests of Jewish people. What started as a boycott of Jewish businesses culminated in the wholesale genocide of Jewish men, women, and children.

We have to ask ourselves, What should have been done, and what must we do now? The windows of Jewish businesses are being broken today, and synagogues are being attacked. In the space of a few days in 2014 several synagogues in Paris were attacked during anti-Israel demonstrations. In one case two hundred Jewish people were trapped inside while a pro-Palestinian mob protested outside.[29] A leader in France's Jewish community compared the incident to Kristallnacht. Abe Foxman, the Anti-Defamation League's National Director Emeritus, warned that "the similarities cannot be ignored." Jewish people in Germany have similar concerns. After synagogue bombings and public chants of "Jews to the gas," a Jewish leader in Germany said, "These are the worst times since the Nazi era."[30]

Please listen to what I'm about to say: most Germans, Austrians, and residents of the Sudetenland paid little attention to Kristallnacht, or they saw it as the work of a few fanatics. Five years earlier the government restricted employment in the civil service and eventually prohibited non-Aryan educators from working.[31] In the absence of resistance the net of oppression tightened against law-abiding Jewish people, and the hatred became a contagion.

Can we afford to assume that the BDS movement is only a boycott and things will get better? No, we cannot. And for the record, neither Kristallnacht, the Holocaust, nor BDS were or are about achieving a two-state solution. They are about anti-Semitism. BDS leaders use the rhetoric of religious and moral authority to condemn Israel in sermons, essays, press releases, reports, and other publications. The Palestinians are portrayed as powerless, oppressed people who must be defended against a bully—Israel. These anti-Israel sentiments mask the real issue, which is anti-Jewish hatred.

A few years ago I was part of a delegation from more than

thirty-five nations that visited an Israeli factory targeted by the BDS movement. The plant employed an equal number of Jewish people and Arabs. Management provided Muslim staffers with a private, enclosed area for appointed times of prayer. When we talked to some of the Arab employees (both men and women), they told us how much they loved working there and said they made a better living in that factory than they could have made elsewhere. Unfortunately the business had to relocate due to BDS and settlement issues. Neither Jewish nor Arab people in that area have the opportunity to earn the good wages they once enjoyed.

You might be surprised to hear that the primary driver of BDS is a confederation of Palestinian groups supported not by weak, helpless people but by a contingent of international financiers and universities.[32] Divestment drives are becoming more frequent on campuses.[33] Even the World Council of Churches is actively involved in the BDS movement.[34]

## MAKING THE LIE STICK

Ever since May 14, 1948, nations have stood against the reborn Jewish nation. The spirit of Amalek is at work, as it has been for millennia. In just seventy-plus years Israel has seen her share of kinetic war. Perhaps the greater war, however, has been the one fought with words and ideas such as Israel's "apartheid," Israel the "occupier," "illegal" settlements, "Palestinian refugees," and the "Gaza blockade." Saying something doesn't make it true. However, Nazi propagandists allegedly said, "If you tell a lie big enough and keep repeating it, people will eventually come to believe it."[35]

There is truth in that statement. A lie can be perpetuated when dark forces systematically shield it from the light. Tyrannical states like Nazi Germany use their great power to repress the truth. Why? Because it is the mortal enemy of the lie. In the end the truth wins, but the lies of anti-Semitism have survived for millennia.

It is easy to stir hatred. Long before anyone accused Israel of occupying the land, long before any walls and settlements were built, and long before ideas such as "land for peace" were considered, a religious leader flew to Berlin and urged Adolf Hitler to execute his evil plan: the leader was the Grand Mufti of Jerusalem, a high-ranking Muslim. According to an associate of Adolf Eichmann, the Grand Mufti "played a role in the decision of the German Government to exterminate the European Jews" and saw it as "a comfortable solution of the Palestine problem." The Mufti "was one of Eichmann's best friends" and pushed him to "accelerate the extermination."[36]

The spirit of Amalek has been at work since the earliest days of Judaism. Current Palestinian leaders from Fatah to Hamas are heirs of the Grand Mufti and his Nazi friends, just as they were the heirs of anti-Semites who went before them. In 2006 the last election for the Palestinian Legislative Council voted Hamas, a political party and terrorist organization, into power. The following are key quotes and claims from the Hamas charter:

- "Israel, by virtue of its being Jewish and of having a Jewish population, defies Islam and the Muslims."
- "The time [to implement Allah's promise] will not come until Muslims will fight the Jews (and kill them); until the Jews hide behind rocks and trees, which will cry: O Muslim! there is a Jew hiding behind me, come on and kill him!"
- "We must spread the spirit of Jihad among the...Umma [the Muslim community], clash with the enemies and join the ranks of the Jihad fighters."
- Essential to achieving the aims of the charter are "fundamental changes in educational curriculi" that are geared toward Islamic purity.
- The charter includes this pledge: "I swear by that who holds in His Hands the Soul of Muhammed!

> I indeed wish to go to war for the sake of Allah!
> I will assault and kill, assault and kill, assault
> and kill."[37]

Does it sound to you like Hamas is after "land for peace"? It doesn't to me.

## THE SPIRIT OF AMALEK AND GENERATIONAL CURSES

God warned His people, "Remember what Amalek did to you on the way as you were coming out of Egypt....You shall not forget" (Deut. 25:17, 19).

Paul wrote, "We do not wrestle against flesh and blood, but against principalities, against powers, against the rulers of darkness of this age, against spiritual hosts of wickedness in the heavenly places" (Eph. 6:12). The battle is never with people. Our opponents are principalities, powers, and the rulers of darkness who manipulate and deceive human beings. It is the enemy who comes "to steal, and to kill, and to destroy" (John 10:10).

As we trace the curse of Amalek all the way to Abraham, Isaac, Ishmael, Esau, and Esau's grandson Amalek, we will see the spirit's movements in world history. We are talking here about a generational curse passed from person to person and generation to generation. However, the Hebrew word for *generation* is *dowr*, which does not suggest a strictly physical or chronological link.[38] Esau and Hitler did not share the same physical DNA, nor were their lives in any way adjacent in time. But both men had the same spiritual DNA. That is what "coded" their hatred for the Jewish people.

Are you ready to track Amalek through history? I promise it will be eye-opening!

### Isaac and Ishmael

Have you ever seen DNA on display, perhaps in a family where the dad has bright red hair and five redheaded children? Or maybe you're a mom with big, brown eyes and your children look like you. Spiritual DNA can also be apparent. The spiritual

DNA of violence and hatred began with Abraham's first son, Ishmael, who was born not to Abraham's wife, Sarah, but to Sarah's maid, Hagar, who was from Egypt. Remember: the first people to oppress the Israelites were the Egyptians, who enslaved them for hundreds of years.

We sometimes treat Ishmael as Abraham's unimportant son, but he is very important—so important that God named him and promised that he would become a multitude.

> Then the Angel of the LORD said to [Hagar], "I will mul-
> tiply your descendants exceedingly, so that they shall not
> be counted for multitude." And the Angel of the LORD
> said to her: "Behold you are with child, and you shall
> bear a son. You shall call his name Ishmael, because the
> LORD has heard your affliction."
> —GENESIS 16:10–11

Ishmael means "God will hear."[39] It was a marvelous promise— a generational blessing—for Ishmael and all his descendants. But God also told Hagar that Ishmael "shall be a wild man; his hand shall be against every man, and every man's hand against him. And he shall dwell in the presence of all his brethren" (Gen. 16:12). Ishmael would constantly quarrel, even with his own descendants. That was part of his spiritual DNA.

There is something hidden in the original Hebrew concerning Ishmael's younger brother Isaac. In English Genesis 21:8 says that Isaac "grew and was weaned. And Abraham made a great feast on the same day that Isaac was weaned." The Hebrew for *weaned* is *gamal*.[40] One of its characters has a long "neck"; it represents a camel and suggests travel or movement.[41] The short version of the story is that when Isaac became *gamal*, he was also "cam-eled." That means that he was old enough not to be at his mother or father's side 24/7. The great feast was not really about the end of his breastfeeding but about his being old enough to live some-what independently while keeping the values his parents had taught him.

This would explain why Sarah no longer wanted Ishmael around Isaac. Notice what triggered her concern: "Sarah saw the son of Hagar the Egyptian, whom she had borne to Abraham, *scoffing*" (Gen. 21:9). This made Sarah angry enough to tell Abraham, "Cast out this bondwoman and her son; for the son of this bondwoman shall not be heir with my son, namely with Isaac" (Gen. 21:10).

That's pretty drastic. But why did Sarah react so strongly to Ishmael's attitude? The Hebrew for *scoffing* in Genesis 21:9 is *tsachaq*, a root that also means to laugh.[42] According to ancient Jewish wisdom, the kind of joking or mocking described by this term relates to death, sex, and faith, which are hallmarks of the Amalek spirit. (We will see more on this later.) Exodus 32:6 says, that after making the golden calf (a religious reference), the Israelites "sat down to eat and to drink, and rose up to play." *Play* here is also *tsachaq*. It referred to "drunken immoral orgies and sexual play."[43] Are you seeing the sex-faith connection so far? Their actions were mocking faith in the God of Israel.

This word is also used in Genesis 19:14, where Lot told his sons-in-law to flee Sodom because the Lord was going to destroy the city, and they thought he was joking. The sons-in-law thought Lot was making a perverse joke about death.

Obviously Ishmael didn't tell his brother some goofy jokes; he told vulgar jokes mocking death, sex, and faith. Sarah was angry because of this and because he was attempting to corrupt his younger brother.

In case you are wondering how death, sex, and faith are connected to a spiritual curse that was passed down from Ishmael's time, the answer is hidden in the Bible. For example, the Torah reveals something deep in Ishmael's character by hiding his name in the following verses:

- Deuteronomy 17:12: "Now the man who acts presumptuously and *will not heed* [will not listen to] the priest..."

- Deuteronomy 18:19: "It shall be that whoever *will not hear* [will not listen to] My words…"
- Deuteronomy 21:18. "If a man has a stubborn and rebellious son who will not obey the voice of his father or the voice of his mother, and who, when they have chastened him, *will not heed* [will not listen]…"

In all three verses the Hebrew word translated "heed" or "hear" is *shama*, which means to hear.[44] Remember that Ishmael's name means God will hear. Well, his name also comes from the word *shama*. Rabbi Lapin walked me through this, so stick with me as I walk you through it.

The above verses tie Ishmael's name to a person who will not listen to the priest, to God, or to his parents. Ishmael was going to have a problem with any type of authority. That explains why it is so hard to achieve a peace plan in the Middle East!

In July 2000 President Bill Clinton, Israeli Prime Minister Ehud Barak, and Yasser Arafat met at Camp David to negotiate peace. Arafat came with a list of demands, but even as his demands were being met, he refused the deal. "Enraged, President Clinton banged on the table and said: 'You are leading your people and the region into a catastrophe.'…'[Arafat] did not negotiate in good faith; indeed, he did not negotiate at all. He just kept saying no to every offer, never making any counterproposals of his own.'"[45] The spirit of Ishmael governed Yasser Arafat.

Let me show you another secret hidden in God's Word. It is found in the description of Hagar and Ishmael as they left Abraham's home:

> The water in the skin was used up, and she placed the boy under one of the shrubs. Then she went and sat down across from him at a distance of about a bowshot; for she said to herself, "Let me not see the death of the boy." So she sat opposite him, and lifted her voice and wept.
> —Genesis 21:15–16

How far away from her dying son did Hagar sit? A hundred yards? Fifty feet? No, a bowshot away. Scripture defines the distance in terms of Ishmael's weapon of choice. Verse 20 tells us that Ishmael became an archer. The Bible does not describe him as a father or shepherd or merchant. It describes him in terms of his weapon.

Have you ever seen Arab men celebrating in the street? How do they do it? Often it's by firing guns into the air. When Yasser Arafat was invited to speak at the United Nations in 1974, he demonstrated his desire for peace by wearing a pistol on his belt. He did not take it off until he stepped up to the rostrum.[46] This characteristic goes back to Ishmael.

Remember that when we talk about Ishmael, we are not necessarily talking about Islam. Muhammad was not born until AD 571, more than two thousand years after Ishmael. What we are talking about is Ishmael's aggressive spirit, which was also found in Amalek, the grandson of Esau, who vowed to wipe out the Jewish people. (Esau married an Ishmaelite woman.) Ishmael's descendants would not only fight others, but they would fight among themselves. A prime example is the never-ending feud between Shiites and Sunnis.

### Jacob, Esau, and Amalek

Before we move into later centuries, let me briefly mention the twin brothers Jacob and Esau. As the oldest, Esau was entitled to the birthright blessing, but he sold it to his brother for a bowl of lentils. Then Isaac, their father, laid hands on Jacob and gave him Esau's blessing. Esau hated his brother for this and fully intended to kill him. So Jacob fled for his life. And who did I say Esau's grandson was? Amalek, who worked ceaselessly to wipe out Jacob's descendants. In fact the Amalekites were the first people to attack the Israelites in the wilderness.

### Amalek in modern times

Please bear in mind as we explore the Amalek spirit that I am pointing out *the spirit* behind anti-Semitism. Many of us were not alive during the Holocaust, but a spirit was at work in Hitler and his gang. In the century before Hitler was born, Rabbi Eliyahu Kagan of Lithuania expressed his belief "that the Germans descend from that evil nation [Amalek]—a nation differing fundamentally from the rest of mankind, evil at its very core (even if not visibly on its surface)."[47]

Rabbi Kagan was not condemning the German people or suggesting that Germans are born anti-Semites. That would be a lie! He was pointing out how the Amalek spirit pounces on opportunities, always waiting to take root somewhere and continue its mission. Am I condemning the German people? Certainly not! Nor would I suggest that every person of Germanic ancestry is an anti-Semite. I am simply tracing the spiritual maneuverings of Amalek and the places where the spirit has turned up.

I have no desire to waste good ink on Hitler. However, we need to acknowledge (1) his mission to exterminate the Jewish people, and (2) his belief that Germany would reign as the world's top superpower for a thousand years. Hitler wrote about this in his 1925 book *Mein Kampf* (*My Struggle*, or *My Fight*). He also blamed the Jewish people for the world's ills and claimed that Jewish people were part of a conspiracy to rule the earth and its financial system. He called this conspiracy "the Jewish peril."

To better understand Hitler's deep hatred of the Jewish people, just study his mentor, Dietrich Eckart, who published *Plain German* (*Auf Gut Deutsch*), a periodical of anti-Semitic rants.[48] Hitler was also very fond of the fiercely anti-Semitic composer Richard Wagner and his hate-filled opera *Der Ring des Nibelungen* (*The Ring of the Nibelung*), in which Wagner portrays Jewish people as evil dwarfs who hoard gold and live underground.[49]

The death-sex-faith connection with the Amalek spirit is evident in the Wagner's opera, often referred to as *The Ring*. Allow me to highlight an important aspect of the opera: in addition to its hatred of the Jewish people, there is a theme in the lyrics that speaks of "light-bringing love, and laughing death."[50] From the Amalek perspective, death laughs and is something to be laughed at. That reminds me of suicide murderers. We'll talk more soon about how they laugh at death, strap bombs around their chests for the sake of Islam, and blow themselves up, just for the chance to kill Jewish people and other "infidels." After they complete their missions, their parents and families are given cash for their "heroic" sacrifices. This is the curse of Amalek, and you can trace its main features every single place that it manifests.

Hitler also made virtual suicide pacts for the sake of killing Jewish people. In June 1941 he decided that instead of invading England for a likely victory, he would invade the Soviet Union. He acted like a man oblivious to the lessons of Napoleon's defeat in Russia. The Russian winter literally froze and starved German soldiers to death. They were also out of fuel and ammo. Hitler's military leaders suggested a plan to send provisions or relieve the men of their mission.[51] Trains being used to transport Jewish people to concentration camps could easily have been loaded with fresh troops and supplies. But Hitler, who frequently declined the advice of his military experts, refused to change his approach in the Soviet Union. Instead of heeding the counsel of others, he frequently responded in fits of rage.[52] He was determined to destroy the Soviet Union and its Jewish population.

*The demonic spirit of Amalek twisted Hitler's thinking.* The same spirit works through the leaders of Iran and other nations who sponsor and incite terrorism against the Jewish people. God's Word warns that Amalek's spiritual descendants are welcoming their own destruction: Even "[Balaam] looked on Amalek, and he took up his oracle and said, 'Amalek was first among the nations, but shall be last until he perishes'" (Num. 24:20). The Amalek spirit opposes what the Bible foretells and what we are standing up for: the ending of division and the entry of the "one new man" (Eph. 2:14–15).

### Sex, death, and the spirit of Amalek

The Amalek spirit is connected with sex and death. We see both in the story of King Saul and Agag, king of the Amalekites. The prophet Samuel told King Saul to fight Amalek and completely destroy the Amalekites and all they had. I always found this a little disturbing. But Saul was not only fighting a people; he was fighting the Amalek spirit whose mission was to wipe out every Jewish person everywhere. Keep that in mind as you read Samuel's marching orders to King Saul:

> Thus says the LORD of hosts: "I will punish Amalek for what he did to Israel, how he ambushed him on the way when he came up from Egypt. Now go and attack Amalek, and utterly destroy all that they have, and do not spare them."
>
> —1 SAMUEL 15:2–3

Saul then attacked Amalek, and God gave him a great victory. But instead of utterly destroying the Amalekites and their goods, Saul spared their king's life and kept their best livestock and other valuables.

> He also took Agag king of the Amalekites alive, and utterly destroyed all the people with the edge of the sword. But Saul and the people spared Agag and the best of the sheep, the oxen, the fatlings, the lambs, and all that was good, and were unwilling to utterly destroy them.
>
> —1 SAMUEL 15:8–9

The next morning, God told Samuel, "I greatly regret that I have set up Saul as king, for he has turned back from following Me, and has not performed My commandments" (1 Sam. 15:11). Why was God so upset? I believe it was because Saul squandered the chance to break the Amalek curse once and for all. Remember God's warning centuries earlier: "The LORD will have war with Amalek from generation to generation" (Exod. 17:16). Saul's decision prolonged that war, and his disobedience was serious enough for God to reject him.

Saul tried to convince Samuel that he saved the plunder so he could sacrifice it to the Lord (1 Sam. 15:21), but Samuel didn't buy his excuse:

Has the LORD as great delight in burnt offerings and sacrifices, as in obeying the voice of the LORD? Behold, to
obey is better than sacrifice, and to heed than the fat of
rams. For rebellion is as the sin of witchcraft, and stub-
bornness is as iniquity and idolatry. Because you have
rejected the word of the LORD, He also has rejected you
from being king.

—1 SAMUEL 15:22–23

Here's where we see the generational curse of Amalek directly
connecting to sex and death. Watch: God stripped the throne
from Saul and raised up David to be king. That morning, Samuel
handled what Saul left undone: he killed Agag himself. You
would think that brought an end to the Amalek curse, right?
Saul had already killed every Amalekite except for Agag. But
there is something hidden in God's Word that explains how the
curse was able to continue.

Scripture says that Samuel killed Agag *the next morning*. That
means Agag spent the overnight in captivity. Why would God's
Word provide that detail? The answer is in the Book of Esther,
which says, "After these things King Ahasuerus promoted
Haman, the son of Hammedatha, *the Agagite*" (Est. 3:1).

Haman, who hated Mordecai and all the Jewish people and
tricked King Ahasuerus into signing a decree to annihilate them,
was a descendent of Agag! But how could that be? "According to
an unidentified midrash, Agag fathered a son" during the night
he spent in Saul's custody. That son "became the progenitor of
Haman."[53] Rabbinic tradition holds that Agag raped and impreg-
nated the servant girl who delivered his final dinner to his cell.[54]
That's how Amalek's seed was alive in Haman.

### Seventy-two virgins and the spirit of Amalek

The death-sex-faith connection is alive for today's radical
Islamists too. They believe that when a male martyr for Islam
(faith) dies killing "infidels" (death), he will be rewarded with
seventy-two virgins in paradise (sex). This is the spirit of Amalek!

In a 2001 interview Hamas terrorist Muhammad Abu Wardeh, who recruited other terrorists for suicide bombings in Israel, said, "I described…how God would compensate the martyr for sacrificing his life for his land. If you become a martyr, God will give you 70 virgins, 70 wives and everlasting happiness."[55] Wardeh actually shortchanged his recruits by two virgins, but I digress.

Mohammed Atta, the lead hijacker on September 11, 2001, has been portrayed as a sexually active "party animal" who indulged himself the night before the attacks. This flies in the face of his being considered a devout Muslim.[56] Like Agag, Atta and his cohorts were influenced by the Amalek spirit, the curse with a bizarre connection between sex and death.

## The Haman-Nuremberg connection

Haman's story provides another fascinating link between the Amalek curse and the Nazis. When God destroyed Haman's plot to hang Mordecai and kill the Jewish people, He turned Haman's plans completely upside down. In Esther chapter 7 Haman was hanged on the gallows Haman built for Mordecai; his ten sons were also hanged (Est. 9:14). It is one of my favorite stories in the Bible, and it is what we celebrate during Purim.

On October 16, 1946, shortly after the Nuremberg Trials ended, ten prominent Nazi leaders were hanged.[57] Before his execution Nazi propagandist Julius Streicher "shouted out the words 'Heil Hitler' and 'Purimfest.'"[58] He was well aware of what Purim meant to the Jewish people, but in the end, his rant and the ten hangings only affirmed another defeat for the spirit of Amalek!

There is a parallel here. Haman's ten sons were hanged just as the ten evil sons of Nazi Germany were hanged. There were actually eleven hangings planned after Nuremberg, but Reichstag president Hermann Göring committed suicide beforehand by swallowing a cyanide tablet he had kept hidden.[59]

Here's the really interesting detail: Jewish wisdom tells us that the same thing happened when Haman's sons were hanged. There were eleven sons, but one committed suicide. Rabbi Daniel Lapin is among those who believe that "incongruities" in the Hebrew text suggest this.[60] The listing of Haman's sons in the Hebrew includes three extra-small letters, which was customary but for reasons that were not always understood. The small letters are *taf, shin,* and *zayin,* whose combined numerical value is 707. It turns out that these letters prophesied a later defeat of Amalek, with the 707 indicating the Hebrew year 5707—the year 1946, when ten Nazis were executed and one died by his own hand![61]

One more fact: because the Nuremberg trial was a military tribunal, executions should have been "by firing squad, or by electric chair as practiced in America. However, the court specifically prescribed hanging."[62] It was a precise replay of the Purim story!

### Nazi dreams and September 11, 2001

The spirit of Amalek is the glue that binds together anti-Semites who don't even know each other. The 2005 documentary film *Obsession* shows a terrorist training camp and reveals the jihadists' hatred for the Jewish people. The film also connects the Nazi era to today's Islamism, showing "a modern rally in Lebanon where Muslims are giving a Nazi salute."[63] Not surprisingly, the film also touches on the Grand Mufti of Jerusalem and his cheerleading for Hitler's Final Solution.

Keep in mind that the 9/11 plot was hatched in Hamburg, Germany. In his book *Jihad and Jew-Hatred: Islamism, Nazism, and the Roots of 9/11*, Matthias Küntzel explains that the idea of using suicide pilots in New York City was not birthed in the twenty-first century. He writes that "the idea of using suicide pilots to obliterate the skyscrapers of Manhattan originated in Berlin." Nazi architect, Albert Speer, said Hitler was never as exuberant as when he talked about leveling New York, which Nazis saw as "the center of world Jewry," with "the military headquarters of Judas" being on Wall Street. Hitler planned "to teach the Jews a lesson in the form of terror attacks on American metropolises."[64] He never accomplished this mission, but his spiritual disciples, the radical Islamists and jihadists of 9/11, did.

As I wrote this chapter, a friend texted me breaking news about a gunman in Germany who killed two people near a synagogue in Halle. The Yom Kippur observance was underway, so dozens of Jewish people were inside the building when the fully-armed man in military gear attempted to shoot down the synagogue door. Failing to gain entry, he shot a woman in front of the synagogue and a man in a kebab shop.[65] You can't make this stuff up. The spirit of Amalek inspires horrible acts.

## STAND UP! SPEAK UP!

The spirit of Amalek is not about a particular race or nationality. The Amalek DNA is spiritual. As of this writing, I have been to Israel thirty-six times and made good friends who are Jewish, Christian, and Arab. I have sipped coffee with Jewish and Arab friends at the same table. And why not? The bloodlines of Ishmael, Esau, and Amalek are crossed, meaning they and the Jewish people had common ancestors. The Amalek inheritance is a spiritual matter.

When Tiz and I had a tour group in Jerusalem a few tears ago, we made our usual stop in the Old City of Jerusalem. It's a fun day for everyone, and the markets are great. While the women went into the shops, some of the men, my son, Luke, and I stood talking just inside the Jaffa Gate. Out of nowhere a young man approached us and said, "We will slit the throats of every Jew and Christian and make your wives and daughters our slaves."

Wow! He left as quickly as he came, and we just stood there, stunned.

What caused his rage? His message reminded me of when Ishmael spoke in vulgar words to his brother, Isaac. We were Jewish and Christian people he'd never met before. We were spending money in the mostly Arab quarter, and our wives were shopping in mostly Arab markets. Yet all he could think about was slitting the throats of people like us.

The young man's goal was perverse, and his statement was religious, not political. He did not mention Americans, Europeans, or Israelis; he named Jews and Christians. He talked about making slaves of our wives and daughters. His brief rant covered sex, death, and religion. It was the spirit of Amalek!

I often ask my Jewish friends, "Why have the Jewish people been hated by so many for so long?" Almost always they answer in a kind, politically correct way. But the question remains: Of all the people in world history, why the Jewish people? It would almost be understandable for an ignorant person to reject people from other countries, cultures, races, or political parties—*almost*. The United States has its own embarrassing history of discrimination against blacks and immigrants. But how does one strain of hatred continue worldwide for thousands of years? What caused so many nations over so many centuries to hate the Jewish people so much? It's not because of where they came from, because Jewish people have lived in almost every nation of the world. It can't be the color of their skin, because Jewish people are black, white, and brown. Yet Hitler and much of the German nation did the most ungodly, unimaginable things to Jewish men, women, and children.

Paul said, "We do not wrestle against flesh and blood" but against dark spiritual forces (Eph. 6:12). He did not, however, call us to remain silent. I implore you to stand up and speak up against anti-Semitism in all its forms. Scripture says, "For Zion's sake I will not keep silent, for Jerusalem's sake I will not remain quiet, till her vindication shines out like the dawn, her salvation like a blazing torch" (Isa. 62:1, NIV).

Open your mouth, speak, and pray—not only for Israel's Jewish population but for every person who lives in the Promised Land. That's how you can play a very big part in breaking the curse of Amalek. Let everyone know that it is the devil who comes to steal, kill, and destroy, but it is Jesus who gives abundant life. Just think how the world would change if those who have been taught to love death realized that the idea was not from God.

We need to break our silence for Zion's sake but also for our own. Jesus said that peacemakers are blessed (Matt. 5:9). God is ready to release His power and blessings, but it's our move. God is calling us to take our places in fulfilling a living prophecy—the defeat of the Amalek spirit. I know firsthand that when you play your part, you will see God's blessing increase. I believe 100 percent that my family has received two lifesaving miracles because of God's great love, mercy, and compassion, and because we are blessing Israel. I will share those miracles in the next chapter.

So get ready. Pray that those who have been taught to love death would learn to love life instead.

The best *is* yet to come!

# PART II

## THE PATH FORWARD

CHAPTER 8

# REPAIRING THE BREACH

*Those from among you shall build the old waste places; you shall raise up the foundations of many generations; and you shall be called the Repairer of the Breach, the Restorer of Streets to Dwell In.*
—Isaiah 58:12

IT WAS A day that I will never forget: May 14, 2018, the seventieth anniversary of Israel's rebirth and the day the United States opened its embassy in Jerusalem. It was a bold move, and it showed Israel and the world that the United States stands with the people and nation of Israel.

The next afternoon five of us walked over to Ben Yehuda Street for a bite to eat. As we talked about the great miracle we had witnessed the day before, one of my friends received a text from his wife. She felt that God had given her a word for me, so he read it aloud from his phone: "The lion is going to roar, and the roar will be heard around the world."

The scene is as fresh in my memory as if it happened yesterday. I remember exactly where we were—the exact table and the exact pizza place. At first we thought the text was about the Jerusalem embassy, with the roar and the lion representing Jerusalem and all of Israel. The world had in fact heard the "roar" of the embassy's move.

However, the text was about something else altogether, and it would change my life. Just a minute or two after the text my phone rang. It was my son, Luke. "Dad, we need to pray," he said. "Something is wrong with Lion, and we are on the way to the hospital."

**143**

Lion is Luke and Jen's son and our grand sugar. He was seven months old and, as every parent knows, infants get sick from time to time. I also remembered that Tiz and I were extra cautious as first-time parents. When the pacifier fell on the ground, we either trashed it or boiled it into oblivion. I admit that by the second or third baby, I was known to wipe the fallen pacifier on my pants and get on with it.

Luke and Jen were first-time parents, so I expected them to overreact a little. I wasn't too alarmed about Lion. I figured the illness would pass and everything would be fine.

But everything wasn't fine. By the time I returned to the States, Lion had undergone more tests, and the doctors' reports scared us. Hearing me say that, you might be thinking, "But, Pastor, God has not given us the spirit of fear."

You are absolutely right. The spirit of fear does not come from God. But can I be totally honest with you? When you hear the *c* word connected to your seven-month-old grand sugar, the first thing that hits you is fear. You have to handle your fear by faith, but it's a process. In fact Tiz and I plan to write a book about the spiritual warfare that's involved.

But let's get back to "the lion's roar." Lion's doctors needed one more test to know for sure what the problem was. Luke, Jen, and baby Lion were staying at the hospital, and people around the world were praying. On the morning we were to receive the test results, our entire church staff went with Tiz and me to the hospital and remained in the lobby, praying.

Tiz and I and the rest of our family went up to the room to wait with Luke and Jen. The doctors arrived earlier than expected, so when we walked in, Luke and Jen already had the results. The scene broke our hearts. Jen was sobbing. Huge tears were running down Luke's face as he held baby Lion, who was sound asleep. Lion's doctors, nurses, and even the chaplain stood silent.

"Luke," I asked, "what's wrong?" My son answered, but because he was crying, I couldn't understand him. I asked again but still could not make out his words.

Then he managed to say, "Dad, it's not good." I could hear the heartbreak in his voice.

We all turned back to the doctors, who told us something no one should ever have to hear: "Lion has a very rare form of leukemia."

I consider myself to be a pretty tough guy. I was raised as an inner-city kid in South St. Louis. I've seen and heard plenty. But when I heard those words, I thought they would knock me to the ground.

Then I heard myself say, "Let's pray."

I know how sad this story sounds. And it was sad. But hang on. It gets better!

First, however, we had to go through a rough patch. Lion's chances of survival were worse than "not good." The doctors needed still another test to determine whether he had what they called a negative gene. Having that gene would be very bad news. What they didn't tell us is that almost everyone has it.

Several weeks later we got the results: no bad gene! But here's the greater miracle: baby Lion has a certain good gene that doctors had never seen in a child his age! They ran the test again to make sure they got it right. They even consulted with children's cancer researchers around the world to make sure they weren't missing something.

Some of the team at the hospital called the good gene the "Lion gene" or the "God gene." It raised Lion's survival odds from almost nothing to 95 percent! Not long ago we celebrated the second birthday of our happy, healthy grand sugar. Lion is a miracle of God, and his healing is a roar that was heard around the world.

## I WILL BLESS THOSE WHO BLESS YOU

This is a time of miracles. No matter what you are facing, God can do a miracle for you that no one has ever seen! If He did for us, it can happen to you.

When we shared Lion's illness at the church and on our television program, we got tens of thousands of responses from people around the world. Obviously we heard from Christians, but we also heard from Jewish people. Many were people we had never met, but some were friends and acquaintances who knew us because of our ministry's work for Israel. Many of our Jewish friends believed that God would heal Lion because of our *zechut*, which is a kind of merit or reward for doing good deeds.[1] Others went to their synagogues or to the Western Wall to give *tzedakah*, or charity, in Lion's name.[2]

Let me show you something that can change your life. The Hebrew word for *blessing* is *b'rakha*.[3] From Rabbi Daniel Lapin I have learned that the Hebrew language consists of letters and a mathematical code known as *gematria*. Therefore, words, names, and phrases have numerical values that reveal the Scriptures' deeper secrets.[4] For instance, in the Hebrew, *b'rakha* contains three letters: *bet*, *reish*, and *kaf*. Each letter's numerical value doubles the letter that comes before it in the Hebrew alphabet. That means all three letters speak of a doubling.[5] *B'rakha* is a picture of God doubling His blessing in your life!

And what is the avot of all blessing? It is God's promise to bless us when we bless Israel. I believe doing this will launch us into another promise: "It shall come to pass in the last days, says God, that I will pour out of My Spirit on all flesh" (Acts 2:17).

## TIKKUN OLAM

I said earlier that our works cannot save us. We are saved by grace, through Christ's work on the cross. Ephesians 2:8–9 is clear: "For by grace you have been saved through faith, and that not of yourselves; it is the gift of God, not of works, lest anyone should boast."

As a covenant people saved by grace, is anything required of us by God? *Covenant* in the Hebrew is *berit*, a "treaty, compact, agreement between two parties…a solemn, binding arrangement between two parties and entails a variety of responsibilities, benefits, and penalties."[6] There is God's side of the covenant, and there is ours. Ours is *tikkun olam*, which is about repairing a broken world.[7] Although the term has become popular, true tikkun olam is more than a nice phrase. It is the mission of every living human being. And it has to do with the relationship between faith and works, which James describes:

> What does it profit, my brethren, if someone says he has faith but does not have works? Can faith save him? If a brother or sister is naked and destitute of daily food, and one of you says to them, "Depart in peace, be warmed and filled," but you do not give them the things which are needed for the body, what does it profit? Thus also faith by itself, if it does not have works, is dead.
>
> —JAMES 2:14–17

Like everything that God's Word teaches, tikkun olam presents a physical and a spiritual reality. James said that our faith needs to produce something. That "something" is good works. Let's assume that you are a Christian farmer. You buy the best land and the best tractors, trucks, and plows you can find. You make sure your land has plenty of water, and you buy the very best seed. You check *The Farmer's Almanac*, and it predicts a bumper crop.

So what's next? Do you sit on your porch and pray that God will give you a great harvest? Well, yes and no. You should absolutely pray for God to bless whatever you put your hands to. The following passage says God will do it.

> The LORD…will bless you in the land which the LORD your God is giving you….The LORD will open to you His good treasure, the heavens, to give the rain to your land in its season, and to bless all the work of your hand.
>
> —DEUTERONOMY 28:8, 12

God gives you the land, sends bounty from His heavenly storehouse, and gives you the rain. But "the work of your hand" is your part. Everything comes by faith: the land, the equipment, the seed, the rain. But you have to *do* the farming. Faith without works is dead.

A couple of days after baby Lion got sick, God spoke to his father (my son, Luke) and my son-in-law (Brandon, our worship leader), both on the same day. Jen was at the hospital with the baby. Luke had gone home to meet a guy who was previously scheduled to paint Lion's nursery. Luke tried to tell the man that Lion was in the hospital, but the man spoke almost no English. Yet the man managed to tell Luke to read the story in Joshua chapter 5. Amazingly Brandon got the same word from God that day.

> It came to pass, when Joshua was by Jericho, that he lifted his eyes and looked, and behold, a Man stood opposite him with His sword drawn in His hand. And Joshua went to Him and said to Him, "Are you for us or for our adversaries?"
>
> So He said, "No, but as Commander of the army of the LORD I have now come."
>
> And Joshua fell on his face to the earth and worshiped, and said to Him, "What does my Lord say to His servant?"
>
> Then the Commander of the LORD's army said to Joshua, "Take your sandal off your foot, for the place where you stand is holy." And Joshua did so.
>
> —JOSHUA 5:13–15

When Joshua saw the walls of Jericho, it was nothing like the walls we see today. Jericho's walls were massive: "A reconstruction…shows a stone revetment ten feet high…and a plastered slope…running to a height of 35 feet…above the revetment. On its crest there is a high wall of brick; this brick wall thus stands back from the stone wall at the bottom of the slope a distance of 65 feet."[8]

In other words, the wall was virtually impenetrable! Imagine how Joshua felt as he assessed the situation. Then suddenly a Man stood opposite him with His sword drawn. When Joshua asked whose side the Man was on, He said, "I'm not on either side, but I have come."

When Luke asked me what I thought God was saying to us

through this passage, my answer was simple: "I believe He is saying, 'The battle is not yours. It's Mine. I will win the battle for you.'"

Notice, however, that the Man in Joshua 5 did not say, "Just go home now. I got this." He said, "There's a battle, and I will win it for you. But here's what you must do. This is your part."

> You shall march around the city, all you men of war; you shall go all around the city once. This you shall do six days. And seven priests shall bear seven trumpets of rams' horns before the ark. But the seventh day you shall march around the city seven times, and the priests shall blow the trumpets. It shall come to pass, when they make a long blast with the ram's horn, and when you hear the sound of the trumpet, that all the people shall shout with a great shout; then the wall of the city will fall down flat. And the people shall go up every man straight before him.
>
> —Joshua 6:3–5

Faith without works is dead. Why else would the Israelites need to march around the walls? Why did Peter need to catch the fish and find a coin in its mouth to pay taxes? Why didn't the Lord just hand Peter the coin? And if God wanted Goliath dead, why did David need his sling and stone? Couldn't God have struck the giant down for him?

God's plan is *covenant*—His part and our part. When He gave baby Lion the "God gene" that saved his life, we still needed great doctors to do their part. The battle is the Lord's, but we have to put our hands to the plow. I believe Jesus had to shed blood from His hands for that reason—to "bless all the work of your hand" (Deut. 28:12).

Currently our ministry provides more than fifty thousand meals each month to children in Africa. We know that many kids are starving there, so the need is obvious. But what if we did what James warned against and said, "Oh my, that's terrible. Tell them we are praying for them, and we know God will provide."

God will provide—but through us. If all we do is pray, our faith is as dead as a doornail. Paul said that "we are His workmanship, created in Christ Jesus *for good works*, which God prepared beforehand" (Eph. 2:10). God partners with us in tikkun olam. So what does that mean to you? According to ancient Jewish wisdom, your soul stood before God before you were born, and He gave you a mission to accomplish. The world should change because you are here.

## LET THERE BE LIGHT

There is something else I want you to know about good works: they are connected to God's light. Listen to what Rabbi Jesus said:

> You are the salt of the earth; but if the salt loses its flavor, how shall it be seasoned? It is then good for nothing but to be thrown out and trampled underfoot by men. You are the light of the world. A city that is set on a hill cannot be hidden. Nor do they light a lamp and put it under a basket, but on a lampstand, and it gives light to all who are in the house. Let your light so shine before men, that they may see your *good works* and glorify your Father in heaven.
>
> —MATTHEW 5:13–16

This is one of the most important things I can share with you. We are to be the light of the world and glorify God. But how? By *doing* (there it is again!) good works! We can't earn God's grace. We do good things to show the world His goodness. In other words, when we feed African children instead of just praying for them, we glorify Him.

So what did it mean when Jesus said that we are the light? If you keep in mind the Jewishness of Jesus, any discussion of light has to go back to the beginning:

> God said, "Let there be light"; and there was light. And God saw the light, that it was good; and God divided the light from the darkness. God called the light Day, and

> the darkness He called Night. So the evening and the
> morning were the first day.
>
> —GENESIS 1:3–5

God's first words in creating the heavens and the earth were "Let there be light." What do you picture when you read those words? You know it was dark, and then it wasn't. But what about the source of that light? In verse 3 God said, "Let there be light." But He didn't create the sun, moon, and stars until verses 14 through 19. It seems strange, but what point would there have been in turning on the lights when there was nothing and no one to see them?

Here's the key to the mystery. In the original Hebrew Genesis 1:1 can be read this way: "When God was about to create heaven and earth…"[9] So, before God even started creating, He set a mandate: "Let there be light." In Hebrew the word for *secret* is *raz*,[10] which has the same numerical value as *'or*, the Hebrew word for *light*.[11] The secret is that everything God creates should become light. In creating light, God created goodness. So He separated good from evil, or light from darkness. He called the good *Day* (with a capital *D*), and He called the darkness *Night* (with a capital *N*). Nowhere else in Scripture are these words capitalized in the middle of a sentence.

Now you can understand what Jesus meant when He said, "You are the light of the world." The world is supposed to "see your *good works* and glorify your Father in heaven" (Matt. 5:16). They see God's light when you tikkun olam (make the world a better place)!

## DON'T WORRY! SEEK!

If you have asked Jesus into your heart, you are no longer a Gentile living outside the covenant promises. People outside of that covenant relationship worry about the things they need. But Jesus told us that God already knows everything we need.

> Therefore do not worry, saying, "What shall we eat?" or
> "What shall we drink?" or "What shall we wear?" For

after all these things the Gentiles seek. For your heavenly Father knows that you need all these things. But
seek first the kingdom of God and His righteousness,
and all these things shall be added to you.

—MATTHEW 6:31–33

The key to having your needs met is to seek the kingdom first.
That is what Jesus did in the Garden of Gethsemane when He
said, "Not My will, but Yours, be done" (Luke 22:42). We can
simply ask, "Father, what is Your will for my life?" He will answer
through His Word.

In Matthew 6 Jesus also told us to seek God's righteousness.
Here is yet another connection to the biblical secret of light. The
Hebrew word for *righteousness* is *tzedakah*.[12] It is commonly
used to signify charity, acts of kindness, and justice. We don't
have to worry about what we eat, what we wear, or where we live
because we are in covenant with God. His part in the covenant
is to give us "all these things" (Matt. 6:33). Our part is to repair
a broken world.

Seeking the kingdom is the best way to live! If you want to
know how to love God, Jesus said, "Love your neighbor." And
instead of worrying and praying for God to meet your needs,
just ask Him, "Where can I be a blessing today?" These are the
things we do when we are saved by grace. We partner with God
to repair our broken world.

Tiz and I do our best to live this way. When we go to Israel, we
look for ways to be a blessing. That is God's will for us! But Israel
is not the only place where God directs us to do good works.
In 2010 Haiti was hit by a devastating earthquake. I received a
phone call from a Christian man in Haiti who was doing what
he could to help those poor people. To this day I don't know how
he got my phone number. He told me he had several tons of food
on the docks at Miami, but he had no way of getting the food to
starving Haitians.

His question was simple: "Can you help?"

I told him that it would be our pleasure but I would come to

Haiti to see that the food arrived and was distributed to those in need. When my son, Luke, and I and two of our pastors, Jon and Scott, arrived in Port-au-Prince, we were unprepared for what we saw. The devastation was horrible! For three days we passed out food. The needs were so great that UN security troops came to help and protect us.

After three days the food ran out, and it was time to fly home. We were tired, filthy, and feeling as though we had barely scratched the surface of the people's needs. As we finished up, a doctor who had come to Haiti from the Dominican Republic asked us when we would be leaving for home. I told her we had to be at the airport in four hours. She asked if we would accompany her to a small church in the mountains so she could show us something. We agreed to go. But because the streets were clogged with ruins, the thirty- or forty-minute drive took two hours.

When we arrived at the tiny church on the side of a very steep mountain, the doctor introduced us to the pastor, who led us to the side of the humble building. There we saw forty-three babies and small children sitting under rusted tin panels that leaned against the side of the church. The children had no shoes and were wearing almost no clothes. They were understandably filthy and very hungry.

The doctor explained that many children roamed the streets because they were orphaned by the earthquake. Human traffickers made the most of the situation, so the pastor rescued children and took them to his church. Sadly he had no provisions for them. The children had also developed a skin disease from the constant moisture, so that needed attention. In all honesty we were in a tight place financially. But we had already learned that wherever God guides, He provides.

You might be wondering why the pastor didn't house those kids in his little church. He did at first, but his church organization told him it was a house of God, not an orphanage. Their response is a perfect example of James' warning about seeing someone in need and just saying, "Depart in peace, be warmed and filled." The pastor was in a tough spot, and now the Lord had put us in an awkward position. The need was obvious: sheets of rusted metal for a home with nothing but mud for a floor, one pot of rice over an open fire, a filthy hole in the ground for a toilet—it was dire.

I asked our new friends what it would cost to build the kids a home. When they gave me a number, I looked at Luke, Scott, and Jon. Each of them nodded in agreement. We had to do something, and God would provide!

We would build the kids a home with separate rooms for boys and girls, a kitchen for cooking, a dining room for eating and studying, and toilets and showers. We made these decisions as we stood on the mountainside, but we had no idea where the water would come from. The pastor had already shown us a buried water tank with about an inch of filthy water in it. When money was available, they would pay for a truck to haul in water. However, the road was little more than a goat path. In the rainy season the truck could not get up the mountain.

That meant we would need to dig a well. We consulted with several Christian well-digging teams. They all said we couldn't get water from a mountain of solid rock. So we hired two local guys with a small pick and hammer to chisel away at the rock. After getting through fifty feet of it, they still hadn't hit water. The cost of the home we promised those kids was more than five times what we expected to spend. We were out of money and out of ideas. But we thought, "What good would the home be without clean water to make the toilets and showers work?"

All I could say was, "Let's keep digging and praying."

Two feet farther down the persistent workers hit a small underground river that runs through the granite mountain. God brought us water from the rock! It was more clean water than we could ever use, but a few days later typhoid hit Haiti. Having a good water supply not only saved the children's lives but also the lives of everyone who came to get pure, clean water for their homes and families. Only God knows how many lives that well saved.

Tikkun olam!

## ONE LIFE AT A TIME

Remember the saying, "If you save one life, God sees it as saving the whole world." Whenever we help someone, God's blessing is on us. It is the key to being blessed. But remember that the avot is in blessing Israel. That includes Jerusalem, which David mentioned, saying, "Pray for the peace of Jerusalem: 'May they prosper who love you'" (Ps. 122:6).

A new relationship with Israel and the Jewish people starts with prayer but ends with works. Jesus said, "Assuredly, I say to you, inasmuch as you *did* it to one of the least of these My brethren, you did it to Me" (Matt. 25:40). I believe this is one of the most important scriptures about the return of the Messiah. It says that when the King comes, He will tell those whom the Father has blessed, "Inherit the kingdom prepared for you from the foundation of the world" (Matt. 25:34).

Doesn't that sound like Paul's words about being "created...for good works, which God prepared beforehand" (Eph. 2:10)? It does to me! Now, here is what Jesus said those good works would look like:

> I was hungry and you gave Me food; I was thirsty and you gave Me drink; I was a stranger and you took Me in; I was naked and you clothed Me; I was sick and you visited Me; I was in prison and you came to Me.
> —Matthew 25:35–36

In Matthew 25:40 Jesus said, "My brethren, you did it to Me." In other words, "When you served My brethren, you served Me." But who are Jesus' brethren? Obviously He was talking about all of us, but the context of what Jesus said in Matthew 25 was the Jewish people. To be a blessing means fulfilling Bible prophecy and facilitating healing between Jewish and Christian people. As Isaiah wrote, "Those from among you shall build the old waste places; you shall raise up the foundations of many generations; and you shall be called the Repairer of the Breach" (Isa. 58:12).

What exactly does that mean? Let's begin with the vocabulary:

*breach* is "the act of breaking; or state of being broken; a rupture; a break; a gap; the space between the severed parts of a solid body parted by violence;...the violation or non-fulfillment of a contract."[13] Next let's consider the factors that created the breach between Christian and Jewish people:

- blaming the Jewish people for killing Jesus
- the Spanish and Portuguese Inquisitions
- the Holocaust and the world's silence
- the spirit of Amalek (including BDS and all other historical forms of anti-Semitism)

It is time to repair centuries of damage in Jerusalem and around the world. God is waiting to release His end-time power, but we need to become proactive breach repairers. Jesus called us to "love one another" (John 13:34). Do we love the children in Africa and Haiti? Absolutely! Do we pray for them? Every day! But they *know* we love them by the food on their plates, the clothes on their backs, the shoes on their feet, the roofs over their heads, and the gifts they open at Christmastime.

This is how people "see your *good works* and glorify your Father in heaven" (Matt. 5:16).

### Meeting medical needs

Last year in Jerusalem the team from Magen David Adom ("Israel's national ambulance, blood-services, and disaster-relief organization")[14] asked us to make a presentation at the Jaffa Gate. As of this writing, we have purchased five ambulances for use in Israel. They are really ICU units on wheels, and they save lives daily.

Jewish people from all walks of life gathered as we made our presentation. We told Magen David Adom that with God's help we would purchase at least one more ambulance every year. As we shared this promise, I noticed that almost all of the people who stood listening were crying. They didn't know us. They weren't part of the ceremony. They were passersby near the gate.

That night during Shabbat dinner at Josh and Rebecca

Reinstein's home, I told them what happened at the Jaffa Gate. I asked Josh, "Why were these total strangers crying?"

Josh's response hit me hard, as his words often do. "Why were they crying? Imagine feeling totally alone for two thousand years and suddenly realizing that you have friends. Can you imagine how great it feels to know that Christians love us?"

"...that they may see your good works" (Matt. 5:16).

Another way God has allowed us to repair the breach is by partnering with Bnai Zion Medical Center, in Haifa. In recent years we have assisted with several projects involving equipment and a terrorist response room. We are currently helping with an underground emergency operating room that would provide safety during rocket and missile attacks.

When our friends from the hospital heard that Tiz and I were coming to Israel this year, they asked us to bring our whole tour group to the hospital for a special lunch and celebration. Afterward, as buses pulled up to take our people back to the hotel, an ambulance approached with lights flashing and sirens wailing. Tiz and I were still inside the building when the people outside shouted for us to come.

We saw ambulance attendants rushing a woman into the emergency room. Then we saw the writing on the ambulance door. It said, "Larry and Tiz Huch—New Beginnings Ministries." Our friends and partners had purchased that unit! How powerful it was to see a Jewish sister's life being affected and possibly saved by our donation. We all cried with joy and praised the Lord.

When half of our group had boarded the bus, another ambulance arrived. This time Tiz and I were outside with Dr. Amnon Rofe, the hospital's former CEO. Jokingly I said, "It's probably one of ours."

It was! But here's the thing: the ambulances are not the hospital's property. They make runs to other hospitals too. Seeing two of them in a few minutes' time was amazing. Dr. Rofe said, "What are the odds of that happening? Possibly hundreds of ambulances pull up every week. And both of these were from your partners and ministries."

The staff were so blessed to see this. They knew we partnered with the hospital but had no idea of the other work we were doing in Israel.

## The little children!

In the same area of Haifa there is a children's home called Ahava Village for Children and Youth, where wonderful people care for 250 needy children. We have helped with several projects at Ahava. Several years ago we learned that the terrorist group Hezbollah stores approximately 120,000 rockets in Lebanon, which is within striking distance of Haifa.[15] A rocket or missile can strike Haifa within seconds of being launched.[16] There was also concern about chemical weapons being added to the cache, including missiles made in Iran.[17]

The children's home needed eighteen bomb shelters to protect the children and staff. I am very proud to say that our friends and partners stepped up. Today Ahava's residents can rest safely in eighteen shelters that also serve as sleeping quarters. If, God forbid, an attack came by night or day, the children would be protected. Talk about repairing the breach!

## Partnering in the promises

So much of what Jewish people need is centered on their return to Israel from all over the world. Therefore, I believe that repairing the breach means facilitating the second exodus. Let's refresh ourselves on what the prophets have said about the return of the Jewish people to their land:

> Fear not, for I am with you; I will bring your descendants from the east, and gather you from the west; I will say to the north, "Give them up!" and to the south, "Do not keep them back!" Bring My sons from afar, and My daughters from the ends of the earth.
> —ISAIAH 43:5–6

Thus says the Lord GOD, "Behold, I will lift My hand in an oath to the nations, and set up My standard for the

peoples; they shall bring your sons in their arms, and your daughters shall be carried on their shoulders."
—ISAIAH 49:22

"Therefore behold, the days are coming," says the LORD, "that it shall no more be said, 'The LORD lives who brought up the children of Israel from the land of Egypt,' but, 'The LORD lives who brought up the children of Israel from the land of the north and from all the lands where He had driven them.' For I will bring them back into their land which I gave to their fathers."
—JEREMIAH 16:14–15

The word *nations* in Isaiah 49:22 does not mean places with fixed borders and governments. Here the word refers to Gentiles. Obviously the Gentiles will not physically carry the Jewish people, but we can partner with Israel to bring their sons and daughters home. The prophecy from Amos 9 also talks about the Gentiles being involved:

"On that day I will raise up the tabernacle of David, which has fallen down, and repair its damages; I will raise up its ruins, and rebuild it as in the days of old; that they may possess the remnant of Edom, and all the Gentiles who are called by My name," says the LORD who does this thing.
—AMOS 9:11–12

The Gentiles destroyed both temples and ran the Jewish people out of Israel. Therefore they must be part of repairing the breach. But Amos 9:14 also mentions the Jewish people's part. Amos said they would plant vineyards and restore the waste places. God's people will be fruitful in the land!

Several years ago Tiz and I heard about families who were literally causing the desert to bloom outside of Ma'ale Amos, the city of the prophet Amos. Ma'ale Amos is about twenty kilometers southeast of Jerusalem, in what the world named the West Bank. We arranged to meet there with the farm's leader, Yosi.

When we arrived, we had to go through a large security gate. It's a dangerous place to live, no less raise a family, so everyone carried weapons for self-defense. I asked Yosi, "Why here? The land is full of rocks. There's no water. Nothing grows easily, and it's not the safest place to live. So why *here*?"

Yosi's emotional response moved me deeply. "Right here, where your feet are standing, Pastor Larry, David tended his father Jesse's sheep. Right here! The prophet Amos stood on this very hill and prophesied that we would return, that we would plant, and it would grow. Pastor Larry, you can taste God in this place; you can smell God in this place."

He was right. Since then we have partnered with the group, planting not only vineyards but thousands of olive trees. We were told that the olive oil used in the second temple for anointing and for the menorah came from this area. The Jewish people believe that when the temple is rebuilt, the oil will come from the trees planted in this soil.

"I will bless those who bless you..."

## REWARDS, MIRACLES, AND REVIVAL

Are we right to think that doing good deeds causes God to reward us? The answer is *yes*. God made us to expect and desire His rewards. That is part of our spiritual DNA. We know that someday in heaven God will reward us according to what we have done.

In current usage *reward* refers to something given in return for something else. Biblically and otherwise, it's "a recompense for worthy acts or retribution for wrongdoing."[18] There are rewards for good deeds and evil ones. We can think of this in terms of Genesis 12:3: "I will bless [give a positive reward to] those who bless you, and I will curse [negatively recompense] him who curses you [Israel]."

The Bible has a lot to say about rewards. Here are just a few scriptures, as examples:

> The LORD rewards every man for his righteousness and his faithfulness.
>
> —1 SAMUEL 26:23, ESV

> The LORD rewarded me according to my righteousness; according to the cleanness of my hands He has recompensed me.
>
> —PSALM 18:20

> Surely there is a reward for the righteous; surely He is God who judges in the earth.
>
> —PSALM 58:11

> His master replied, "Well done, good and faithful servant! You have been faithful with a few things; I will put you in charge of many things. Come and share your master's happiness!"
>
> —MATTHEW 25:23, NIV

> God "will repay each person according to what they have done."
>
> —ROMANS 2:6, NIV

> Whatever you do, work at it with all your heart, as working for the Lord, not for human masters, since you know that you will receive an inheritance from the Lord as a reward.
>
> —COLOSSIANS 3:23–24, NIV

We can agree that God rewards us according to our deeds. In light of Bible prophecy and world events, I believe the Messiah's coming is near. But if I'm wrong, we can enjoy an appointed time of blessings during which God will pour out living waters on those who thirst for His powerful move. Revival, the anointing, and His power will fall on our children and our children's children.

> And it shall come to pass afterward that I will pour out My Spirit on all flesh; your sons and your daughters shall prophesy, your old men shall dream dreams, your young

men shall see visions. And also on My menservants and on
My maidservants I will pour out My Spirit in those days.

—JOEL 2:28–29

The Hebrew word translated "pour" in Joel 2 is *shaphak*, which also means to gush.[19] God is not talking about a sprinkle or a few drops but a flood of God's power coming every which way. My own life testifies to this. I already mentioned that I was raised in South St. Louis, in an unchurched family. I went from the inner city to college. I was there to play football, but I also turned to drug use and became a drug dealer. Then I moved to the country of Colombia, where I lived as a drug trafficker and addict who shot up as many as ten or twelve times a day.

When I came back to the United States, I learned that I'd been selling drugs to an undercover DEA agent and had seven warrants out for my arrest. So I left town with two friends and ended up in Flagstaff, Arizona, where we rented a little old house in the red-light, drug-infested part of town.

One day as I sat on our front porch smoking dope, I noticed a young Mexican guy walking down the street. He kept looking back at me and walking up and down the block. After two or three trips he stopped, took a deep breath, and headed right for me. He stopped at the porch steps and said, "I have never done this before, but I couldn't leave until I told you that Jesus is the One you're looking for."

All that time, I thought the guy was summoning up the courage to come over and buy some drugs. Instead he told a long-haired, dope-smoking guy with earrings about Jesus! I laughed, but he wouldn't go away. He wanted me to go to church with him. I thought, "Can you picture me in church? I'm a *drug addict*."

The guy saved my life. His name is Bill, and he's my hero. He came over to my place every day. Finally I said, "OK. I'll go to church." I actually said it to get him off my back. But that night, I went to church, and during what I thought was a silly little Christian movie, I received Jesus as my Lord and Savior.

What I'm about to say will bother some people. I understand, but I'll say it anyway. When I went to the altar to pray at that little wooden church, not one person prayed with me. They saw a hippie with long hair, earrings, and bare feet and figured that a guy like me wouldn't make it anyway. So they passed me by. I thank God that He looks on the inside of a person, not just the outside.

I knew nothing about the Bible or church or salvation or Jesus. I didn't know what to say or how to pray. I only knew what I saw in the movie that night. It was *Gospel Road: A Story of Jesus*, with Johnny Cash. At the end of the film I saw Jesus dying on the cross at Calvary. But then I saw Him dying on the cross in the streets of a couple of modern cities. Somehow I understood that Jesus didn't only come for the good people in church but also for people from the streets, like me.

I knelt at that altar alone and said, "Jesus, if You're real, be real to me."

The love of God hit me so hard, I began to cry. Street guys don't cry in public, but God had touched my heart. I remember the pastor (who became *my* pastor) putting his arm around me and saying, "God really touched you, didn't He?"

I pushed his hand away and said, "Well, somebody did."

I experienced the power and love of God and became His child, but I was still a drug addict. People have told me, "Then you weren't really saved."

But I was! I was saved by grace, not works.

A few weeks later an evangelist came to our church for a week. He called me out and prophesied that I would go around the world and be used by God. I thought, "Me? The long-haired drug addict?"

Then he said, "You want everything that God has to offer you, don't you?"

I answered, "If it comes from God, not you." You can tell that I still didn't trust church people!

It didn't bother him a bit. He just said, "Then receive it," and touched my head.

No one was there to catch me. I felt like I floated through the air, and I landed three or four rows back, flat on my back and speaking in tongues. I was so embarrassed to be laid out and speaking that way! I wanted to get up, but I couldn't. The whole thing was humiliating, but it was also life changing.

The evangelist stood over me and said aloud, "Lord, don't let him up until he knows it's You and the Holy Spirit."

The next morning, I was still high, but for the first time in years it wasn't from drugs. My normal routine was to start the day by rolling a joint. But as I began rolling one, I looked at my friends and said, "I don't think I want this stuff anymore. I don't want to ruin what I'm feeling right now."

From that moment, I quit thinking about drugs. It was a miracle! After being drug-free and consistently in church, prayer, and my Bible for a couple of months, I started sensing the call of God on my life. Then one Sunday morning the devil tried to attack me. As I listened to my pastor's teaching, I suddenly felt as though a needle had stuck my vein. I felt the drugs going in and tasted them in my mouth, just like when I was using. In that moment, I felt an overwhelming desire for drugs.

All I could do was pray. I cannot tell you one word my pastor said that morning. I only knew that if God didn't help me right then and there, I would leave the church and be back to my old life.

When the pastor was done preaching, the whole church went to the altar and prayed. In the same instant, everyone began praising God and felt His power sweeping through the room. It touched everyone. I won't try to explain it because I had never seen it before and have never seen it since. But young and old became "drunk" in the Spirit. Nobody faked it. It was not orchestrated. We were simply under the influence of the Spirit of the living God, just like what happened on the day of Pentecost. Some people laughed. Some wept with joy. Some sang. One lady cried out, "Are we in heaven?"

It was a supernatural visitation of the Holy Spirit, and when I stood up, the sensation of the needle and the desire for drugs was gone once and for all. Satan was defeated!

Jesus sent us the Holy Spirit because He is the power of God. A few years ago my mom (who is now ninety-two years young) was visiting us in Dallas. She told Tiz something that I had never heard her say before. She said, "When Larry came back from Colombia and moved to Arizona, I was sure I would never see him alive again. I thought he would either be killed in a drug deal or die from an overdose. Only God could have changed him."

God did not make me a drug addict or dealer. Satan is the one who comes "to steal, and to kill, and to destroy" (John 10:10). But God continues to use my testimony to spark faith in others. His Word says that "all things work together for good to those who love God, to those who are the called according to His purpose" (Rom. 8:28). Whenever someone asks me to pray about a drug addiction, I can say beyond a shadow of a doubt that God can set that person free, just as He set me free. Whatever Satan means for evil, God can reverse and bring good from it.

We have seen thousands of people from around the world get delivered from drugs and other addictions because their faith was sparked by what God did for me or someone else they know. He has done it countless times, but He is also getting ready to do a new thing. He told us so in Haggai.

> "The silver is Mine, and the gold is Mine," says the LORD of hosts. "The glory of this latter temple shall be greater than the former," says the LORD of hosts. "And in this place I will give peace," says the LORD of hosts.
> —HAGGAI 2:8–9

Think about the question the imprisoned John the Baptist sent to Jesus: "Are You the Coming One, or do we look for another?" (Matt. 11:3). Jesus answered, "Go and tell John the things which you hear and see: The blind see and the lame walk; the lepers are cleansed and the deaf hear; the dead are raised up and the poor have the gospel preached to them" (Matt. 11:4–5). God will show today's world who He is by signs, wonders, and miracles, just as Jesus did in John the Baptist's day.

We have talked about the great outpouring of the Spirit that will happen before Jesus' second coming. Haggai said the latter glory would be greater than anything before it. His prophecy also promised that God would give His people peace. The Hebrew word for *peace* is *shalom*, which means "peace, harmony, wholeness, completeness, prosperity, welfare, and tranquility."[20] In other words, nothing will be missing or broken in our lives.

The world needs to see what John's disciples saw: signs, wonders, and miracles. That is the end-time blessing of God! To receive it, we must bless Israel. For centuries we moved away from the avot of blessing, and the further away we moved, the weaker we became. But if we return to Him—if we teshuva— He will return to us in might and power, and we will live under heaven's open windows. Returning to Him is the trigger to the great end-time outpouring of His Spirit.

You might ask, "Pastor Larry, do you really believe that?"

Absolutely! I believe it because God said it would happen, but also because Tiz and I are living in end-time miracles! God didn't make me a drug addict, but He delivered me and used my testimony to save others. God didn't make baby Lion sick, but the unusual gene God gave him is a miracle, and it's being heard around the world. These miracles enable us to say, "Don't give up. God can do something no one has ever seen before!"

We know that God will reward us in heaven someday, but He will reward us now, here on earth too. God will reward your zechut in this life, just as I believe He rewarded ours. He wants to bless you with miracles, but they are not only for you. My friend Joseph once prophesied to me that our miracles reveal who God is, and they give other people faith. They are signs that reveal the force that is behind your victory. That force is God's power. He gives miracles and holds them high for all to see.

## ANOTHER PRAISE

I can't close this chapter without sharing one more amazing miracle in our family. When I started writing this book, my family had a great need. I mentioned that Tiz and I had planned to write a book about what we learned through baby Lion's story.

Well, as we began that book, Tiz became ill. Within five days of her initial doctor appointment, she was in the hospital having very serious cancer surgery.

Yet again we were given little hope. Not only was Tiz's future in question but also the future of our children and grandchildren. Doctors were almost certain that Tiz had a bad gene that would complicate her situation. That same gene would likely have been passed down through the family, which could mean problems for our kids and grandkids.

Thankfully the first test found that Tiz did not have that very negative gene. One of the hospital team members pointed toward heaven and said, "Tiz, only He could have done this."

But one of Tiz's best doctors wasn't so sure about the test results. Based on what he knew, it made no sense for Tiz *not* to have the bad gene. So, three weeks later, after Tiz was retested, more test results confirmed that she did not have the gene. That was amazing news because it meant her treatment would probably work, and our children and grandchildren would be spared future health crises!

Today Tiz today is 100 percent cancer free! To God be all the glory! We are thankful not only to Him but also to everyone involved in Tiz's treatment.

You and I serve a mighty God! No matter what you pray for, no matter what the need is, no matter how impossible it seems, God can do the unimaginable for you. So I encourage you to partake of this end-time flood of His power, anointing, and miracles. Stand up for Israel. Speak up for Israel. Bless Israel. Do it, and almighty God will do what no one else can. "No eye has seen, no ear has heard, and no mind has imagined what God has prepared for those who love him" (1 Cor. 2:9, NLT).

Stay with me now because we are about to see what's ahead: the latter rain fulfillment and the coming of the Messiah!

CHAPTER 9

# ONE NEW MAN AND THE MESSIAH'S COMING

*For He Himself is our peace, who has made both one, and
has broken down the middle wall of separation, having
abolished in His flesh the enmity, that is, the law of commandments contained in ordinances, so as to create in
Himself one new man from the two, thus making peace.*
—EPHESIANS 2:14–15

D O YOU REMEMBER the young Muslim man who approached
me and others inside the Jaffa Gate and promised to slit
every Christian and Jewish throat?

Minutes before that happened, I had another memorable
encounter. Bear in mind that it was Sukkot, and Jerusalem was
packed shoulder to shoulder with people from all over the world.
As our group exited David's tomb and headed for some shopping, someone grabbed my arm. Surprised, I turned to see an
Orthodox rabbi dressed in an ornate robe, round fur hat, and
full beard. Smiling warmly, he said, "Come inside our sukkah."

A sukkah is a temporary booth built for the Feast of
Tabernacles, and this one was filled with Jewish men. It was
obvious to everyone that we were a Christian group, yet the rabbi
invited me to join the celebration of God's appointed time.

As we entered the sukkah, the rabbi asked me where I lived. I
told him I was from Dallas, Texas. "Great," he said, "and what do
you do for a living?"

I thought, "Oh, here it comes. When I tell him I'm a Christian pastor, our friendly visit could be over." Of course, I told him anyway.

"That's great!" he shouted. Then he grabbed a kippah (a man's skull cap) and put it on my head. Next he wrapped my shoulders in a tallit and handed me the lulav and etrog, two of the plants that are waved during Sukkot.[1] Then he gave me a warm hug, and we all began to dance arm in arm, in a circle, to celebrate God's goodness.

This, my friend, was an end-time miracle! The coming together of Jewish people and Gentiles is like a worldwide fire fueled by the Holy Spirit. To experience it in Jerusalem is indescribable. There is no city in the world like it, especially on the Sabbath. People gather from around the world to pray. Light shines on the ancient walls that once held the temple. And day by day Jewish people and Christians walk together! It is *beautiful*!

## BREAKING DOWN DIVISION

A year or so after meeting this rabbi, we took another group to Israel. After a Sabbath dinner we walked through the Old City to the Western Wall to pray. If you have been there, you know that men and women pray separately. So Tiz took the women, and I took the men to a synagogue that is under the Old City. Once there, we prayed with our Jewish brothers.

As we left the synagogue, someone touched my arm. It was the Orthodox rabbi I had met the year before! Seeing our Christian group leaving David's tomb probably did not seem unusual to him, but seeing us praying in a synagogue, on the Sabbath, at the Western Wall (the holiest place in all of Judaism)—that was another story!

After a few moments of small talk, the rabbi pulled me aside. "Tell me, Pastor, what do you teach in your church that causes you and your people to love Israel and come pray with us on Shabbat?"

I told him that we teach the Jewish roots of the Bible and celebrate Shabbat, Rosh Hashanah, and Yom Kippur. He gave me a big hug and said, "What you are teaching will pave the way for the Messiah's coming." Then he gave me his phone number and home address and said, "Please, the next time you come to Israel, come to my home for dinner."

What Paul prophesied is happening: Jesus has "broken down the middle wall of separation" and created "in Himself one new man" (Eph. 2:14–15). In my opinion the prophecy of the "one new man" is the most important in God's Word. That kind of unity will produce great power. Yes, Jesus has already paid for this miracle, but the physical remains of the wall won't come down on their own. We must pull them down, and Paul tells us how:

> Be strong in the Lord and in the power of His might. Put on the whole armor of God, that you may be able to stand against the wiles of the devil. For we do not wrestle against flesh and blood, but against principalities, against powers, against the rulers of the darkness of this age, against spiritual hosts of wickedness in the heavenly places.
>
> —Ephesians 6:10–12

We sometimes gloss over the "wiles of the devil" that Paul mentioned. They are simply strategies, schemes, devices, and tricks. Satan's mode of operation is to capitalize on our vulnerabilities. Therefore, to divide and conquer is one of his most powerful tools. He uses it to break up relationships, organizations, nations, and churches. But he uses it perhaps most powerfully to divide Christians and Jewish people. Division fragments our power and makes us more vulnerable to attack.

How foolishly we have fallen into this trap! How many church splits or family splits have you seen? The division damages everyone involved. Do you know how many church denominations exist? Numbers vary, but the *World Christian Encyclopedia* documents thirty-three thousand.[2] That fits the devil's strategy perfectly and increases his ability to influence us.

The day after I gave my life to the Lord in Flagstaff, Arizona,

I told some of my coworkers about it. The owner of the business overheard me and wanted to know which denomination I had joined. Not having any church experience, I didn't know what she meant. When she asked a second time, all I could say was, "The one with Jesus in it."

Imagine how we could touch the world if we took Paul's words to heart:

> There is one body and one Spirit, just as you were called in one hope of your calling; one Lord, one faith, one baptism; one God and Father of all, who is above all, and through all, and in you all.
> —EPHESIANS 4:4–6

## SYNERGY AND UNITY

Around the time when Jesus first appointed His twelve disciples, He gave us the avot concerning unity. The scribes had just accused Him, saying, "He has Beelzebub," and, "By the ruler of the demons He casts out demons" (Mark 3:22). Jesus responded with truth:

> So He called them to Himself and said to them in parables: "How can Satan cast out Satan? If a kingdom is divided against itself, that kingdom cannot stand. And if a house is divided against itself, that house cannot stand. And if Satan has risen up against himself, and is divided, he cannot stand, but has an end."
> —MARK 3:23–26

Whether Satan divides your house or God's house, "that kingdom cannot stand." Why? Because it loses what any group thrives on: *synergy*. The word comes from two Greek words: *syn* (meaning together) and *ergon* (meaning work).[3]

Here's how synergy works from a biblical perspective: "Five of you shall chase a hundred, and a hundred of you shall put ten thousand to flight; your enemies shall fall by the sword before you" (Lev. 26:8). Here's a practical example: Imagine that you are moving to a new home. Could you do the move by yourself? Maybe. But how would things go with five, ten, or even twenty friends helping out? How might their strength and ability lighten the load? And what about the tricks of the trade they've learned along the way? Wouldn't learning from their experiences and shortcuts make your move easier?

I tell myself all the time, "If I think I know everything, it just proves that I haven't learned anything yet." When I look back forty years to some of what I thought was true—well, all I can say is, "Thank God for His amazing grace!"

I believe growth comes when we are open and respectful toward others. Some years ago Tiz and I were in Denver for a Christian booksellers' convention. I had done a Christian TV interview and then stopped at our hotel room to change my clothes. Tiz called and asked, "Where are you?"

When I told her that I would be back at the convention center soon, she said, "Well, come as quickly as you can. There is someone here who wants to talk to you."

As it turned out, the person who wanted to talk to me was one of Hollywood's biggest celebrities and one of the kindest, humblest people I have ever met. She was interested in talking about some of my other books, so Tiz and I flew out a few weeks later to meet her and several other people in show business. They had all read my book on breaking generational curses and said it greatly impacted them. The woman who invited us had also been on a recent talk show when the subject of heaven came up.

They just wanted to hear our thoughts about these things. So when they asked for my opinion, I asked a question of my own: "How do you make heaven your home?"

Everyone at the table said, "Through the grace of God and Jesus Christ."

Whether they answered exactly as we would or not, their answer was good enough for us. They were from a denomination with which mainstream Christianity sometimes takes issue. But we were there to help, not divide. If that upsets you, remember what Paul said about fancy words and doctrinal differences:

> When I first came to you, dear brothers and sisters, I didn't use lofty words and impressive wisdom to tell you God's secret plan. For I decided that while I was with you I would forget everything *except Jesus Christ*, the one who was crucified.
> —1 CORINTHIANS 2:1–2, NLT

Unity is what matters. When we got bad news about baby Lion, tens of thousands of people prayed for us and believed God for Lion's miracle. Not once did we question their doctrines or denominations. The family of God came together—Jewish and Gentile people alike—to stand with us. They tore down walls of separation to do it. God came out of the holy of holies and healed our grand sugar. The same thing happened when we needed a miracle for Tiz. That is the power of unity. Look at just a few of the things Scripture has to say about it:

> In Judah the hand of God was on the people to give them unity of mind to carry out what the king and his officials had ordered, following the word of the LORD.
> —2 CHRONICLES 30:12, NIV

> How good and pleasant it is when God's people live together in unity!
> —PSALM 133:1, NIV

> Now John answered Him, saying, "Teacher, we saw someone who does not follow us casting out demons in Your name, and we forbade him because he does not follow us."
> But Jesus said, "Do not forbid him, for no one who works a miracle in My name can soon afterward speak evil of Me. For he who is not against us is on our side."
> —MARK 9:38–40

Just as a body, though one, has many parts, but all its many parts form one body, so it is with Christ. For we were all baptized by one Spirit so as to form one body—whether Jews or Gentiles, slave or free.

—1 CORINTHIANS 12:12–13, NIV

Make every effort to keep the unity of the Spirit through the bond of peace.

—EPHESIANS 4:3, NIV

No one has ever seen God; but if we love one another, God lives in us and his love is made complete in us.

—1 JOHN 4:12, NIV

## WHAT GOD HATES AND LOVES

We can be too quick to complain. "They're not doing it right!" we say. "They're not part of our denomination." But what does the Lord say? "If they're not against us, they are for us."

Several years ago I had dinner with a good Jewish friend in Israel who loves Christians. When he posed a tough question, I knew it was sincere. "Pastor Larry," he said, "what should I say when Jewish people ask, 'If Christians have the love of God in their hearts, why do they think He is a mean God, and more importantly, why are they so mean to each other?'"

Sometimes we show the world a distorted picture of the Prince of Peace! There are countless examples, but one is really to the point. At the Church of the Holy Sepulchre in Jerusalem, custody is shared by Greek Orthodox, Armenian Orthodox, and Roman Catholic denominations. Amazingly none of these groups have possession of the building's keys. Instead the keys are entrusted to a Muslim family that serves as the church's "neutral guardian."[4] They are the Joudeh family, and they claim to have played this role since "the time of Saladin, the Muslim conqueror who seized the holy city from the Crusaders in 1187." However, the existing records only date back to the sixteenth-century.[5]

Most Israelis believe that this odd arrangement is the best way to keep Christian groups from fighting over the church. They might be right. Several years ago Israeli police broke up a fight between Greek Orthodox and Armenian monks, and "dozens of worshippers traded kicks and punches."[6] I realize that this might be an extreme example. But whether our conflicts are revealed with fists or words, we have to stop. We cannot fight in the name of the Prince of Peace.

The devil has a plan to divide us, but God wants us united. Discord, to God, is an abomination.

> These six things the LORD hates, yes, seven are an abom-
> ination to Him: a proud look, a lying tongue, hands that
> shed innocent blood, a heart that devises wicked plans,
> feet that are swift in running to evil, a false witness who
> speaks lies, and one who sows discord among brethren.
>                                        —PROVERBS 6:16–19

Imagine being in a room when the Lord says, "I hate the things I'm about to show you." That would get your attention! But when He says, "The last item on My list is an abomination to Me," that would stop you cold.

The Hebrew word translated "abomination" here is *tow'ebah*, which describes "a disgusting thing…[such as] unclean food, idols…[or] wickedness."[7] Discord is an abomination because it does exactly what the devil wants: it divides and conquers. No wonder the Bible has so much to say about it:

> Now I plead with you, brethren, by the name of our
> Lord Jesus Christ, that you all speak the same thing, and
> that there be no divisions among you, but that you be
> perfectly joined together in the same mind and in the
> same judgment….Is Christ divided? Was Paul crucified
> for you? Or were you baptized in the name of Paul?
>                                 —1 CORINTHIANS 1:10, 13

> I, therefore, the prisoner of the Lord, beseech you to walk
> worthy of the calling with which you were called, with

all lowliness and gentleness, with longsuffering, bearing with one another in love, endeavoring to keep the unity of the Spirit in the bond of peace. There is one body and one Spirit, just as you were called in one hope of your calling; one Lord, one faith, one baptism; one God and Father of all, who is above all, and through all, and in you all.

—EPHESIANS 4:1–6

But avoid foolish disputes, genealogies, contentions, and strivings about the law; for they are unprofitable and useless. Reject a divisive man after the first and second admonition, knowing that such a person is warped and sinning, being self-condemned.

—TITUS 3:9–11

These are grumblers, complainers, walking according to their own lusts; and they mouth great swelling words, flattering people to gain advantage. But you, beloved, remember the words which were spoken before by the apostles of our Lord Jesus Christ: how they told you that there would be mockers in the last time who would walk according to their own ungodly lusts. These are sensual persons, who cause divisions, not having the Spirit.

—JUDE 16–19

Jude said that those who sow division don't have the Holy Spirit! As long as we remain divided, we forfeit the victory Jesus purchased with His blood. What if we tore down the walls of division instead and became God's mighty army of peacemakers? God says *a lot* about that!

Depart from evil and do good; seek peace and pursue it.

—PSALM 34:14

Behold, how good and how pleasant it is for brethren to dwell together in unity! It is like the precious oil upon the head, running down on the beard, the beard of

Aaron, running down on the edge of his garments. It is like the dew of Hermon, descending upon the mountains of Zion; for there the LORD commanded the blessing—life forevermore.

—PSALM 133:1–3

Blessed are the peacemakers, for they shall be called sons of God.

—MATTHEW 5:9

Therefore if you bring your gift to the altar, and there remember that your brother has something against you, leave your gift there before the altar, and go your way. First be reconciled to your brother, and then come and offer your gift.

—MATTHEW 5:23–24

The kingdom of God is not meat and drink; but righteousness, and peace, and joy in the Holy Ghost.

—ROMANS 14:17, KJV

Let us pursue what makes for peace and for mutual upbuilding.

—ROMANS 14:19, ESV

Finally, brethren, farewell. Become complete. Be of good comfort, be of one mind, live in peace; and the God of love and peace will be with you.

—2 CORINTHIANS 13:11

The wisdom that is from above is first pure, then peaceable, gentle, willing to yield, full of mercy and good fruits, without partiality and without hypocrisy. Now the fruit of righteousness is sown in peace by those who make peace.

—JAMES 3:17–18

Wow! God tells us that when brothers and sisters dwell in unity, the Lord will command His blessing of life forevermore!

This is the same God who commanded light, life, sun, moon, stars, rivers, mountains, and all of creation to exist—and they did. When God sees us living in unity, He will command His blessing over every area of our lives. And when He commands it, nothing can stop it!

## RESTORATION: ISRAEL AND THE CHURCH

Tiz and I believe that end-time prophecy is too often presented in a doom-and-gloom way. When we read prophecy correctly, it portrays great hope and joy. As I often say, "I read the end of the Book, and we win." Just read Peter's words as he quoted the prophet Joel on the day of Pentecost:

> It shall come to pass in the last days, says God, that I will pour out of My Spirit on all flesh; your sons and your daughters shall prophesy, your young men shall see visions, your old men shall dream dreams. And on My menservants and My maidservants I will pour out My Spirit in those days.
>                                                              —Acts 2:17–18

No doom and gloom there! Nor did Peter say what might come to pass or what he and Joel hoped would happen. Peter said what *will* happen. Every Christian has at least heard this amazing prophecy, but do we recognize the signs of its fulfillment? Do we know what precedes this great outpouring? It's almost hidden, but take a look at what Peter said about the times of refreshing:

> …that He may send Jesus Christ, who was preached to you before, whom heaven must receive until the times of restoration of all things, which God has spoken by the mouth of all His holy prophets since the world began.
>                                                              —Acts 3:20–21

Peter said the sign of the outpouring and of the Messiah's coming would be the restoration foretold by the prophets. *Restoration* is "the action of returning something to a former owner, place, or condition."[8] We've already seen the land of Israel restored to its former owners, as Ezekiel, Isaiah, and Jeremiah prophesied. Step one in the restoration of all things is happening right now, and Isaiah said that we, the church, would be part of its fulfillment!

> Thus says the Lord GOD: "Behold, I will lift My hand in an oath to the nations, and set up My standard for the peoples; they shall bring your sons in their arms, and your daughters shall be carried on their shoulders."
> —ISAIAH 49:22

This prophecy is *huge*. When we bless Israel, God breaks the curses passed down from our spiritual fathers, and the blessings can be released in full. Every year, with the help of our partners, our ministry helps thousands of Jewish people return to the nation of Israel. We do it because they need the help *and* because it is important for Gentiles to step up and help the Jewish people make this journey. That is just one way to be part of God's restoration plan.

Another sign of God's restoration is one I mentioned previously but only in passing. When the Jewish people were scattered around the world, they not only lost their land, but because they needed to fit into other countries and communities, they lost their language also. Except during a few religious celebrations, the Hebrew language had fallen out of use. Amazingly Zephaniah prophesied long ago, "I will restore to the peoples a pure language" (Zeph. 3:9). In other words, the Jewish people would get their language back.

When the Jewish people began arriving in Israel in the late 1800s and early 1900s, those already in the land spoke mostly Ladino, Arabic, and Yiddish.[9] But Eliezer Ben-Yehuda envisioned restoring the Hebrew language. It would mean starting virtually from scratch, which was amazing all by itself. But there was something even more amazing: Zephaniah 3:8 (the verse before the prophecy about a pure language) is the only verse in the entire Hebrew Bible that contains every single letter of the Hebrew alphabet.[10] The sign of the future miracle had been encoded in the ancient text!

The end of Zephaniah 3:9 explains the importance of a unified language: it is so "they all may call on the name of the LORD, to serve Him with one accord." It is another aspect of unity, and it is part of your restoration story also.

Let's do a very quick recap of what has happened so far: In 1948 we saw the restoration of the land to the people. We have seen the people restored to the land of Israel. The Hebrew language has been restored. Jerusalem was restored in 1967, just as Jesus prophesied in Luke 21:24. For the record Jesus' prophecy spoke of a doom-and-gloom period for Jerusalem, because Rome destroyed it and the second temple, and the Jewish people were either slaughtered or taken as slaves. From that time forward Jerusalem was in Gentile hands. But in the same breath Jesus jumped ahead two thousand years to when the times of the Gentiles in Jerusalem were fulfilled. So doom and gloom were followed by restoration.

Remember what Judah ben Samuel prophesied: The Ottomans would rule the land of Israel for eight jubilees, until 1917. Then Jerusalem would be a no-man's-land for fifty years (until 1967), when it was restored. All of what Jesus and ben Samuel prophesied about Jerusalem's restoration happened. Add to that what happened in 2018, when the United States moved its embassy from Tel Aviv, the capital designated by the world, to Jerusalem, which the Jewish people always considered to be their capital. That is the restoration of all things!

From AD 70 on, the Jewish people and the land of Israel endured some very dark times. But the church suffered losses too. We lost our Jewish roots. Many church services were held in Latin, which few people understood. And for centuries common people were forbidden to know God's Holy Word. However, as the prophets' words of restoration for the Jewish people are fulfilled, the church's restoration is also happening. The church is

awakening to the fact that we were grafted into the nation and
people of Israel.

## THE TABERNACLE OF DAVID

As you have seen, one of the most important prophecies we have
studied is from Amos 9, which is cited in Acts 15. (This prophecy
is directly tied to the creating of "one new man," which Paul later
prophesied in Ephesians 2:15.)

> "On that day I will raise up the tabernacle of David,
> which has fallen down, and repair its damages; I will
> raise up its ruins, and rebuild it as in the days of old;
> that they may possess the remnant of Edom, and all the
> Gentiles who are called by My name," says the LORD
> who does this thing.
> —AMOS 9:11–12

> Then all the multitude kept silent and listened to
> Barnabas and Paul declaring how many miracles and
> wonders God had worked through them among the
> Gentiles. And after they had become silent, James
> answered, saying, "Men and brethren, listen to me:
> Simon has declared how God at the first visited the
> Gentiles to take out of them a people for His name. And
> with this the words of the prophets agree, just as it is
> written: 'After this I will return and will rebuild the tab-
> ernacle of David, which has fallen down.'"
> —ACTS 15:12–16

In Acts 15 the first leaders of what we now know as Christianity
met in the Jerusalem Council and discussed how they ought to
handle the Gentiles who followed Jesus' teachings. James told the
group that the influx of Gentiles was God's handiwork, and he
quoted the prophet Amos to back up his remarks.

Let's examine this prophetic word. First both Amos and
James talked about the coming of the Messiah and the building

of David's tabernacle. Notice that neither passage mentions the building of the third temple, or even the tabernacle of Moses, but only the tabernacle of David. I believe the third temple will be built at some point, because Daniel and Ezekiel said it would happen. But I also believe that the Lord could come at any time.

Why is that important? For many spiritual reasons obviously—but my point here is about the timing of the third temple and Jesus' return. First of all the Al-Aqsa Mosque now sits on the Temple Mount. Second the Muslim people are unlikely to surrender the site easily. Third Jewish scholars believe the third temple will measure nine million square cubits, which is thirty-six times larger than the second temple.[11] (How is that going to work?) Next we need to ask what the third temple will look like, what materials will be used, and how long it will take to build it.

The Bible says the Messiah will come in the twinkling of an eye. I believe that what is impossible for man is totally possible for God. He could speak the temple into existence with one word. But these logistical questions are worth asking. We also need to consider the fact that God's Word tells us to look for the tabernacle of David.

So, what about David's tabernacle? We know it was nothing fancy, basically a tent that housed the ark of the covenant. It had an open space for worshippers with no wall of separation.[12] In fact the absence of a dividing wall may be the most important point about the tabernacle's restoration. Without a wall of separation one new man is possible. That is unity! Because God promised to command His blessing when we become unified, I believe these facts are keys.

In David's tabernacle God walked among His people 24/7. There was no single day of the year during which only one man could enter the holy of holies. God's presence filled the music, worship, prayers, miracles, and intercession. We know from 1 Chronicles chapter 25 that David appointed praise and worship teams that rotated around the clock. I believe this describes what will happen when the promise of one new man is fulfilled: God will walk among us with signs, wonders, and miracles!

So can Jewish people and Gentiles ever worship God together again? Absolutely, and there is proof: (1) God said it would happen, (2) it already happened with David, (3) it happened in the Book of Acts, and (4) it is beginning to happen with us, the last church.

### Restoring the fivefold ministry

There is another aspect of restoring the tabernacle of David. It is the latter rain restoration of the fivefold ministry of apostles, prophets, evangelists, pastors, and teachers, *and* the gifts of the Spirit found in 1 Corinthians 12. Here is what Paul said about the fivefold ministry:

> He himself gave some to be apostles, some prophets, some evangelists, and some pastors and teachers, for the equipping of the saints for the work of the ministry, for the edifying of the body of Christ, till we all come to the unity of the faith and of the knowledge of the Son of God, to a perfect man, to the measure of the stature of the fullness of Christ; that we should no longer be children, tossed to and fro and carried about with every wind of doctrine, by the trickery of men, in the cunning craftiness of deceitful plotting.
> —EPHESIANS 4:11–14

Peter told us to add knowledge to our faith (2 Pet. 1:5). We do this in part by reading the Scriptures through the eyes of a Jewish Jesus (and Moses and Paul). We can understand the fullness of Christ when we know and understand the wisdom of the Old Testament prophets. Adding Jewish wisdom to what we have learned as Christians is key to restoring the fivefold ministry! The point is to build on the "foundation of the apostles and prophets" with Jesus Christ as "the chief cornerstone" (Eph. 2:20). In Him the whole building is fitted together and "grows into a holy temple in the Lord" (Eph. 2:21).

As Christians we already have the teachings of the apostles, but that is only half of the building. To become complete, we also need the wisdom and knowledge of the prophets and Jesus

Christ. He is the One who brings us together and never divides us! Jesus unifies Jewish and Gentile people, and together they become the spiritual tabernacle of David.

## BE THE GOOD SAMARITAN

I'm sure you remember Rabbi Israel Meir Lau, whom I have already mentioned. After speaking at a conference in Japan, he was asked to meet with a ninety-four-year-old man who was the "de facto leader of Japan's sixty million Buddhists." The man told Rabbi Lau that he had long hoped to meet him and would be ready to "depart this world for a better place" now that he had done so.[13]

The monk explained that in his youth he did not "know any Jews" or "anything about Judaism." However, he had read *The Protocols of the Elders of Zion*, which Hitler cited in *Mein Kampf*. He added that, although Japan sided with Germany in the war, they had no part in Hitler's Final Solution. However, in forcing the United States into war, the Japanese indirectly helped the Germans to slaughter Jewish people, because US resources spent fighting Japan could have been used to aid the Jewish people. He therefore considered himself guilty of murdering the rabbi's parents. This gentle soul then asked the rabbi to forgive him. Rabbi Lau was very gracious but explained that forgiveness was not necessarily his to grant.[14]

No one is free to stand idly by when innocent blood is shed! This idea is found even in the laws of great nations. In the United States we have Good Samaritan laws. In some states these laws prohibit doing nothing when another person is in danger. These laws get their name from the parable of the good Samaritan, which Jesus told after this exchange with a lawyer:

> Behold, a certain lawyer stood up and tested Him, saying, "Teacher, what shall I do to inherit eternal life?"
>
> He said to him, "What is written in the law? What is your reading of it?"
>
> So he answered and said, "'You shall love the LORD your God with all your heart, with all your soul, with

all your strength, and with all your mind,' and 'your neighbor as yourself.'"

And He said to him, "You have answered rightly; do this and you will live."

But he, wanting to justify himself, said to Jesus, "And who is my neighbor?"

—LUKE 10:25–29

"Who is my neighbor?" What a great question, and what a great answer Jesus gave him! It was not only for the lawyer in the story. It was for all of us! Most of us are familiar with what Jesus said next, but I urge you to read it with fresh eyes.

Jesus answered and said: "A certain man went down from Jerusalem to Jericho, and fell among thieves, who stripped him of his clothing, wounded him, and departed, leaving him half dead. Now by chance a certain priest came down that road. And when he saw him, he passed by on the other side. Likewise a Levite, when he arrived at the place, came and looked, and passed by on the other side. But a certain Samaritan, as he journeyed, came where he was. And when he saw him, he had compassion. So he went to him and bandaged his wounds, pouring on oil and wine; and he set him on his own animal, brought him to an inn, and took care of him. On the next day, when he departed, he took out two denarii, gave them to the innkeeper, and said to him, 'Take care of him; and whatever more you spend, when I come again, I will repay you.' So which of these three do you think was neighbor to him who fell among the thieves?"

And he said, "He who showed mercy on him."

Then Jesus said to him, "Go and do likewise."

—LUKE 10:30–37

Jesus said we are to "go and do likewise." Samaritans and Jewish people were not exactly friends in Jesus' day. That is what makes the message so clear. To be a true child of God is not to be outwardly religious but inwardly caring. The priest and the Levite were not. True religion is helping those in need no matter who they are. If Jesus made this point involving Samaritans and Jewish people, how much more relevant is it for Christians and our Jewish brothers and sisters? After all we truly are family, with Abraham as our father.

## A COMMON ROOT

Christians and Jewish people have more in common than you might think. A Jewish friend who is an artist in Jerusalem painted a picture for Tiz and me and our ministry. It shows an ancient olive tree in the Garden of Gethsemane that divides (from one root and one trunk) into two equally healthy trees. Amazingly, the two trees reconnect to form one tree, which speaks of Jewish people and Gentiles becoming one new man.

In the painting you can look through the space below where the trees rejoin and see the Eastern Gate, or Golden Gate, which is Shaar HaRachamim, the Gate of Mercy. The Book of Ezekiel contains several references to a gate that faces east. (See, for example, Ezekiel 10:19; 11:1; and 43:4.) My point here is that Judaism and Christianity grow from the same root. The enemy has tried to divide us for too long. So let's remember some of the important things that Jewish people and Christians have in common:

1.  Jesus was born Jewish, both in His ethnic background and His religious thoughts and practices.

2.  The word *gospel* means good news, an idea presented in the Book of Isaiah:[15] "How beautiful upon the mountain are the feet of him who brings good news, who proclaims peace, who brings glad tidings of good things, who proclaims salvation, who says to Zion, 'Your God reigns!'" (Isa. 52:7).

In the Hebrew *basar* means "to announce (glad news)."[16]

3. The Torah and Jesus connect our points of faith. To the Jewish people the Torah is a connection to God. To Christian people Jesus is the living Word and our connection to the Father: "In the beginning was the Word, and the Word was with God, and the Word was God.... And the Word became flesh and dwelt among us, and we beheld His glory, the glory as of the only begotten of the Father, full of grace and truth" (John 1:1, 14).

4. Jewish people pray to the God of Abraham, Isaac, and Jacob. Through Jesus we also have access to the Father. When Jesus' disciples asked Him how they should pray, He said: "When you pray, say: Our Father in heaven" (Luke 11:2).

   Jesus also said that He is the door to the Father (John 10:7–9; 14:6). When Jesus died on the cross, the curtain to the holy of holies was torn open so we could come boldly before God's throne, where Jesus is sitting at the Father's right hand, making intercession for us (Rom. 8:34).

5. Every Jewish person leaves Egypt at Passover and longs for Jerusalem. Every Christian goes to Calvary, also in Jerusalem.

6. Fifty days after Passover every Jewish person celebrates Shavuot. On the same day, Christians celebrate "when the Day of Pentecost had fully come" (Acts 2:1).

Remember what Dr. Brad Young said: "The religion of the Jews in the first century is the root which produced the fruit of Christian faith. Faith in Jesus, however, has sometimes made it difficult for Christians to understand and appreciate the faith of Jesus. The religion of Jesus and his people was Judaism."[17]

I like what Tiz says: "Let's stop focusing on where we disagree, and let's focus on our places of agreement." That is the place to start!

## END-TIME WEALTH TRANSFER

Once we tear down the man-made wall that has divided us, we can use our energy to rebuild the tabernacle of David—the place without walls where God will walk among us. Amos indicated that we Gentiles would be a part of this miracle of unity (Amos 9:12). We will also receive great blessings and rewards from God because of the part we will play. Amos provides a powerful picture of what that will look like:

> "Behold, the days are coming," says the LORD, "when the plowman shall overtake the reaper, and the treader of grapes him who sows seed; the mountains shall drip with sweet wine, and all the hills shall flow with it."
> —AMOS 9:13

The Lord is speaking about a time of profound and even instant prosperity. The end-time transfer of wealth will be among the signs, wonders, and miracles that usher in the Messiah's coming.

At the time of Amos' prophecy Israel was very prosperous, mostly because Israel-Judah relations had improved, and Aram (Syria) had been subdued by Israel's king.[18] Great outpourings of God's power are often coupled with prosperity. Perhaps the greatest example we have of this is in the first Exodus when God's people went from being impoverished slaves to being people of wealth in an instant.

> Now the children of Israel had done according to the word of Moses, and they had asked from the Egyptians articles of silver, articles of gold, and clothing. And the LORD had given the people favor in the sight of

the Egyptians, so that they granted them what they requested. Thus they plundered the Egyptians.
                                    —EXODUS 12:35–36

The "word of Moses" here refers to Moses' earlier instructions from God:

I will give this people favor in the side of the Egyptians; and it shall be, when you go, that you shall not go empty-handed. But every woman shall ask of her neighbor, namely, of her who dwells near her house, articles of silver, articles of gold, and clothing; and you shall put them on your sons and on your daughters. So you shall plunder the Egyptians.
                                    —EXODUS 3:21–22

This was the first wealth transfer. I know a lot of people get nervous when the subjects of wealth and prosperity come up. But a revival from God brings with it the finances to take His power to the world. Other people call the Exodus wealth transfer a fairy tale. But present-day Egyptians apparently don't see it that way. When interviewed by the Egyptian weekly *Al-Ahram Al-Arabi*, Dr. Nabil Hilmi, dean of the faculty of law at the University of Al-Zaqaziq, revealed that he and "a group of Egyptians living in Switzerland [had] opened the case of the so-called 'great exodus of the Jews from Pharaonic Egypt.'"[19]

Dr. Hilmi and the other plaintiffs accused the ancient Israelites of leaving Egypt "in the middle of the night" with gold, jewelry, and other priceless valuables. I kid you not! The headline of the article in which the interview was excerpted is "Egyptian Jurists to Sue 'The Jews' for Compensation for 'Trillions' of Tons of Gold Allegedly Stolen During Exodus From Egypt."[20]

I don't know whether the Jewish people left Egypt with trillions of tons of gold. That sounds like a lot to carry across the desert. But God's Word says that Israel "plundered" the Egyptians. One Bible version says, "They picked those Egyptians clean" (Exod. 12:36, MSG).

Dr. Hilmi's lawsuit sounds bizarre, but it's real. Claims in an ancient Egyptian court case were defeated by the Jewish advocate when he argued for back wages to be paid to six hundred thousand slaves who served Pharaoh over a period of four hundred years.[21] The case, heard by Alexander the Great, was dropped like a hot potato, as it should have been.

The Israelites plundered the Egyptians in part to fulfill God's promise to Abraham: "Your descendants will be strangers in a land that is not theirs.…Afterward they shall come out with great possessions" (Gen. 15:13–14). In Chassidic thought the wealth transfer in the Book of Exodus paralleled the Israelites' spiritual riches in coming back to God. God told Moses to tell Pharaoh, "Let My people go," so they could serve God in worship (Exod. 9:1). God made sure they left with riches, but they misused them and created a golden calf (Exod. 32:1–4).

According to Exodus 25:1–8 the purpose of the wealth transfer from the unrighteous to God's people was to provide for a sanctuary where God could be close to His children. He made sure they had plenty of gold, silver, and bronze; blue, purple, and scarlet yarn and fine linen thread; and oil and spices for anointing and for incense before they left Egypt. Remember that this happened in addition to other signs, wonders, and miracles, especially the ten plagues that showed Pharaoh who was really God.

I declare to you that "Jesus Christ is the same yesterday, today, and forever" (Heb. 13:8). What He did before, He will do again. There is no lack of wealth in the world, but a lot of it is in the wrong hands. Just look at Las Vegas. CNBC reported in 2011 that the worldwide casino industry was expected revenue of $144 billion that year.[22] There is plenty of money, and God will transfer it into the hands of people who will tikkun olam.

## MALACHI AND OUR MONEY

Let's take another look at Malachi to find hidden keys to our personal prosperity and the end-time transfer of wealth. Remember the backstory o Malachi's writings. The Jewish people had just returned from the Babylonian captivity, and men such as Ezra, Nehemiah, and Malachi formed the Great Assembly to seek God's wisdom for the returnees.

One of the reasons Babylon defeated the Jewish people involved their money. God had blessed and prospered Israel so greatly that they felt no need to obey God's laws concerning shmitta (or shemittah), which means to release.[23] Shmitta is the agricultural seventh year—the Sabbath year when fields are left fallow. It is a kind of tithe.

> Six years you shall sow your field, and six years you shall prune your vineyard, and gather its fruit; but in the seventh year there shall be a sabbath of solemn rest for the land, a sabbath to the LORD. You shall neither sow your field nor prune your vineyard. What grows on its own accord of your harvest you shall not reap, nor gather the grapes of your untended vine, for it is a year of rest for the land.
>
> —LEVITICUS 25:3–5

Shmitta taught every Jewish person to trust Jehovah Jireh, their provider, who would make good on His promise, even when they observed the agricultural Sabbath.

> So you shall observe My statutes and keep My judgments, and perform them; and you will dwell in the land in safety. Then the land will yield its fruit, and you will eat your fill, and dwell there in safety. And if you say, "What shall we eat in the seventh year, since we shall not sow nor gather in our produce?" Then I will command My blessing on you in the sixth year, and it will bring forth produce enough for three years.
>
> —LEVITICUS 25:18–21

Shmitta focused on trust, but it also gave the Jewish people time to focus on their personal relationship with God. As is true of all human beings, prosperity tempted many Jewish people to stray from God and from shmitta. In disregarding His Word, they walked into the very trap God had warned them about; they put their trust in their labor rather than their Maker.

> Then you say in your heart, "My power and the might of my hand have gained me this wealth." And you shall remember the LORD your God, for it is He who gives you power to gain wealth, that He may establish his covenant which He swore to your fathers, as it is this day.
> —DEUTERONOMY 8:17–18

I pray that we would take to heart the lessons the Israelites learned. I encourage you to read all of Deuteronomy chapter 8, especially verses 6 through 19. God is essentially saying, "Listen, I'm going to bless you. You won't lack anything. But when your stomachs are full, when you've built beautiful homes, when you prosper in your jobs and businesses, don't forget who empowered you to gain this wealth."

Unfortunately the Israelites did forget, and so they were overcome. Seventy years later God said, "Return to Me, and I will return to you" (Mal. 3:7). In other words, "It's your move. I'm waiting for you to come back."

Imagine their response: "Wow, Lord, that sounds great!" But they needed more input, so they asked, "In what way shall we return?" (Mal. 3:7).

You would expect God to say, "Quit sinning. Quit worshipping idols," or something along those lines. But no. God brought up their tithes and offerings. My purpose here is not to teach about tithing but about reading God's Word through the eyes of the Jewish prophets. The goal is to add their wisdom and knowledge to our faith.

We know that the tithe belongs to God. But what did Malachi mean by "offerings"? As you read, remember that God was speaking to Jewish people who knew things that Gentiles did not yet know. While they were in the wilderness, they learned that about giving beyond the tithe:

> Three times a year all your males shall appear before
> the LORD your God in the place which He chooses: at
> the Feast of Unleavened Bread [Passover, or Pesach],
> at the Feast of Weeks [Shavuot], and at the Feast of
> Tabernacles [Sukkot]; and *they shall not appear before
> the LORD empty-handed.*
> —DEUTERONOMY 16:16, EMPHASIS ADDED

If we listen only with Gentile ears, we could mistakenly believe
that the three feasts and the giving of offerings have nothing to
do with us. But watch this: "The LORD spoke to Moses, saying,
'Speak to the children of Israel, and say to them: "The feasts of
the LORD, which you shall proclaim to be holy convocations,
these are *My* feasts"'" (Lev. 23:1–2, emphasis added).

God said the feasts are His. Many Christians say, "The feasts
are not for us; they are Jewish feasts." It is true that God gave
the feasts to the Jewish people first. But now they are ours also,
because we have been grafted into the promises of Abraham.

## RUMOR AND SHADOW

There's a certain rumor that relates to the Book of Malachi. We
have touched on it in a way, but I'd like to finish it off, right here,
right now.

When I first became a Christian, I heard sermons on Malachi
all the time. I was taught that the Jewish people never returned
(teshuva) as God commanded them to do. But that's not true. We
have proof in the New Testament that they did—by gathering for
the feasts and by giving the tithes and offerings God prescribed in
Leviticus and restated more generally in Malachi. These include
offerings to be given three times a year, at the three feasts named
in Deuteronomy 16:16: Passover, Shavuot, and Sukkot.

Let me give you a quick summary that proves the Jewish
people returned in obedience to God's call in Malachi:

- The Last Supper occurred during the Feast of
  Passover. Jesus said, "I have eagerly desired to eat

this Passover with you before I suffer" (Luke 22:15,
NIV). Not only did Jesus keep the Passover, but so
did all the Jewish people. The scene of Jesus' triumphant entry to Jerusalem proves my claim:
"The next day the great crowd that had come for
the festival heard that Jesus was on his way to
Jerusalem. They took palm branches and went out
to meet him, shouting, 'Hosanna! Blessed is he
who comes in the name of the Lord! Blessed is the
King of Israel!'" (John 12:12–13, NIV).

- Fifty days after Passover the Feast of Shavuot,
  or Pentecost, proved that the Jewish people had
  returned to God.

   Remember that Jesus commanded His disciples not to leave Jerusalem until the power of God
   fell on them on Shavuot. Then, "when the Day of
   Pentecost had fully come, they were all with one
   accord in one place. And suddenly there came a
   sound from heaven, as of a rushing mighty wind,
   and it filled the whole house where they were sitting" (Acts 2:1–2).

   Devout Jewish people from every nation were
   gathered in Jerusalem. They had returned, just as
   God commanded. They were "devoted, dedicated,
   reverent, God-fearing."[24] The Greek suggests
   that they were "taking hold of what is good" and
   having "godly respect for the things of God."[25]

- Finally there is the Feast of Sukkot, which is
  described in Leviticus:

   "Also on the fifteenth day of the seventh month,
   when you have gathered in the fruit of the land,
   you shall keep the feast of the LORD for seven
   days; on the first day there shall be a sabbath-
   rest, and on the eighth day a sabbath-rest....You
   shall keep it as a feast to the LORD for seven days

in the year. It shall be a statute forever in your
generations. You shall celebrate it in the seventh
month. You shall dwell in booths for seven days.
All who are native Israelites shall dwell in booths,
that your generations may know that I made the
children of Israel dwell in booths when I brought
them out of the land of Egypt" (Lev. 23:39, 41–43).
God's people had indeed returned, and Sukkot
proves it.

No devout Jewish person would show up empty-handed for
any of these feasts. They came together as a people and gave their
offerings.

Now for the shadow—actually several shadows, beginning
with the feasts. As amazing as the feasts are, they are but "a
shadow of things to come" (Col. 2:17). That does not mean they
are insignificant. Even a shadow is substantial when God is
involved. Just ask Peter and the sick people in Jerusalem!

Believers were increasingly added to the Lord, multitudes of both men and women, so that they brought
the sick out into the streets and laid them on beds and
couches, that at least the shadow of Peter passing by
might fall on some of them. Also a multitude gathered
from the surrounding cities to Jerusalem, bringing sick
people and those who were tormented by unclean spirits,
and they were all healed.

—Acts 5:14–16

Peter's shadow had the same net effect as the laying on of
hands. The Passover was the shadow of God's ultimate forgiveness, mercy, and power. When Jesus died and rose again, the
shadow of once-a-year forgiveness became the forgiveness that
is forever. The annual blessing of Shavuot was also shadow until
"the Day of Pentecost had fully come" (Acts 2:1). Now God's Spirit
is with us and in us forever.

There are more shadows. Just before Sukkot and Yom Kippur

is Rosh Hashanah, which is a shadow of the rapture. Yom Kippur is a shadow of the second coming. Sukkot, the Feast of Tabernacles, is a shadow of the marriage supper of the Lamb, which is celebrated for seven days amid great joy and happiness. This is when hundreds of thousands of Jewish people entered the Pool of Siloam and walked the Pilgrimage Road singing, "This is the day the LORD has made; we will rejoice and be glad in it" (Ps. 118:24).

The seventh day of Sukkot is the greatest day of all, and it illustrates God's love being poured out on us, with Jesus in the middle of it all.

> When His brothers had gone up, then He also went up to the feast, not openly, but as it were in secret. Then the Jews sought Him at the feast, and said, "Where is He?"
> …Now about the middle of the feast Jesus went up into the temple and taught.…On the last day, that great day of the feast, Jesus stood and cried out, saying, "If anyone thirsts, let Him come to Me and drink. He who believes in Me, as the Scripture has said, out of his heart will flow rivers of living water."
> —JOHN 7:10–11, 14, 37–39

For much more on these topics, I encourage you to go to my website, https://larryhuchministries.com, and check it out.

## THE SECOND COMING AND OPEN WINDOWS

You now know this drill very well: every teaching in God's Word has a physical or earthly side and a spiritual side. In addition a lesser and a greater message are usually rolled into one. This is true of what Malachi prophesied, saying, "Behold, I send My messenger, and he will prepare the way before Me" (Mal. 3:1).

We established earlier that the messenger who prepared the way for Jesus' first coming was John the Baptist, who also baptized Him. He was the "voice of one crying in the wilderness," according to Matthew 3:3 and Isaiah 40:3. Now stay with me here, and my point will become clear. Malachi 3:1 says, "The Lord, whom you seek, will suddenly come to His temple." This is not speaking of Jesus' first coming, because there was nothing sudden about that event.

So, as we have already seen, Malachi spoke to the first coming of Christ but also the second. The duality of Malachi's message also applies to the portion about the windows of heaven. To see this, we need to first look at the parable of the sower and the seed. Then we can make the connection to Malachi.

> Then [Jesus] spoke many things to them in parables, saying, "Behold, a sower went out to sow. And as he sowed, some seed fell by the wayside; and the birds came and devoured them. Some fell on stony places, where they did not have much earth; and they immediately sprang up because they had no depth of earth. But when the sun was up they were scorched, and because they had no root they withered away. And some fell among thorns, and the thorns sprang up and choked them. But others fell on good ground and yielded a crop: some a hundredfold, some sixty, some thirty. He who has ears to hear let him hear!"
> —MATTHEW 13:3–9

Jesus spoke here about having physical and spiritual ears, and we definitely need our spiritual ears to understand this passage. He spoke about the "good ground" and about the thirtyfold, six-tyfold, and one hundredfold harvest. Did He pull those numbers out of the air? No. He was speaking about something every Jewish person understood: the three offerings the Jewish people gave at three different feasts—Passover, Shavuot, and Sukkot. Giving at these feasts three times a year would release a blessing, building from thirtyfold to sixtyfold to one hundredfold (unlimited blessing).

This was separate from the tithe, but it was connected to the opening of the windows of heaven, the channel of divine flow described by Malachi:

> Prove me now herewith, saith the LORD of hosts, if I will not open you the windows of heaven, and pour you out a blessing, that there shall not be room enough to receive it. And I will rebuke the devourer for your sakes, and he shall not destroy the fruits of your ground; neither shall your vine cast her fruit before the time in the field, saith the LORD of hosts. And all nations shall call you blessed.
> —MALACHI 3:10–12, KJV

Please hear me: God is good *all* the time, but there are His appointed times, His moadim, when His blessings exceed all other times. Tiz says that Texas has the same sun in January and in August. But while August can be blistering hot, temperatures can dip below freezing in January. What's the difference? The sun is closer in August than it is in January. It's the same sun; it's just closer. God is the same God all year round, but at His moadim His power and blessings are closer. Scripture affirms that such times exist.

> There is an appointed time for everything, and there is a time for every event under heaven....He has made everything appropriate in its time.
> —ECCLESIASTES 3:1, 11, NASB

> Seek the LORD while He may be found, call upon Him while He is near.
> —ISAIAH 55:6

In the Book of Genesis God revealed His seasons. "Then God said, 'Let there be lights in the firmament of the heavens to divide the day from the night; and let them be for signs and seasons, and for days and years" (Gen. 1:14). If we take the English word *seasons* at face value, we think of winter, spring, summer, and fall. That would be the physical or lesser understanding. But the spiritual understanding is the greater, and it relates to God's moadim.

A Hebrew-minded rendition of Genesis 1:14 might read like this: "and let them be for signs and for festivals and for days and for years." In Psalm 104:19 "[God] appointed the moon for seasons." God was talking about His moadim.

## KEY SCRIPTURES FOR TODAY

You might be wondering, "Why haven't I been told about these things before?" I believe God sets certain revelations aside and uncovers them at special times in history. We are in one of those times now, and the following passages of Scripture are important for today.

> O LORD, my strength and my fortress, my refuge in the
> day of affliction, the Gentiles shall come to you from
> the ends of the earth and say, "Surely our fathers have
> inherited lies, worthlessness and unprofitable things."
> Will a man make gods for himself, which are not gods?
> Therefore behold, I will this once cause them to know, I
> will cause them to know My hand and My might; and
> they shall know that My name is the LORD.
> —JEREMIAH 16:19–21

According to Jeremiah, God would not only return the Jewish people to the Promised Land (restoring both the people and the land), but He would also bring the Gentiles back to their Jewish roots and restore to them the promises and power of God.

Look at what the prophet Zechariah wrote:

> Thus says the LORD of hosts: "In those days ten men
> from every language of the nations shall grasp the sleeve
> of a Jewish man, saying, 'Let us go with you, for we have
> heard that God is with you.'"
> —ZECHARIAH 8:23

The "sleeve of a Jewish man" is *kanaph* in the Hebrew, which means wing.[26] This is the corner of the Jewish prayer shawl, the tallit. The shawl's four corners connect our prayers with God's

promises. In grasping the sleeve of a Jewish man, we add to our
faith the ancient knowledge of the prophets. This is one way in
which God is opening Gentile eyes and returning the church to
its Jewish roots. All of this is part of the restoration of all things,
mentioned in Acts:

> Those things which God foretold by the mouth of all
> His prophets, that the Christ would suffer, He has thus
> fulfilled. Repent therefore and be converted, that your
> sins may be blotted out, so that times of refreshing
> may come from the presence of the Lord, and that He
> may send Jesus Christ, who was preached to you before,
> whom heaven must receive until the times of restoration
> of all things, which God has spoken by the mouth of all
> His holy prophets since the world began.
> —ACTS 3:18–21

God is not restoring the things that man or our religious insti-
tutions have contrived. He is restoring what the prophets and
apostles, with Jesus as chief cornerstone, have established. These
things remove the wall of separation and make the Jewish people
and Gentiles one new man, the living tabernacle of David.

We saw earlier the opening of the windows of heaven and the
rebuking of the devourer in Malachi chapter 3. Now let me share
a passage from Malachi that is less frequently taught:

> "You shall trample the wicked. For they shall be ashes
> under the soles of your feet on the day that I do this,"
> says the LORD of hosts. "Remember the law of Moses,
> My servant, which I commanded him in Horeb for all
> of Israel, with the statutes and judgments. Behold, I will
> send you Elijah the prophet before the coming of the
> great and dreadful day of the LORD. And he will turn
> the hearts of the fathers to the children, and the hearts
> of the children to the fathers, lest I come and strike the
> earth with a curse."
> —MALACHI 4:3–6

There's a lot to unpack here. First we are to "remember the law of Moses" and distinguish it from legalism. The Torah is not legalistic but instructive. Second we will see the hearts of the fathers returning to the children and vice versa. From the natural perspective we pray that all fathers and children will love each other. From the spiritual point of view we see the one new man arising as the dividing wall comes down. In this context the fathers are the Jewish people and the nation of Israel, who gave birth to Christianity, their "child." Then God says that if this doesn't happen, He will "strike the earth with a curse." That is another way of saying, "I will bless those who bless you, and I will curse him who curses you."

We cannot begin to imagine God's great blessing as Jewish people and Gentiles become one new man!

## WHAT IF?

As we close, let's take a final look at the words of Amos.

> "On that day I will raise up the tabernacle of David, which has fallen down, and repair its damages; I will raise up its ruins, and rebuild it as in the days of old; that they may possess the remnant of Edom, and all the Gentiles who are called by My name," says the LORD who does this thing....I will plant them in their land, and no longer shall they be pulled up from the land I have given them," says the LORD your God.
>
> —AMOS 9:11–12, 15

First the prophet says that God "will raise up the tabernacle of David...and rebuild it as in the days of old." The rebuilt tabernacle won't have a dividing wall, because the original had none. Because there will be unity, God will pour out His blessing. Second the prophet says God will include Gentiles in bringing back the Jewish people to their own land. Third the prophet says Jewish people will never be forced to leave their land again. God has given it back to them forever.

There is a fourth aspect of the prophecy that we haven't looked at yet. It is in Amos 9:12, where the Gentiles are also mentioned, and it says, "...that they may possess the remnant of Edom." Some interpret the word Edom as meaning all of humankind because the word is related to the words 'adom and 'adam. But Edom, which means red, was biblically connected to Esau, who was born red all over and was both Jacob's brother and the father of the Edomites.

> So when her days were fulfilled for her to give birth, indeed there were twins in her womb. And the first came out red. He was like a hairy garment all over, so they called his name Esau.
> —Genesis 25:24–25

In Genesis 25:30 (KJV) Esau asked for "red pottage," which is the Hebrew 'adom.[27] We saw how Esau's hatred for Jacob (Israel) manifested powerfully in the life of his grandson Amalek. In his own anger Esau married into the family of Ishmael, Abraham's firstborn (Gen. 28:8–9). We know that Ishmael was circumcised as a young man, and God granted him great favor and made him into a numerous people (Gen. 16:9–12). We also know that his name means God will hear. But we have also seen that Ishmael had issues with authority. The question today is, If God speaks to Ishmael's descendants, will they listen?

Earlier we saw three scriptures from Deuteronomy that indicated they would not listen or submit to authority:

- Deuteronomy 17:12: "Now the man who acts presumptuously and *will not heed* [will not listen to] the priest..."
- Deuteronomy 18:19: "It shall be that whoever *will not hear* [will not listen to] My words..."
- Deuteronomy 21:18. "If a man has a stubborn and rebellious son who will not obey the voice of his father or the voice of his mother, and who, when

> they have chastened him, *will not heed* [will not listen to]..."

Here is my question for you: Could prayer and a miracle of God change the Ishmaelites' attitude toward authority? Before you respond, consider what happened when Abraham died:

> Then Abraham breathed his last and died in a good old age, an old man and full of years, and was gathered to his people. And his sons Isaac and Ishmael buried him in the cave of Machpelah, which is before Mamre, in the field of Ephron the son of Zohar the Hittite.
> —Genesis 25:8–9

Both Isaac and Ishmael attended their father's burial. We tend to ignore this detail, but I believe God is revealing a miracle in it. Abraham was 175 years old when he died. That means Isaac was 75 and Ishmael was 89. Tradition assumes that the brothers had been separated for 50 years at that point.

Yet here we see them together again. Could it be that the love they felt for their father caused them to come together in peace? The famous teacher Rashi told us that when the brothers came together, Ishmael repented. Ishmael was the elder son, yet he acknowledged Isaac as the favorite son and the heir. "Rashi also notes that Yitzchak's name precedes that of Yishma'el, and comments, 'From here we learn that Yishma'el did teshuva and allowed Yitzchak to go before him.'"[28]

Could this happen again? God's Word says it can: "Say to your brethren, 'My people,' and to your sisters, 'Mercy is shown'" (Hos. 2:1). A favorite scripture for Christians is also the church's unofficial mission statement: "Repent ye therefore, and be converted" (Acts 3:19, KJV). The word translated "converted" in Acts 3 "has the same meaning as shalem,"[29] a word that is sometimes used in Aramaic versions of the Scriptures to express the idea. Have you noticed what it sounds like? Yes! The Hebrew word *shalom*, which means peace.

It could be that God is telling all of us—whether Jewish, Christian, Muslim, or anything else—that it is time to return and submit to His Holy Word. Isn't that His message anyway? And don't the names Ishmael (God will hear) and Israel (God will rule) both contain El, the name of God Himself? Remembering this is important because these two major figures play an enormous role in Bible and world history.

Yes! Let's pray that God will hear the prayers of Ishmael and his descendants will hear the voice of the God who rules! There is nothing God cannot do. He will fulfill His plan for the whole world and for Israel and for the Jewish people. Let this be your prayer:

> There stand the thrones for judgment, the thrones of the house of David. Pray for the peace of Jerusalem: "May those who love you be secure. May there be peace within your walls and security within your citadels." For the sake of my family and friends, I will say, "Peace be within you."
> —PSALM 122:5–8, NIV

The exact moment that I wrote these last words, my son and daughter-in-law brought baby Lion to our house. It was late in the evening and I was a little surprised to hear them coming through the door. It was also during the final months of Lion's treatment, and I knew they'd had a doctor's appointment that day. I could tell by their faces that they had something exciting to share. As Lion ran into my office and jumped up on my lap, Luke and Jen smiled from ear to ear.

Lion had a port in his chest that led to his heart. It was supposed to stay in for five more months. But his health was so good that the doctors decided to remove the port the next day. He wasn't going to need it anymore! It came out five months early because our wonderful God always does "exceedingly abundantly above all that we ask or think" (Eph. 3:20)!

So why are you hearing about Lion's miracle again? Because

when you see or hear of a miracle in someone else's life, God is telling you, "You're next!" This testimony is assigned to you. What miracle do you need? Whatever it is, stand up for Israel and watch almighty God stand up for you!

Meanwhile make the following words your banner:

> For Zion's sake I will not be silent, and for Jerusalem's sake I will not keep still, until her righteousness shines like a bright light, her salvation like a blazing torch.
>
> —Isaiah 62:1, BSB

Truly your best is yet to come! Baruch Hashem!

# NOTES

## CHAPTER 1

1. David Van Biema, "Re-Judaizing Jesus," in "10 Ideas That Are Changing the World," *Time*, March 13, 2008, http://content.time.com/time /specials/2007/article/0,28804,1720049_1720050_1721663,00.html.
2. Van Biema, "Re-Judaizing Jesus."
3. Van Biema, "Re-Judaizing Jesus."
4. "What Does the Name 'Jesus' Mean?," Christianity.com, accessed March 31, 2020, https://www.christianity.com/jesus/is-jesus-god/names-of -jesus/what-does-the-name-jesus-mean.html.
5. Dan Hummel, "The New Judaizers: How American Pentecostals Are Adopting Jewish Trappings in Their Theology, Practices and Politics," *Jerusalem Post*, March 10, 2018, https://www.jpost.com/Magazine/The- new-Judaizers-540415.
6. Hummel, "The New Judaizers."
7. Joseph Klausner, *Jesus of Nazareth: His Life, Times, and Teaching* (New York: Macmillan, 1929), 374. Hummel mentions "Jacob Klausner" but seems to be speaking of Joseph Klausner.
8. Hummel, "The New Judaizers."
9. Brad H. Young, *Jesus the Jewish Theologian* (Grand Rapids, MI: Baker Academic, 1995), https://books.google.com/ books?id=sbBM7w74E3wC&q.
10. "What Is Tzitzit (and Tallit)?," Chabad.org, accessed March 31, 2020, https://www.chabad.org/library/article_cdo/aid/537949/jewish/What-Is -Tzitzit-and-Tallit.htm.
11. Blue Letter Bible, s.v. "*pentēkostē*," accessed March 31, 2020, https://www.blueletterbible.org/lang/lexicon/lexicon. cfm?Strongs=G4005&t=KJV.
12. "The Many Parallels of Sinai and Pentecost," Acts 242 Study, February 8, 2012, http://acts242study.com/they-many-parallels-of-sinai-and- pentecost/. Because I agree with the calculations presented in this article, I have presented its case here.
13. "The Many Parallels of Sinai and Pentecost," Acts 242 Study.
14. Beth Messiah Messianic Synagogue, "Moadim (The Appointed Times)," Beth Messiah Messianic Synagogue, September 10, 2019, http:// bethmessiah .life/2019/09/moadim-the-appointed-times/.
15. Blue Letter Bible, s.v. "*towrah*," accessed March 31, 2020, https://www .blueletterbible.org/lang/lexicon/lexicon.cfm?Strongs=H8451&t=KJV.
16. "The Letter Yod," Hebrew for Christians, accessed March 31, 2020, https://www.hebrew4christians.com/Grammar/Unit_One/Aleph-Bet/ Yod/yod.html.

17. "Where the 'Christian' Name Really Came From," *Relevant*, April 8, 2013, https://relevantmagazine.com/god/where-christian-name-really-came/.

18. W. D. Davies, *Paul and Rabbinic Judaism: Some Rabbinic Elements in Pauline Theology*, 4th ed. (Philadelphia: Fortress Press, 1980), xxxvi, https://archive.org/details/paulrabbinicjuda0000davi.

19. Julian Sinclair, "Pirkei Avot," The Jewish Chronicle, accessed January 21, 2020, https://www.thejc.com/judaism/jewish-words/pirkei-avot-1.2573. See also Naftali Silberber, "Why Is the Tractate Named 'Fathers'?" Chabad.org, accessed March 31, 2020, https://www.chabad.org/library/article_cdo/aid/517534/jewish/Why-is-it-Named-Fathers.htm.

20. Young, *Jesus the Jewish Theologian*, preface.

## CHAPTER 2

1. Blue Letter Bible, s.v. "*barak*," accessed April 1, 2020, https://www.blueletterbible.org/lang/lexicon/lexicon.cfm?Strongs=H1288&t=KJV.

2. Jeff A. Benner, "Bless," Ancient Hebrew Research Center, accessed April 1, 2020, https://www.ancient-hebrew.org/definition/bless.html . See also Blue Letter Bible, s.v. "*Běrakah*," accessed April 1, 2020, https://www.blueletterbible.org/lang/lexicon/lexicon.cfm?Strongs=H1293&t=KJV.

3. Blue Letter Bible, s.v. "*arar*" accessed April 1, 2020, https://www.blueletterbible.org/lang/lexicon/lexicon.cfm?Strongs=H779&t=KJV.

4. George J. Zemek, *The Word of God in the Child of God: Exegetical, Theological, and Homiletical Reflections From the 119th Psalm* (Eugene, OR: Wipf and Stock, 2005), 108, https://www.amazon.com/Word-God-Child-Theological-Homiletical/dp/1597523801.

5. Pope Paul VI, "Declaration on the Relation of the Church to Non-Christian Religions: Nostra Aetate," October 28, 1965, http://www.vatican.va/archive/hist_councils/ii_vatican_council/documents/vat-ii_decl_19651028_nostra-aetate_en.html.

6. James Carroll, *Constantine's Sword: The Church and the Jews* (Boston: Mariner, 2002), 37–57.

7. Justin Martyr, *Dialogue with Trypho*, chapter 29, Early Christian Writings, accessed April 1, 2020, http://www.earlychristianwritings.com/text/justinmartyr-dialoguetrypho.html.

8. Justin Martyr, *The First Apology of Justin*, chapter 49, Early Christian Writings, accessed April 1, 2020, http://www.earlychristianwritings.com/text/justinmartyr-firstapology.html.

9. David Zaslow, *Jesus First-Century Rabbi* (Brewster, MA: Paraclete Press, 2014), chap. 14, https://books.google.com/books?id=PPYcAgAAQBAJ&pg.

10. Irenaeus, *Against Heresies*, 3.21, https://archive.org/details/SaintIrenaeusAgainstHeresiesComplete/page/n185/mode/2up.

11. Origen, *De Principiis*, 3.21, http://www.newadvent.org/fathers/04123.htm.

12. Origen, *Against Celsus*, 2.8, https://archive.org/details/FathersOfTheThirdCenturyVol.4OfTheAnte-niceneFathers/page/n871/mode/2up.

13. Edward H. Flannery, *Anguish of the Jews: Twenty-Three Centuries of Anti-Semitism*, rev. ed. (Mahwah, NJ: Paulist Press, 1985), 50, https://www.amazon.com/Anguish-Jews-Twenty-Three-Centuries-Antisemitism/dp/0809143240.

14. Martin Luther, "On the Jews and Their Lies," 1543, https://web.archive .org/web/20110219063044/http://www.humanitas-international.org/ showcase/chronography/documents/luther-jews.htm.

15. Yosef Eisen, "The Bloody Crusades," Chabad.org, accessed April 2, 2020, https://www.chabad.org/library/article_cdo/aid/2617029/jewish/The -Bloody-Crusades.htm.

16. Eisen, "The Bloody Crusades."

17. August C. Krey, The First Crusade (Princeton, NJ: Princeton University Press, 1921), 260, https://archive.org/details/firstcrusade00krey/ page/260/mode/2up/search/blood.."

18. Eisen, "The Bloody Crusades."

19. Christopher Tyerman, *God's War: A New History of the Crusades* (Cambridge, MA: Belknap Press, 2006), 282, https://archive.org/details /godswarnewhistor00tyer/page/281/mode/2up.

20. Eisen, "The Bloody Crusades."

21. Blue Letter Bible, s.v. "*plēthynō*," accessed April 2, 2020, https://www .blueletterbible.org/lang/lexicon/lexicon.cfm?Strongs=G4129&t=KJV.

22. Hila Ratzabi, "What Were Pogroms?," My Jewish Learning, accessed April 2, 2020, https://www.myjewishlearning.com/article/what-were -pogroms/.

23. Joseph Jacobs, "Aaron of Lincoln," *Jewish Encyclopedia*, accessed February 4, 2020, http://jewishencyclopedia.com/articles/66-aaron-of-lincoln.

24. Council Fathers, "Fourth Lateran Council: 1215—Constitutions," Papal Encyclicals Online, accessed April 2, 2020, https://www. papalencyclicals.net/councils/ecum12-2.htm.

25. Yosef Eisen, "Life Under the Church," Chabad.org, accessed February 4, 2020, https://www.chabad.org/library/article_cdo/aid/2617030/jewish/ Life-Under-the-Church.htm.

26. Council Fathers, "Fourth Lateran Council"; Eisen, "Life Under the Church."

27. Yosef Eisen, "Ten Anti-Semitic Myths," Chabad.org, accessed April 2, 2020, https://www.chabad.org/library/article_cdo/aid/2617031/ jewish/10-Anti-Semitic-Myths.htm.

28. Walter Laqueur, "The Many Lives of the 'Protocols of the Protocols of the Elders of Zion,'" *Mosaic*, December 4, 2017, https://mosaicmagazine. com/essay/history-ideas/2017/12/the-many-lives-of-the-protocols-of-the-elders-of-zion/; Eisen, "Ten Anti-Semitic Myths."

29. "Children's Memorial," Yad Vashem, accessed April 2, 2020, https:// www.yadvashem.org/remembrance/commemorative-sites/children-memorial.html.

30. David M. Halbfinger, Michael Wines, and Steven Erlanger, "Is B.D.S. Anti-Semitic? A Closer Look at the Boycott Israel Campaign," *New*

*York Times*, July 27, 2019, https://www.nytimes.com/2019/07/27/world/middleeast/bds-israel-boycott-antisemitic.html.

## CHAPTER 3

1. Jonathan Sacks, "Can a Country Be Born in a Day?," Aish.com, April 13, 2002, https://www.aish.com/h/iid/48906257.html.
2. Sacks, "Can a Country Be Born in a Day?"
3. "Yom Hazikaron in Jerusalem 2020," iTravelJerusalem, accessed April 2, 2020, https://www.itraveljerusalem.com/article/day-of-remembrance-in-jerusalem/.
4. "Yom Hazikaron in Jerusalem 2020," iTravelJerusalem.
5. Robert C. Diprizio, ed., *Conflict in the Holy Land: From Ancient Times to the Arab-Israeli Conflicts* (Santa Barbara, CA: ABC-CLIO, 2020), 154, https://www.google.com/books/edition/_/RNjKDwAAQBAJ?ght; MJL, "Terrorism in Israel: Questions and Answers," My Jewish Learning, accessed April 2, 2020, https://www.myjewishlearning.com/article/terrorism-in-israel-questions-and-answers/. The first figure was tabulated as of 2014; the second as of 2017.
6. Gene Currivan, "Zionists Proclaim New State of Israel; Truman Recognizes It and Hopes for Peace: Tel Aviv Is Bombed, Egypt Orders Invasion," *New York Times*, May 15, 1948, https://archive.nytimes.com/www.nytimes.com/library/world/480515israel-state-50.html.
7. One for Israel, "Can a Nation Be Born in a Day? Celebrating Israel's Independence Day," One for Israel, accessed April 2, 2020, https://www.oneforisrael.org/top-articles/can-a-nation-be-born-in-a-day/.
8. "Proclamation of the New Jewish State," *New York Times*, May 15, 1948, https://archive.nytimes.com/www.nytimes.com/library/world/480515israel-proclamation.html.
9. Billy Crone, *The Final Countdown Tribulation Rising, Volume 1: The Jewish People & the Antichrist* (n.p.: Get a Life Ministries, 2019), 103, https://www.google.com/books/edition/_/r3mIDwAAQBAJ?hl=en&gbpv=0. Crone talks about Israel's startups and its role as an innovator.
10. "Ezekiel," Biblica, accessed April 2, 2020, https://www.biblica.com/resources/scholar-notes/niv-study-bible/intro-to-ezekiel/.
11. Yehuda Altein and Alex Heppenheimer, "The Prophet Ezekiel," Chabad.org, accessed April 2, 2020, https://www.chabad.org/library/article_cdo/aid/112374/jewish/The-Prophet-Ezekiel.htm.
12. Tzvi Freeman, "What Is Emunah?," accessed April 2, 2020, https://www.chabad.org/library/article_cdo/aid/1398519/jewish/Emunah.htm.
13. Tzvi Freeman, "What Is Bitachon?," accessed April 2, 2020, https://www.chabad.org/library/article_cdo/aid/1405289/jewish/Bitachon.htm.
14. Vanessa Romo, "Trump Formally Recognizes Israeli Sovereignty Over Golan Heights," NPR, March 25, 2019, https://www.npr.org/2019/03/25/706588932/trump-formally-recognizes-israeli-sovereignty-over-golan-heights; Matthew Lee, "US Angers Palestinians With Reversal on Israeli Settlements," *U.S. News & World Report*, November 19, 2019,

https://www.usnews.com/news/politics/articles/2019-11-18/us-to-soften-position-on-israeli-settlements-in-west-bank.

15. Dave Lawlor, "Trump Presents Middle East Peace Plan, Green Lights Israeli Annexations," Axios, updated January 28, 2020, https://www.axios.com/white-house-israel-palestinian-peace-plan-middle-east-6660aa93-d289-4b7a-aeca-5ee6a37dccc3.html.

16. See Ticia Verveer, "The Ancient Cry of the Shofar," *Times of Israel*, September 7, 2018, https://blogs.timesofisrael.com/the-ancient-cry-of-the-shofar/.

17. Benjamine Glatt, "Uncovering the Divine Spirit During the Six Day War," *Jerusalem Post*, June 7, 2017, https://www.jpost.com/Christian-News/Uncovering-the-divine-spirit-during-the-Six-Day-War-496091.

## CHAPTER 4

1. "The Exodus Song (This Land Is Mine)," Songfacts, accessed April 2, 2020, https://www.songfacts.com/facts/pat-boone/the-exodus-song-this-land-is-mine.

2. Marcy Oster, "Pat Boone Donates 'Exodus' Song Lyrics to Yad Vashem," Jewish Telegraphic Agency, February 13, 2013, https://www.jta.org/2013/02/13/israel/pat-boone-donates-exodus-song-lyrics-to-yad-vashem; "The Exodus Song," Songfacts.

3. Ziva Dahl, "The Big Lie: Anti-Semitism and the 'Occupied Palestinian Territories,'" Observer, April 8, 2016, https://observer.com/2016/04/the-big-lie-anti-semitism-and-the-occupied-palestinian-territories/.

4. Lois Tverberg, "Shema—Hear and Obey," En-Gedi Resource Center, June 30, 2015, https://engediresourcecenter.com/2015/06/30/shema-hear-and-obey/.

5. Paul J. Kissling, *Genesis*, The College Press NIV Commentary, vol. 1 (Joplin, MO: College Press Publishing, 2004), 327, https://books.google.com/books?id=lotBnvqdmeQC&q.

6. "Israel: Origins of the Name 'Palestine,'" Jewish Virtual Library, accessed April 2, 2020, https://www.jewishvirtuallibrary.org/origin-of-quot-palestine-quot.

7. United Nations Security Council, Resolution 242 (1967), S/RES/242 (1967) (November 22, 1967), https://unispal.un.org/DPA/DPR/unispal.nsf/0/7D35E1F729DF491C85256EE700686136.

8. "The Siege of Masada: Story & Symbolism of the Masada Fortress," DeadSea.com, accessed April 3, 2020, https://www.deadsea.com/articles-tips/history/story-masada-siege-symbolic-meaning/. See also Si Sheppard, *The Jewish Revolt, AD 66–74* (Oxford, UK: Osprey Publishing, 2013), 83.

9. Tony Bunting, s.v. "Siege of Masada," in *Encyclopaedia Britannica*, March 28, 2017, https://www.britannica.com/event/Siege-of-Masada.

10. Benjamin Kerstein, "The Bar-Kochba Revolt," Ancient History Encyclopedia, August 30, 2018, https://www.ancient.eu/The_Bar-Kochba_Revolt/.

11. Joshua J. Mark, "Palestine," Ancient History Encyclopedia, October 25, 2018, https://www.ancient.eu/palestine/.

12. "Israel," Jewish Virtual Library.

13. Howard Grief, "Legal Rights and Title of Sovereignty of the Jewish People to the Land of Israel and Palestine Under International Law," Israel Forever Foundation, accessed April 3, 2020, https://israelforever.org/interact/blog/legal_rights_jewish_people_land_of_israel/.

14. "Faisal-Weizmann Agreement," United Nations, January 3, 1919, https://unispal.un.org/DPA/DPR/unispal.nsf/0/5BFF833964EDB9BF85256CED00673D1F. See also Dan Adler, "Why You Should Know San Remo," Israel Forever Foundation, accessed April 3, 2020, https://israelforever.org/interact/blog/why_you_should_know_san_remo/.

15. "Faisal-Weizmann Agreement," United Nations.

16. Adler, "Why You Should Know San Remo."

17. "The Palestine Mandate," The Avalon Project, July 24, 1922, https://avalon.law.yale.edu/20th_century/palmanda.asp.

18. "Rare Seal Bearing Biblical Name Found in City of David Excavation," Israel Ministry of Foreign Affairs, March 31, 2019, https://mfa.gov.il/MFA/IsraelExperience/History/Pages/Rare-seal-bearing-biblical-name-found-in-City-of-David-excavation-31-March-2019.aspx.

19. "Rare Seal Bearing Biblical Name Found in City of David Excavation," Israel Ministry of Foreign Affairs.

20. "Rare Seal Bearing Biblical Name Found in City of David Excavation," Israel Ministry of Foreign Affairs; Amanda Stiver, "In the News: Ancient Seal Found in Jerusalem," Beyond Today, July 19, 2012, https://www.ucg.org/vertical-thought/in-the-news-ancient-seal-found-in-jerusalem.

21. Yaakov Katz, "New Discovery in Jerusalem's City of David: 2,000-Year-Old Pilgrimage Road," *Jerusalem Post*, June 30, 2019, https://www.jpost.com/Magazine/Ascending-a-2000-year-old-Pilgrimage-Road-593766.

22. Jennifer Guetta-Peersmann, "Pool of Siloam," Jennifer Guetta, accessed February 22, 2020, http://jenniferguetta.com/pool-of-siloam/.

23. Guetta-Peersmann, "Pool of Siloam"; Israel Today Staff, "Your Guide to the Jerusalem's New Pilgrims' Path," Israel Today, July 12, 2019, https://www.israeltoday.co.il/read/your-guide-to-the-jerusalems-new-pilgrims-path/.

24. Katz, "New Discovery in Jerusalem's City of David: 2,000-Year-Old Pilgrimage Road."

25. Julie Stahl, "New Discovery on Jerusalem Pilgrimage Road Proves It Was Built by the Man Who Crucified Jesus," CBN News, October 22, 2019, https://www1.cbn.com/cbnnews/israel/2019/july/lsquo-the-beating-heart-of-jerusalem-rsquo-newly-discovered-pilgrimage-road-gives-glimpse-into-life-during-jesus-rsquo-time.

26. Amanda Borschel-Dan, "Tiny First Temple Seal Impression Found With Name of Bible-Era Royal Steward," *Times of Israel*, September 9, 2019, https://www.timesofisrael.com/

tiny-first-temple-seal-impression-inscribed-with-biblical-royal-stewards-name/.

27. Doron Spielman, "Israeli and American Dignitaries Unveil the Pilgrimage Road," *Times of Israel*, June 30, 2019, https://blogs.timesofisrael.com/israeli-and-american-dignitaries-unveil-pilgrimage-road/.

28. "Ambassador Friedman's Remarks at Christians United for Israel Summit 2019," U.S. Embassy in Israel, accessed April 3, 2020, https://il.usembassy.gov/ambassador-friedmans-remarks-at-christians-united-for-israel-summit-2019/.

29. "US Officials Inaugurated 'Fake' Archaeology Project: Senior Palestinian," France 24, July 1, 2019, https://www.france24.com/en/20190701-us-officials-inaugurated-fake-archaeology-project-senior-palestinian.

## CHAPTER 5

1. Morgan Hines and Bill Keveney, "Alex Borstein's Powerful Emmys Speech Grabs Attention: 'Step Out of Line, Ladies,'" *USA Today*, updated September 23, 2019, https://www.usatoday.com/story/entertainment/tv/2019/09/22/emmys-alex-borstein-tells-grandmas-holocaust-story-survival/2415239001/.

2. Hines and Keveney, "Alex Borstein's Powerful Emmys Speech Grabs Attention."

3. Yossi Lew, "What Does 'Aliyah' Mean?," Chabad.org, accessed April 3, 2020, https://www.chabad.org/library/article_cdo/aid/1584066/jewish/What-Does-Aliyah-Mean.htm.

4. Jeff A. Benner, "Wisdom, Knowledge and Understanding," Ancient Hebrew Research Center, accessed April 3, 2020, https://www.ancient-hebrew.org/studies-words/wisdom-knowledge-and-understanding.htm.

5. "Elul and the Days of Awe: The Season of Judgment, Mercy, Repentance, and the Return of Yeshua," The Messianic Prophecy Bible Project, accessed February 24, 2020, https://free.messianicbible.com/holiday/elul-and-the-days-of-awe-the-season-of-judgment-mercy-repentance-and-the-return-of-yeshua/.

6. Jerry Hennig, "Repentance...Teshuvah (Shuwb)," March 19, 2016, https://www.dasydministry.org/-%20New%20Folder/Teshuvah%20repent%20PDF.pdf.

7. Blue Letter Bible, s.v. "*shuwb*," accessed April 3, 2020, https://www.blueletterbible.org/lang/lexicon/lexicon.cfm?Strongs=H7725&t=KJV.

8. Online Etymology Dictionary, s.v. "repent," accessed April 3, 2020, https://www.etymonline.com/word/repent.

9. "Men of the Great Assembly," JewishHistory.org, accessed February 23, 2020, https://www.jewishhistory.org/the-men-of-the-great-assembly/.

10. "Men of the Great Assembly," JewishHistory.org.

11. Benner, "Wisdom, Knowledge and Understanding."

12. Blue Letter Bible, s.v. "*yada`*," accessed April 3, 2020, https://www.blueletterbible.org/lang/lexicon/lexicon.cfm?strongs=H3045&t=KJV;

Blue Letter Bible, s.v. *"yad,"* accessed April 3, 2020, https://www.
blueletterbible.org/lang/lexicon/lexicon.cfm?Strongs=H3027&t=KJV.

13. Benner, "Wisdom, Knowledge and Understanding." See also Blue Letter
Bible, s.v. *"`ayin,"* accessed April 3, 2020, https://www.blueletterbible
.org/lang/lexicon/lexicon.cfm?Strongs=H5869&t=KJV.

14. Blue Letter Bible, s.v. *"nathan,"* accessed April 3, 2020, https://www
.blueletterbible.org/lang/lexicon/lexicon.cfm?Strongs=H5414&t=KJV.

## CHAPTER 6

1. Menachem Posner, "Shofar During the Month of Elul: How and Why,"
Chabad.org, accessed April 3, 2020, https://www.chabad.org/holidays
/JewishNewYear/template_cdo/aid/2306683/jewish/Shofar-During-the
-Month-of-Elul-How-and-Why.htm.

2. Blue Letter Bible, s.v. *"mowpheth,"* accessed April 3, 2020, https://www
.blueletterbible.org/lang/lexicon/lexicon.cfm?Strongs=H226&t=KJV.

3. Blue Letter Bible, s.v. *"`owth,"* accessed April 3, 2020, https://www.blue
letterbible.org/lang/lexicon/lexicon.cfm?Strongs=H4159&t=KJV.

4. Blue Letter Bible, s.v. *"`owth."*

5. Tony Phillips, "A Tetrad of Lunar Eclipses," NASA.gov, March 27, 2014,
https://science.nasa.gov/science-news/science-at-nasa/2014/27mar_
tetrad.

6. John Henry, "Eight Tetrads Since the Day of Christ Falling on the First
and Last of the Seven Feasts of the Lord," Landmark Bible Baptist, last
updated April 30, 2014, http://prophecy.landmarkbiblebaptist.net/Signs
/8Tetrads.html.

7. Henry, "Eight Tetrads Since the Day of Christ Falling on the First and
Last of the Seven Feasts of the Lord."

8. Henry, "Eight Tetrads Since the Day of Christ Falling on the First and
Last of the Seven Feasts of the Lord."

9. "Columbus Day Poem—In 1492, Columbus Sailed the Ocean Blue,"
Scholastic, accessed April 4, 2020, https://www.scholastic.com/content/
dam/teachers/blogs/shari-carter/migrated-files/columbus_day_poem_
ns.pdf.

10. History.com Editors, "Inquisition," History.com, last updated August
21, 2018, https://www.history.com/topics/religion/inquisition. It is
important to note that Muslims were also targeted in the Inquisition.

11. Oliver Dunn and James E. Kelley Jr., trans., *The Diario of Christopher
Columbus's First Voyage to America 1492–1493* (Norman, OK:
University of Oklahoma Press, 1989), 19, https://archive.org/details/
diarioofchristop00colu/mode/2up.

12. "What Is Tisha B'Av?," Chabad.org, accessed April 4, 2020, https://www
.chabad.org/library/article_cdo/aid/144575/jewish/What-Is-Tisha-BAv.
htm.

13. Yosef Eisen, "The Spanish Expulsion," Chabad.org, accessed April 4,
2020, https://www.chabad.org/library/article_cdo/aid/2435008/jewish/
The-Spanish-Expulsion.htm.

14. Eisen, "The Spanish Expulsion."

15. Daymond Duck, "The Prophecy of Ten Jubilees," Prophecy Forum, April 24, 2017, http://prophecyforum.com/bible-prophecy/prophecy-ten-jubilees/.

16. Tim McHyde, "Rabbi Judah ben Samuel's Jubilee Prophecy—Messiah in 2017?," Escape All These Things, September 21, 2013, https://escapeallthesethings.com/judah-ben-samuel-prophecy/.

17. McHyde, "Rabbi Judah ben Samuel's Jubilee Prophecy."

18. Dimo Yascioglu, comment on "Since 'Osman' Is a Turkish Name and the Empire's Name Was 'Osmanlı' in Turkish, Where Does the Word 'Ottoman' Come From?," Quora, May 20, 2019, https://www.quora.com/Since-Osman-is-a-Turkish-name-and-the-empire-s-name-was-Osmanlı-in-Turkish-where-does-the-word-Ottoman-come-from.

19. Duck, "Prophecy of Ten Jubilees."

20. "Ottoman Empire (1301–1922)," BBC, last updated September 4, 2009, https://www.bbc.co.uk/religion/religions/islam/history/ottomanempire_1.shtml.

21. Jill Hamilton, *God, Guns and Israel: Britain, the First World War and the Jews in the Holy City*, 3rd ed. (Gloucestershire, UK: History Press, 2009), chapter 19, https://books.google.com/books?id=aP8SDQAAQBAJ&pg.

22. David B. Green, "Dec. 11, 1917, General Allenby Shows How a 'Moral Man' Conquers Jerusalem," Balfour Project, December 11, 2014, http://www.balfourproject.org/this-day-in-jewish-historygeneral-allenby-shows-how-a-moral-man-conquers-jerusalem/, quoting Gaston Bodart.

23. Peter Hofmann, *Cosmic Crossroad Countdown: The Fig Tree and the Prophetic Generation* (Bloomington, IN: AuthorHouse, 2017), chap. 5, https://books.google.com/books?id=ijwwDwAAQBAJ&pg.

24. "The Miracles of the Six-Day War: Introduction," Chabad.org, accessed April 4, 2020, https://www.chabad.org/multimedia/timeline_cdo/aid/525341/jewish/Introduction.htm.

25. "Israeli History: Six-Day War," Israeli-Weapons.com, accessed April 4, 2020, https://www.israeli-weapons.com/history/six_day_war/SixDayWar.html.

26. I and some of my staff were present at this meeting with presidential candidate Donald J. Trump, former Governor Mike Huckabee, and evangelical leaders on June 21, 2016, in New York City.

27. Lori Hanes, "Glen's Mind Officially Blown: Rabbi Daniel Lapin Boards the Trump Train," Glenn, May 20, 2016, https://www.glennbeck.com/2016/05/20/glenns-mind-officially-blown-rabbi-daniel-lapin-boards-the-trump-train/.

28. Daniel Lapin, interview by Larry Huch, November 5, 2017, New Beginnings Church, Bedford, Texas.

29. Jerusalem Embassy Act of 1995, Public Law 104–45, November 8, 1995, https://www.congress.gov/104/plaws/publ45/PLAW-104publ45.pdf.

30. Jerusalem Embassy Act of 1995.

31. Jerusalem Embassy Act of 1995.

32. Commemorating the 50th Anniversary of the Reunification of Jerusalem, S. Res. 176, 115th Cong., June 5, 2017, https://www.congress.gov/bill/115th-congress/senate-resolution/176/text.

33. H.R.1164–Taylor Force Act, 115the Cong., December 5, 2017, https://www.congress.gov/bill/115th-congress/house-bill/1164.

34. Lara Jakes and David M. Halbfinger, "In Shift, U.S. Says Israeli Settlements in West Bank Do Not Violate International Law," *New York Times*, November 18, 2019, https://www.nytimes.com/2019/11/18/world/middleeast/trump-israel-west-bank-settlements.html.

35. Romo, "Trump Formally Recognizes Israeli Sovereignty Over Golan Heights."

36. R. James Woolsey, "Challenges to Peace in the Middle East," Washington Institute, 1994, https://www.washingtoninstitute.org/policy-analysis/view/challenges-to-peace-in-the-middle-east.

## CHAPTER 7

1. Israel Meir Lau, *Out of the Depths: The Story of a Child of Buchenwald Who Returned Home at Last* (New York: Sterling, 2011), 8.

2. Lau, Out of the Depths, 303.

3. Lau, Out of the Depths, 303.

4. Brendan Cole, "Anti-Semitism Is Worse Today Than During Hitler's Rise, Says Grandson of German Diarist Who Defied Nazis," *Newsweek*, January 27, 2020, https://www.newsweek.com/holocaust-hitler-antisemitism-friedrich-kellner-1484061.

5. "Wilhelm Marr (1819–1904)," Jewish Virtual Library, accessed February 10, 2020, https://www.jewishvirtuallibrary.org/wilhelm-marr.

6. "Wannsee Conference and the 'Final Solution,'" Holocaust Encyclopedia, accessed April 4, 2020, https://encyclopedia.ushmm.org/content/en/article/wannsee-conference-and-the-final-solution.

7. Jon Henley, "Antisemitism Rising Sharply Across Europe, Latest Figures Show," *The Guardian*, February 15, 2019, https://www.theguardian.com/news/2019/feb/15/antisemitism-rising-sharply-across-europe-latest-figures-show.

8. Cnaan Liphshiz, "French Jewish Cemetery Vandalized. Police Say It Wasn't Antisemitic," *Jerusalem Post*, May 28, 2019, https://www.jpost.com/Diaspora/French-Jewish-cemetery-vandalized-Police-say-it-wasnt-antisemitic-590850.

9. Shaun Walker, "Jews in Germany Warned of Risks of Wearing Kippah Cap in Public," *The Guardian*, May 25, 2019, https://www.theguardian.com/world/2019/may/26/jews-in-germany-warned-of-risks-of-wearing-kippah-cap-in-public.

10. "Rejection of Jews Relatively Low Among Both Orthodox Christians and Catholics," Pew Research Center, May 8, 2017, https://www.pewforum.org/2017/05/10/democracy-nationalism-and-pluralism/pf-05-10-2017_ce-europe-08-01/.

11. Schoen Consulting, "Holocaust Knowledge and Awareness Study," Claims Conference, May 2, 2019, http://www.claimscon.org/wp-content

/uploads/2019/04/EXECUTIVE-SUMMARY-WO-WATERMARK-
AUSTRIA-EMBARGOED-UNTIL-5-2-19_.pdf.

12. Hollie McKay, "The Weather Channel Digital Under Fire for
Classifying Jerusalem as the 'State of Palestine,'" FOX News, June 7,
2019, https://www.foxnews.com/tech/weather-channel-digital-under-
fire-classifying-jerusalem-palestine.

13. "City Achieves New Record-Low May in Murder and Shooting Incident
Categories," New York City Police Department, June 4, 2019, https://
www.nyc.gov/site/nypd/news/p0604b/city-achieves-new-record-low-
may-murder-shooting-incident-categories#/0.

14. Stacy Cowley, "Times Apologizes for Publishing Anti-Semitic Cartoon,"
New York Times, April 28, 2019, https://www.nytimes.com/2019/04/28
/business/ny-times-anti-semitic-cartoon.html.

15. Angelique Chrisafis and Haroon Siddique, "Toulouse Shootings:
Mohamed Merah Killed as Siege Ends," The Guardian, March 22, 2012,
https://www.theguardian.com/world/2012/mar/22/toulouse-shootings
-mohamed-merah-killed.

16. James McAuley, "In France, Murder of a Jewish Woman Ignites Debate
over the Word 'Terrorism,'" Washington Post, July 23, 2017, https://
www.washingtonpost.com/world/europe/in-france-the-murder-of-a-
jewish-woman-ignites-a-debate-over-terrorism/2017/07/23/4c79fe28-
6bb9-11e7-abbc-a53480672286_story.html.

17. Philippe Theise, "Hundreds Rally in Paris to Seek Justice for Murdered
Jewish Woman Sarah Halimi," France 24, January 5, 2020, https://www
.france24.com/en/20200105-hundreds-rally-in-paris-to-seek-justice-for
-murdered-jewish-woman-sarah-halimi.

18. "Deadly Shooting at the Tree of Life Synagogue," Anti-Defamation
League, accessed April 4, 2020, https://www.adl.org/education/educator
-resources/lesson-plans/deadly-shooting-at-the-tree-of-life-synagogue.

19. Deanna Paul and Katie Mettler, "Authorities Identify Suspect
in 'Hate Crime' Synagogue Shooting That Left 1 Dead, 3 Injured,"
Washington Post, April 28, 2019, https://www.washingtonpost.com/
nation/2019/04/27/california-synagogue-shooting-multiple-injuries/.

20. "Alleged Poway Synagogue Shooter Yelled That Jews Are 'Ruining the
World,'" Jewish Telegraphic Agency, April 28, 2019, https://www.jta.org
/quick-reads/alleged-poway-synagogue-shooter-lives-with-his-parents-
and-thinks-jews-are-taking-over-the-world.

21. Ewan Palmer, "Neo-Nazis Disrupt Arkansas Holocaust Remembrance
Event to Voice Support for Professor Accused of Anti-Semitism,"
Newsweek, May 7, 2019, https://www.newsweek.com/nazis-arkansas-
holocaust-russellville-acu-professor-1417832.

22. Marc Thiessen, "Why Won't Dems Slam Their Anti-Semitic Fellow
Congresswomen?," New York Post, August 21, 2019, https://nypost.
com/2019/08/21/why-wont-dems-slam-their-anti-semitic-fellow
-congresswomen/.

23. Jonathan Bernis, "What You Need to Know About the BDS Movement," Jewish Voice, accessed April 4, 2020, https://www.jewishvoice.org/read/article/what-you-need-know-about-bds-movement.

24. "Anti-Jewish Boycott," United States Holocaust Memorial Museum, accessed April 4, 2020, https://www.ushmm.org/learn/timeline-of-events/1933-1938/anti-jewish-boycott.

25. "Boycott of Jewish Businesses," United States Holocaust Memorial Museum, accessed April 4, 2020, https://encyclopedia.ushmm.org/content/en/article/boycott-of-jewish-businesses.

26. "Kristallnacht," History, last updated December 6, 2018, https://www.history.com/topics/holocaust/kristallnacht.

27. "Boycott of Jewish Businesses," United States Holocaust Memorial Museum.

28. "Map: Synagogues Destroyed During Kristallnacht," United States Holocaust Memorial Museum, accessed April 4, 2020, https://www.ushmm.org/information/exhibitions/online-exhibitions/special-focus/kristallnacht/synagogues/how-was-kristallnacht-carried-out/map-synagogues-destroyed-during-kristallnacht.

29. Cnaan Liphshiz, "In Riot Outside Synagogue, French Jews Were Left to Protect Themselves," Jewish Telegraphic Agency, July 18, 2014, https://www.jta.org/2014/07/18/global/in-riot-outside-synagogue-french-jews-were-left-to-protect-themselves.

30. Abraham H. Foxman, "Kristallnacht's Lessons for Today," Anti-Defamation League, November 7, 2014, https://www.adl.org/news/op-ed/kristallnachts-lessons-for-today.

31. "Nazi Laws," New York State Department of Financial Services, accessed April 4, 2020, https://dfs.ny.gov/docs/consumer/holocaust/history_art_looting_restitution/Nazi%20Laws/nazi_laws_summary_english.pdf.

32. "Boycott, Divestment, and Sanctions (BDS)," Influence Watch, accessed April 4, 2020, https://www.influencewatch.org/movement/boycott-divestment-and-sanctions/; "What Is BDS?," BDSMovement.net, March 16, 2020, https://bdsmovement.net/what-is-bds.

33. Rachel Zoll, "BDS Push Gains Traction at US Colleges," *Times of Israel*, March 1, 2015, https://www.timesofisrael.com/bds-push-gains-traction-at-us-colleges/.

34. Lahav Harkov, "World Council of Churches Trainees Use Antisemitic Rhetoric, Advocate BDS," *Jerusalem Post*, January 14, 2019, https://www.jpost.com/Diaspora/Antisemitism/World-Council-of-Churches-trainees-use-antisemitic-rhetoric-advocate-BDS-577256.

35. "Joseph Goebbels: 'The Poison Dwarf,'" Holocaust Education and Archive Research Team, accessed April 4, 2020, http://www.holocaustresearchproject.org/holoprelude/goebbels.html.

36. David G. Dalin and John F. Rothmann, *Icon of Evil: Hitler's Mufti and the Rise of Radical Islam* (New York: Random House, 2008), 169, https://www.amazon.com/Icon-Evil-Hitlers-Mufti-Radical/dp/1400066530.

37. Raphael Israeli, trans., "The Charter of Allah: The Platform of the Islamic Resistance Movement (Hamas)," accessed April 4, 2020, https://fas.org/irp/world/para/docs/880818.htm.

38. Blue Letter Bible, s.v. "*dowr*," accessed April 4, 2020, https://www.blueletterbible.org/lang/lexicon/lexicon.cfm?Strongs=H1755&t=KJV.

39. Blue Letter Bible, s.v. "*Yishma`e'l*," accessed April 4, 2020, https://www.blueletterbible.org/lang/lexicon/lexicon.cfm?Strongs=H3458&t=KJV.

40. Blue Letter Bible, s.v. "*gamal*," accessed April 4, 2020, https://www.blueletterbible.org/lang/lexicon/lexicon.cfm?Strongs=H1580&t=KJV.

41. Miriam Feinberg Vamosh, "Word of the Day/Gamal למג‎," Haaretz, September 7, 2012, https://www.haaretz.com/word-of-the-day-gamal-1.5157968.

42. Blue Letter Bible, s.v. "*tsachaq*," accessed April 4, 2020, https://www.blueletterbible.org/lang/lexicon/lexicon.cfm?Strongs=H6711&t=KJV.

43. "Numbers 25 Commentary," Precept Austin, December 12, 2016, https://www.preceptaustin.org/numbers-25-commentary.

44. Blue Letter Bible, s.v. "*shama*," accessed February 29, 2020, https://www.blueletterbible.org/lang/lexicon/lexicon.cfm?Strongs=H8085&t=KJV.

45. Benny Morris, "Arafat Didn't Negotiate—He Just Kept Saying No," *The Guardian*, May 22, 2002, https://www.theguardian.com/world/2002/may/23/israel3.

46. Tamar Sternthal, "Concealed Carry: AP Covers Up Arafat's Gun at the UN," CAMERA, October 2, 2018, https://www.camera.org/article/concealed-carry-ap-covers-up-arafats-gun-at-the-un/.

47. Dovid Rosenfeld, "Chapter 3, Mishna 21(a): Why Not a Good Samaritan?," Torah.org, July 29, 2018, https://torah.org/learning/pirkei-avos-chapter3-21a/.

48. "Dietrich Eckart (1868–1923)," Jewish Virtual Library, accessed April 4, 2020, https://www.jewishvirtuallibrary.org/dietrich-eckart.

49. Peter Brach, "The Anti-Semitic Intention of *The Ring of the Nibelung*: An Evaluation of Jewish Culture and Wagner's Dwarven Characters," University of Texas, accessed April 4, 2020, https://www.laits.utexas.edu/wagner/selectedessays/pdf/brach.pdf.

50. "Siegfried," International Association of Richard Wagner Societies, accessed April 4, 2020, https://www.richard-wagner.org/rwvi/en/about-wagner/the-works/?collection_id=95.

51. "Catastrophe at Stalingrad," The History Place, accessed April 5, 2020, https://www.historyplace.com/worldwar2/defeat/catastrophe-stalingrad.htm; "Invasion of the Soviet Union, June 1941," *Holocaust Encyclopedia*, accessed April 5, 2020, https://encyclopedia.ushmm.org/content/en/article/invasion-of-the-soviet-union-june-1941.

52. "Catastrophe at Stalingrad," The History Place.

53. Yaakov Yosef Reinman, ed., *The Midrash Rabbah* (Jerusalem: Machon HaMidrash HaMevo'ar, 2002), 7, https://books.google.com/books?id=r2UYd3jKvDIC&pg.

54. K. R. Smith, *The Storm Before the Calm: America and Israel at the End of Days* (Bloomington, IN: Westbow Press, 2010), 34, https://www.amazon.com/Storm-Before-Calm-America-Israel/dp/1449702503.

55. Ibn Warraq, "Virgins? What Virgins?," *The Guardian*, January 11, 2002, https://www.theguardian.com/books/2002/jan/12/books.guardian review5.

56. Sonia Phalnikar, "Book Casts Sept. 11 Terrorist in Unexpected Light," DW, April 30, 2004, https://www.dw.com/en/book-casts-sept-11-terrorist-in-unexpected-light/a-1152077.

57. "Nazi War Criminals Executed," History, accessed April 4, 2020, https://www.history.com/this-day-in-history/nazi-war-criminals-executed.

58. "Julius Streicher," Shoah Resource Center, accessed April 4, 2020, https://www.yadvashem.org/odot_pdf/Microsoft%20Word%20-%20 6050.pdf.

59. "High-Ranking Nazi Leader Hermann Göring Dies," History, accessed April 4, 2020, https://www.history.com/this-day-in-history/hermann-goering-dies.

60. Daniel Lapin, "Were Haman's Sons Hanged Twice?," Rabbi Daniel Lapin, June 14, 2018, https://rabbidaniellapin.com/were-hamans-sons-hanged-twice/.

61. Bernhard Rosenberg, "Purim Heroine Esther's Nazi Prophecy," My Central Jersey, March 4, 2015, https://www.mycentraljersey.com/story/life/faith/2015/03/04/purim-heroine-esther-prophesy-nazis/24273719/.

62. Rosenberg, "Purim Heroine Esther's Nazi Prophecy."

63. Mitchell Bard, "Exclusive Book & Movie Reviews: Understanding Islamism Obsession: The Threat of Radical Islam—Peace Arch Home—Entertainment—77 Minutes—2007," Jewish Virtual Library, accessed April 5, 2020, https://www.jewishvirtuallibrary.org/understanding-islamism-a-review-of-quot-obsession-quot.

64. Matthias Küntzel, *Jihad and Jew-Hatred: Islamism, Nazism, and the Roots of 9/11*, trans. Colin Meade (New York: Telos Press, 2007), xix, https://www.amazon.com/Jihad-Jew-Hatred-Islamism-Nazism-Roots/dp/0914386395.

65. "German Halle Gunman Admits Far-Right Synagogue Attack," BBC, October 11, 2019, https://www.bbc.com/news/world-europe-50011898.

## CHAPTER 8

1. Julian Sinclair, "Zechut," The Jewish Chronicle, March 6, 2009, https://www.thejc.com/judaism/jewish-words/zechut-1.8036; Balabusta, "Zechut," *Sabbath Meals*, February 8, 2005, https://sabbathmeals.typepad.com/sabbath_meals/2005/02/zechut.html.

2. Tracey R. Rich, "Tzedakah: Charity," Judaism 101, accessed March 3, 2020, http://www.jewfaq.org/tzedakah.htm.

3. "Hebrew Glossary—B," Hebrew for Christians, accessed April 5, 2020, https://www.hebrew4christians.com/Glossary/Hebrew_Glossary_-_B/ hebrew_glossary_-_b.html.

4. Daniel Lapin, "Color My World," Rabbi Daniel Lapin, February 12, 2013, https://rabbidaniellapin.com/color-my-world/.

5. "Hebrew Numbers," Tex Texin, accessed April 4, 2020, http://www.i18nguy.com/unicode/hebrew-numbers.html.

6. "Covenant—Beriyth (Hebrew Word Study)," Precept Austin, March 1, 2017, https://www.preceptaustin.org/covenant_definition.

7. MJL, "Tikkun Olam: Repairing the World," My Jewish Learning, accessed April 5, 2020, https://www.myjewishlearning.com/article/tikkun-olam-repairing-the-world/.

8. Danielle Park, "Wall of Jericho," Civil Engineer, accessed April 5, 2020, https://www.thecivilengineer.org/online-historical-database-of-civil-infrastructure/item/393-wall-of-jericho.

9. "B'reisheit In the Beginning," ReformJudaism.org, accessed April 5, 2020, https://reformjudaism.org/learning/torah-study/breishit/english-translation.

10. Blue Letter Bible, s.v. "raz," accessed April 5, 2020, https://www.blueletterbible.org/lang/lexicon/lexicon.cfm?Strongs=H7328&t=KJV.

11. Gershom Scholem, "The Meaning of the Torah in Jewish Mysticism," in Essential Papers on Kabbalah, ed. Lawrence Fine (New York: New York University Press, 1995), 204.

12. Rich, "Tzedakah."

13. American Dictionary of the English Language, s.v. "breach," accessed April 5, 2020, http://webstersdictionary1828.com/Dictionary/breach.

14. American Friends of Magen David Adom, "Magen David Adom's Story Is Your Story," accessed April 5, 2020, https://afmda.org/about-us/.

15. Daniel C. Kurtzer, "Israel and Hezbollah: Deterrence and the Threat of Miscalculation," Council on Foreign Relations, September 11, 2017, https://www.cfr.org/report/israel-and-hezbollah-deterrence-and-threat-miscalculation.

16. "National Emergency Preparation," Nefesh B'Nefesh, accessed April 5, 2020, https://www.nbn.org.il/aliyahpedia/government-services/post-aliyah-guides/national-emergency-preparation/.

17. Gideon Kouts/Maariv, "Former Syrian General: Hezbollah Is in Possession of Chemical Weapons," Jerusalem Post, March 8, 2018, https://www.jpost.com/Middle-East/Former-Syrian-official-to-Maariv-Hezbollah-has-chemical-weapons-544567.

18. Definitions, s.v. "reward," accessed April 5, 2020, https://www.definitions.net/definition/REWARD.

19. Blue Letter Bible, s.v. "shaphak," accessed April 4, 2020, https://www.blueletterbible.org/lang/lexicon/lexicon.cfm?Strongs=H8210&t=KJV.

20. Randy Woodley, "Peace, Harmony, Wholeness, Completeness, Prosperity, Welfare, and Tranquility: In Other Word[s]: Shalom," accessed April 5, 2020, https://themorelist.com/blog/2018/3/28/peace-harmony-wholeness-completeness-prosperity-welfare-and-tranquility-in-other-word-shalom.

## CHAPTER 9

1. MJL, "What are the Lulav and Etrog?," My Jewish Learning, accessed April 5, 2020, https://www.myjewishlearning.com/article/lulav-etrog/.

2. David B. Barrett, George T. Kurian, and Todd M. Johnson, eds., *World Christian Encyclopedia*, vol. 1, 2nd ed. (Oxford, UK: Oxford University Press, 2001), 16, https://archive.org/details/worldchristianen0001unse/page/16/mode/2up.

3. Blue Letter Bible, s.v. *"synergos,"* accessed April 5, 2020, https://www.blueletterbible.org/lang/lexicon/lexicon.cfm?strongs=G4904&t=KJV; Blue Letter Bible, s.v. *"syn,"* accessed April 5, 2020, https://www.blueletterbible.org/lang/lexicon/lexicon.cfm?strongs=G4862&t=KJV; Blue Letter Bible, s.v. *"ergon,"* accessed April 5, 2020, https://www.blueletterbible.org/lang/lexicon/lexicon.cfm?strongs=G2041&t=KJV.

4. Oren Liebermann, "Two Muslim Families Entrusted With Care of Holy Christian Site for Centuries," CNN, March 27, 2016, https://www.cnn.com/2016/03/26/middleeast/easter-muslim-keyholder/index.html.

5. Rinat Harash, "Muslim Holds Ancient Key to Jesus' Tomb in Jerusalem," Reuters, November 30, 2017, https://www.reuters.com/article/us-religion-jerusalem-church/muslim-holds-ancient-key-to-jesus-tomb-site-in-jerusalem-idUSKBN1DU17Q.

6. "Monks Brawl at Jerusalem Shrine," BBC News, updated November 9, 2008, http://news.bbc.co.uk/2/hi/middle_east/7718587.stm.

7. Blue Letter Bible, s.v. *"tow'ebah,"* accessed April 5, 2020, https://www.blueletterbible.org/lang/lexicon/lexicon.cfm?Strongs=H8441&t=KJV.

8. Lexico, s.v. *"restoration,"* accessed April 4, 2020, https://www.lexico.com/definition/restoration.

9. Daniel Bensadoun, "This Week in History: Revival of the Hebrew Language," *Jerusalem Post*, October 15, 2010, https://www.jpost.com/Jewish-World/Jewish-News/This-week-in-history-Revival-of-the-Hebrew-language.

10. "Verse-by-Verse Bible Commentary: Zephaniah 3:8," StudyLight.org, accessed April 5, 2020, https://www.studylight.org/commentary/zephaniah/3-8.html.

11. Yehuda Shurpin, "4 Unique Characteristics of the Third Temple," Chabad.org, accessed April 6, 2020, https://www.chabad.org/library/article_cdo/aid/3716004/jewish/4-Unique-Characteristics-of-the-Third-Temple.htm.

12. "The Tabernacle of David," WildOlive, accessed April 6, 2020, http://www.wildolive.co.uk/david%27s_tabernacle.htm.

13. Lau, *Out of the Depths*, 310.

14. Lau, *Out of the Depths*, 310–311.

15. R. C. Sproul, "What Does the Word 'Gospel' Mean in the New Testament?" Ligonier Ministries, December 6, 2019, https://www.ligonier.org/blog/what-does-word-gospel-mean-new-testament/.

16. Blue Letter Bible, s.v. *"basar,"* accessed April 6, 2020, https://www.blueletterbible.org/lang/lexicon/lexicon.cfm?Strongs=H1319&t=KJV.

17. Young, *Jesus the Jewish Theologian*, preface.

18. Nissan Mindel, "The Prophet Amos," Chabad.org, accessed April 6, 2020, https://www.chabad.org/library/article_cdo/aid/112277/jewish/The-Prophet-Amos.htm.

19. Nabil Hilmi, interview, *Al-Ahram Al-Arabi*, August 9, 2003, quoted in "Egyptian Jurists to Sue 'The Jews' for Compensation for 'Trillions' of Tons of Gold Allegedly Stolen During Exodus From Egypt," Memri, August 22, 2003, https://www.memri.org/reports/egyptian-jurists-sue-jews-compensation-trillions-tons-gold-allegedly-stolen-during-exodus. See also "Law of the Land," The Byzantine Forum, August 22, 2003, http://www.byzcath.org/forums/ubbthreads.php/topics/35658/Re:_Jews_sued_for_%27stealing%27_g.

20. Hilmi, interview.

21. Elisha Greenbaum, "The Gold of Egypt," Chabad.org, accessed April 6, 2020, https://www.chabad.org/parshah/article_cdo/aid/352437/jewish/The-Gold-of-Egypt.htm; see also Sefaria, "Sanhedrin 91a, accessed April 14, 2020,. https://www.sefaria.org/Sanhedrin.91a?lang=bi.

22. Ansuya Harjani, "World's Most Expensive Casino Properties," CNBC, May 1, 2011, https://www.cnbc.com/2011/05/01/Worlds-Most-Expensive-Casino-Properties.html.

23. "What Is Shemittah?," Chabad.org, accessed April 6, 2020, https://www.chabad.org/library/article_cdo/aid/562077/jewish/What-Is-Shemittah.htm.

24. Lexico, s.v. "*devout*," accessed April 6, 2020, https://www.lexico.com/synonym/devout.

25. Bible Hub, s.v. "2126. *eulabés*," accessed April 6, 2020, https://biblehub.com/greek/2126.htm.

26. Blue Letter Bible, s.v. "*kanaph*," accessed April 6, 2020, https://www.blueletterbible.org/lang/lexicon/lexicon.cfm?Strongs=H3671&t=KJV.

27. Blue Letter Bible, s.v. "*adom*," accessed April 6, 2020, https://www.blueletterbible.org/nkjv/gen/25/30/t_conc_25030.

28. Chaim Miller, "Yishma'el's Error," adapted from the teachings of Lubavitcher Rebbe, Chabad.org, accessed April 6, 2020, https://www.chabad.org/parshah/article_cdo/aid/760980/jewish/Yishmaels-Error.htm.

29. "Chapter 3: The Secret Language of the Bible," Bridges to Common Ground, accessed April 6, 2020, https://bridgestocommonground.org/deadly-misunderstanding-secret-language-bible/.